The Action Research Guidebook

Third Edition

The Action Research Guidebook

A Process for Pursuing Equity and Excellence in Education

Third Edition

Richard D. Sagor

Charlene Williams

CORWIN
A SAGE Publishing Company

A SAGE Publishing Company

FOR INFORMATION:

Corwin
A SAGE Company
2455 Teller Road
Thousand Oaks, California 91320
(800) 233-9936
www.corwin.com

SAGE Publications Ltd.
1 Oliver's Yard
55 City Road
London EC1Y 1SP
United Kingdom

SAGE Publications India Pvt. Ltd.
B 1/I 1 Mohan Cooperative Industrial Area
Mathura Road, New Delhi 110 044
India

SAGE Publications Asia-Pacific Pte. Ltd.
3 Church Street
#10-04 Samsung Hub
Singapore 049483

Executive Editor: Arnis Burvikovs
Senior Associate Editor: Desirée A. Bartlett
Senior Editorial Assistant: Andrew Olson
Production Editor: Amy Schroller
Copy Editor: Jared Leighton
Typesetter: C&M Digitals (P) Ltd.
Proofreader: Laura Webb
Indexer: Robie Grant
Cover Designer: Michael Dubowe
Marketing Manager: Anna Mesick

Printed in the United States of America

Library of Congress Cataloging-in-Publication Data

Names: Sagor, Richard, author.

Title: The action research guidebook : a process for pursuing equity and excellence in education / Richard D. Sagor, Charlene Williams.

Description: Third edition. | Thousand Oaks, California : Corwin, [2017] | Includes bibliographical references and index.

Identifiers: LCCN 2016039394 | ISBN 9781506350158 (pbk. : alk. paper)

Subjects: LCSH: Action research in education. | Teachers—In-service training.

Classification: LCC LB1028.24 .S33 2017 | DDC 370.72—dc23
LC record available at https://lccn.loc.gov/2016039394

This book is printed on acid-free paper.

16 17 18 19 20 10 9 8 7 6 5 4 3 2 1

Contents

Preface to the Third Edition   ix

Publisher's Acknowledgments   xix

About the Authors   xxi

1. Introduction to Action Research   1

   Why Conduct Action Research?   1
   The Complexity of Routine Instructional Decisions   2
   Key Terms and Concepts   6
   Universal Student Success   12

2. Finding a Focus   14

   Zeroing in on Your Priorities   14
   Using Reflective Writing to Find a Focus   15
   Performance, Process, and Program Targets and
      Action Research by School Leaders   22
   Using a Journal to Identify Action Research Foci   24
   Reflective Interviews   29
   Reflective Interviewing and the Problem of Isolation   30
   Analytic Discourse   31
   Team Reflection   31

3. Refining the Focus   34

   Visualizing Success   35
   Conducting an Instructional Postmortem   36
   Taking Stock of One's Recent Leadership Experience   39
   Comparing Your Experience With the Experience of Others   39
   Developing Criteria to Measure Changes
      With Priority Achievement Targets   45
   Creating Performance Rating Scales   47
   Rating Scales and Program Action Research   50
   The Special Problem of Long-Range Goals   53
   Assessing Rate of Growth   54
   Determining Adequate Yearly Progress in Real Time   54
   Producing Your Own Rate-of-Growth Charts   56
   Ascertaining Rate of Growth in Leadership Projects   58

4. Articulating a Theory of Action   59

   If Not Us, Who?   60
   An Adequate Knowledge Base Already Exists   61
   Going Beyond Proven Practices: Building a Theory of Action   61
   Two Kinds of Variables   64
   Creating Mileposts on the Route to Mastery   65
   Inferring Independent Variables   65
   Using the Priority Pie to Identify, Clarify,
      and Weigh Independent Variables   66
   Using the Priority Pie With Descriptive Research   71

5. Drawing a Theory of Action   73

   Why a Map?   74
   European Explorers as Action Researchers   74
   Building a Graphic Reconstruction   77
   Graphic Reconstructions for Quasi-Experimental Research   78
   Graphic Reconstructions With Descriptive Research   80
   Proofing a Theory of Action for Leadership Projects   88

6. Determining the Research Questions   91

   Three Generic Action Research Questions   92
   Developing Your Own Research Questions   100
   Two-Step Walk-Through   100
   Drafting the Questions   104
   Surfacing Research Questions for Leadership Projects   106

7. Building a Data Collection Plan   107

   Data Collection and the Competing Demands for Your Time   107
   What Qualifies as Teaching?   108
   What Things Qualify as Data?   109
   Data in Descriptive Research   109
   Data in Quasi-Experimental Research   109
   Data Collection and Concerns About Precision   110
   Fishing in a Sea of Data   111
   Securing Research Assistants   112
   Building a Triangulated Data Collection Plan   113
   Data Collection Planning for Leadership Projects   116
   Integrating Efficiencies Into Your Data Collection Work   117
   Using Technology to Compile and Assemble Action
      Research Data   125
   Keeping a Researcher's Journal   126

8. Analyzing the Data   128

   Trend Analysis   129
   Organizing Data to Help Answer the Three Generic Questions   131
   ACR Question 1: What Did We Do?   131
   ACR Question 2: What Changes Occurred Regarding
      the Achievement Targets?   143

ACR Question 3: What Was the Relationship
Between Actions Taken and Any Changes
in Performance on the Targets?   149
Drawing Tentative Assertions   153
Using Member Checking to Add Credibility
to the Tentative Assertions   155
Additional Tools for Qualitative Data Analysis   156
Qualitative Data Analysis Using Bins and a Matrix   158
Low-Tech Strategies for Bins and Matrixes   160
Using a Computer for Bins and Matrixes   162

9. Turning Findings Into Action Plans   167

Modifying Your Theory of Action   167
Data-Based Decision Making   172
Turning Your Findings Into Ed Specs   176
Solicit and Brainstorm Action Alternatives   178
Using Ed Specs to Evaluate Action Alternatives   179
Using Ed Specs to Evaluate Action Alternatives
for Schoolwide Projects   181
Completing the Cycle: Revised Theory of Action 2   182

10. Reporting and Sharing Action Research   184

Common Issues   185
Formats for Reporting   189
Creating a Bank of Abstracts   191
Creating a District Archive   195

11. Conclusion: The School as a Learning Organization   196

The Two Keys: Coherence and Congruence   197
Putting the Pieces Together   198

Resources

Resource A: How to Use the Feedback Forms and
Summary Reports   201
Resource B: Five Characteristics of a Quality
Action Research Project   203
Resource C: Applications for Leadership Projects   206
Resource D: Sample Abbreviated Action Research Reports   218

Glossary   247

References   251

Index   255

Preface to the Third Edition

Readers familiar with the second edition of *The Action Research Guidebook* should find much to their liking in this new edition. The most noticeable changes you will see are in the quality and quantity of examples. You will find many new illustrative examples throughout the text, as well as in the resource section. Not only in many cases will you find these examples to be different from the last edition, but you will see they have been completely redesigned to better illustrate the key action research strategies being discussed. A second major change in the third edition that we think return readers will appreciate is the explicit focus on equity, inclusion, and our role as reflective practitioners in helping all young people achieve excellence in our schools. Lastly, this edition contains several sample abbreviated action research reports (Resource D) that provide helpful models for folks new to action research. We hope you enjoy the changes.

We decided to begin the third edition of *The Action Research Guidebook* with the same sentiment Richard used to open the first edition, with a sincere and heartfelt thank you for making K–12 education your life's work.

There is no better way for us to contribute to society and to the health of our communities than investing in the growth and development of the youth attending our schools. In their book, *Good Work: When Excellence and Ethics Meet*, Howard Gardner, Mihaly Csikszentmihalyi, and William Damon (2001) started by defining the concept of *good work*. They defined it as an endeavor that simultaneously satisfies both meanings of the word *good*. To Gardner et al. (2001), *good work* was work that resulted in a product or service that was not only demonstrably good for society *but* was done well.

From the beginning, the purpose of *The Action Research Guidebook* has been to support educators as they endeavor to do their good work. Over the past fifteen years, we have learned a great deal from the users of the earlier editions of this book and also from our own practice and the experience of our colleagues. In the first two editions, it was inferred and overtly stated that our mission as public school educators was the pursuit of *universal student success*. Clearly, teaching in a system where every child, independent of his or her home or family circumstances, could reasonably expect to leave school armed with the skills, attitudes, and temperament needed to realize his or her dreams would meet the first condition of *good work*. For years, we have witnessed reflective educators succeeding with the second aspect of *good work*—that is, doing their job well. These were the educators who were constantly pushing the edge of the envelope, exploring promising ideas and then systematically using data on their practice to improve their teaching and help their students succeed academically.

EXCELLENCE AND EQUITY

Careful readers of the first two editions of this book will notice a continual refinement of our perspective on strategies that contribute to quality action research. We are pleased to report that our work with educators over the past fifteen years has reinforced our belief in the critical nature of the four stages of the action research process: *Stage 1: Clarifying Vision and Targets; Stage 2: Articulating Theory; Stage 3: Implementing Action and Collecting Data;* and *Stage 4: Reflecting on Data and Planning Informed Action.* For that reason, this third edition of *The Action Research Guidebook*, like the first two, has been built around those four sequential stages.

So in one way, we could say from our perspective, not much has changed over the past fifteen years. Specifically, our view on the importance of assisting educators in developing the skills to do the *good work* that characterizes reflective practitioners has not undergone much change at all. What has changed, however, is our willingness to implicitly assume that everyone shares the same understanding of what constitutes universal student success and, more importantly, that everyone working in our school has reflected on how many of our current instructional practices may actually be contributing to the difficulties many of our students experience at school.

In the nearly two decades that we have been working with teachers on developing the skills of reflective practice, we have witnessed the introduction of plethora of school reform initiatives (starting with "A Nation at Risk," followed by the State Standards Movement, then No Child Left Behind, and now Common Core). Each of these initiatives was sold to parents, educators, and communities as a mechanism to foster universal student success. When listening to the promoters, one might actually conclude that the people pushing these programs truly believed that all that was required to help all children succeed was the implementation of a new set of policies and procedures. Regardless of what the program promoters believed in their hearts, the sad truth is that their prescriptions didn't work as intended.

Sadly, after decades of reform, still the best predictor of a school's achievement test scores is the school's ZIP code. Unfortunately, in spite of years of rhetoric on "school reform," the data are clear: Nothing prepares a young person better for success in our schools than being born a member of the majority culture and/or coming from an affluent family. The truth is that after years of what we were told was a national commitment to a vision of leaving no child behind, pretty much the same students who failed in the past are still being left behind.

What we have learned over recent years is that student and school success are multivariate phenomena. And many of these critical variables that promote opportunity and success need to be addressed both deliberately and simultaneously. As citizens, we need to deal with structural defects in our economy and stem the pervasive epidemic of youth poverty. As educators, we need to continue to push for higher standards as we strive for excellence. We also need to recognize that many of the most powerful factors that influence whether any particular student withers or thrives in an educational environment aren't those things addressed by most state and federal education policies but are things that can be attacked by local districts, schools, and teachers. Elsewhere, Richard has written extensively on the importance of providing young people with feelings of competence, belonging, usefulness, potency, and optimism (CBUPOs). Young people who derive those five feelings through their school experiences develop greater self-esteem and achieve significantly higher academic outcomes (Sagor, 2003; Sagor & Cox, 2004).

Sadly, even with educational reform high on the public agenda for nearly three decades, still, way too many young people never get to enjoy CBUPOs at school. Opportunities for the continuous experience of feelings of competence, belonging, usefulness, potency, and optimism are not distributed equitably in our schools. An upper-middle-class white girl attending a well-funded school in an affluent suburb will be far more likely to spend her schooldays bathing in feelings of competence, belonging, usefulness, potency, and optimism than will a low-income African American boy attending an impoverished school in the inner city. As we said earlier, the issue of educational underperformance is complex and multifaceted and likely won't be fixed with one magic bullet. No Common Core curriculum, no standardized test, and no set of new accountability procedures or sanctions will cause every child to succeed. There is, however, one common denominator that separates the successful students—the students experiencing CBUPOs at school—and the students who are not succeeding. That common denominator is active, meaningful engagement. Simply put, when students are purposefully engaged, they learn; when they are passive, uninvolved, and/or disengaged, they don't. The evidence suggests that disadvantaged, poor, and minority students are significantly less engaged at school than are white advantaged students. In this edition, we have included and you will explore, several examples of teachers and administrators striving to use action research to help them enhance equitable student engagement.

Over the years and across the country, we have repeatedly observed individual teachers and teams of reflective practitioners relentlessly examining the manner in which each of their diverse students experiences their instruction. Those same teachers then use that information to purposefully modify their teaching to ensure that each day, each and every student experiences feelings of competence, belonging, usefulness, potency, and optimism through their schoolwork. In the schools and classrooms where the habit of reflective practice—looking for patterns of engagement and adjusting instruction accordingly—has been internalized, not only are high academic expectations an integral part of the school culture, but these educators and their schools are continuously growing in their cultural competence (Dilworth, 1997; Gay, 2000; Robins, Lindsey, Lindsey, & Terrell, 2002; Singleton & Linton 2006). These observations lead us to the most significant change in this edition of *The Action Research Guidebook*. In the first two editions, the projects and examples we included as illustrations of action research were selected with just one criterion in mind: Did the project or example clearly illustrate the technique under discussion? For the third edition, we have deliberately added a second criterion: Is the particular project we are highlighting or the example we are sharing making use of the action research process to further the twin goals of excellence and equity? We are confident that the examples we decided to use provide effective illustrations of the key strategies and techniques of the four-stage process. In addition, we hope these examples will provide extra value for you and your students, due to the focus on the pursuit of the twin goals of equity and excellence.

In the chapters that follow, you will be getting to know Charlene in another capacity. When not busy authoring books, Charlene had been working full time as one of the senior directors in the Portland (OR) School District. In this capacity, she supervised all of the building administrators in one of the most challenging geographic regions of this large urban school district. Beginning in Chapter 2, you will be invited to peer through a window and observe her reflective practice as she engages with her principals on school improvement. You will have a bird's-eye view while she conducts action research on her own effort to improve her perspective and skills with leadership coaching. In addition, you will learn from the action research conducted by a number of colleagues working in a diverse, urban middle school that we decided to name the AR Academy. At the AR Academy, the school community made a decision to operate as a professional learning community (PLC) (Dufour, Dufour, & Eaker, 2008). The faculty at the AR Academy recently committed itself to the pursuit of high levels of quality student engagement and to have that engagement experienced equitably by all of their students. Throughout the book, you will be encountering four projects conducted at the AR Academy. We will look at the work conducted by the AR Academy principal, Mr. Johnson; two different projects conducted by one of the AR teachers, Ms. Montgomery; and a collaborative action research project being carried out by the AR Academy's PLC team. All five of these studies are different in scope and process; consequently, they illustrate different aspects and uses of the action research process, but they share one common theme: enhancing the quality, quantity, and equitable distribution of high student engagement. We have attempted to capture the full range of educational applications for action research but have decided to do so in the context of the simultaneous pursuit of excellence and equity. In each example, the researchers you will meet are using the same four-stage process; however, you will see them adapting that process in a manner that fits their unique circumstances and priorities. Each example has been drawn from the work of real educators whom we've worked with or observed while they conducted their action research projects. In each case, we have turned these folks into hypothetical examples by liberally combining bits and pieces of different projects to best illustrate the concept.

HOW TO USE THIS BOOK

It was our hope to produce a handbook that would provide the busy educator who wished to experience the action research process with an easy-to-follow template, one that could be readily adapted to a variety of professional interests and foci. We hope we succeeded in accomplishing that goal. But if that were all we did, we would have let ourselves down.

We would simply have written one more step-by-step how-to manual. And by doing so, we would have glossed over the true complexity of the issues educators confront on a daily basis. Since every educational context and every learner is somewhat different, excellent teaching requires constant creative problem solving by the expert in the classroom. Any book that contends to provide a one-size-fits-all prescription for the problems faced by the classroom teacher is ignoring this reality and treating the professional reader in a condescending fashion. In this book, our goal will be to continually provide you with two things:

1. A variety of examples, along with step-by-step instructions for carrying out the action research process

2. A discussion of the rationale for and function of each of the components of the action research process

If you are new to action research, we hope the step-by-step instructions will enable you to have a productive and professionally fulfilling first-time experience with practitioner research. Furthermore, we hope the presentation of the rationale for these procedures will help you creatively incorporate each of the stages of the process into the context of your own work and adapt them to your own priorities. Later, as you become a more experienced action researcher, you will undoubtedly choose to modify and customize many of the strategies presented here, as well as invent new ones, as you mold the four stages of the action research process to achieve your own professional goals.

If you are already an experienced action researcher, we encourage you to look at the activities provided in this book as illustrative suggestions from colleagues. Use this book as a potpourri of ideas, which you might choose to try out as written, or use it to stimulate alternative creative approaches that support your search for answers to the perplexing questions of practice that you are currently struggling with.

As a handbook, this text was written to be used *while* you are working your way through the action research process. We don't recommend that you sit down and read through the entire book at once. Rather, we envision you reading through a section at a time, as you are preparing to work through that stage of your project. The intent of each chapter is to provide concrete strategies for immediate use. Consequently, the book has been organized sequentially, with each activity, as well as each discussion, being conceptually built on what had gone before.

If you are using the handbook in the manner it was intended—as a personal guidebook to provide guidance as you work your way through an action research project—it likely means that there could be several days, weeks, or sometimes even months between the reading of chapters. For this reason, most chapters start with a brief review of previous material to provide continuity.

A WORD ABOUT COLLABORATION

Increasingly, it is expected that our schools will be collaborative workplaces marked by school improvement initiatives driven by collegial teams. More and more schools now describe themselves as professional learning communities. This is a significant change. It wasn't that many years ago that Roland Barth (1980) referred to the typical elementary school as a string of one-room schoolhouses connected by a corridor. It is now far more common to see groups of teachers collaborating as a grade level or through vertical teaming in an effort to discover answers to perplexing issues of practice.

The Action Research Guidebook: A Process for Pursuing Equity and Excellence in Education, third edition, is premised on a belief that all readers (in fact all educators) share the same ultimate vision: fostering universal student success. It is unlikely that any of us will ever consider our work complete until every student is accomplishing everything he or she is capable of accomplishing. Realizing that vision will require attention to three categories of action: changes in our students' and our own *performance*, changes in the *processes* we utilize, and changes in the *programs* we offer. In this book, these three categories of action are called *performance targets*, *process targets*, and *program targets*. While it is possible for individual educators to utilize the action research process to succeed with projects focused on any of these areas, it is becoming increasingly the norm to find teams pursuing this work collaboratively. If you engage in action research collaboratively, you will experience several benefits. For starters, the product of multiple minds is inevitably better than one. Therefore, the very act of including more people and more perspectives in a study will make it more likely that the study will be insightful and robust.

Another benefit of working as a team is that it reduces professional isolation. Some years ago, a long-term study was funded with the goal of tracking a cohort of new teachers as they progressed through their careers (Schlecty & Vance, 1983). The subjects in this study were the most academically able graduates of a prestigious university. These were young people who had an academic pedigree that would have enabled them to pursue any career they chose. They could easily have been accepted into law school, medical school, business school, or engineering. But this group was so motivated by a desire to help young people that they chose a career in education. Sadly, the study was brought to a premature halt because after a few years, virtually every one of these young people had left teaching. Why did this happen? When the researchers checked, they found out it had nothing to do with the remuneration teachers receive, and they found these young people were as concerned about students and their learning as they had been when they entered the classroom. It was the day-to-day work of teaching that drove them away. But what aspect of the day-to-day work was so problematic for these talented young people? As it turned out, they didn't find the work to be boring, routine, or easy. Quite the opposite, they found classroom teaching to be incredibly challenging and complex. What caused them to leave teaching for easier work in other "more prestigious" professions was the loneliness and isolation of teaching. This group of bright and creative young people understood that the challenges faced routinely by classroom teachers are simply too intellectually and emotionally challenging to be solved by any one person working in isolation.

There are several ways you may choose to approach collaborative action research. However, it is strongly suggested that you begin by finding a method of collaboration that will work for you. The three most common forms of collaboration with educational action research are indicated by this continuum.

Type 1 Collaboration	Type 2 Collaboration	Type 3 Collaboration
Same four-stage process	Same four-stage process	Same four-stage process
Same focus	Same focus	Different foci
Same questions	Same questions	Different questions
Same theory of action	Different theories of action	Different theories of action
Same methods	Same methods	Different methods

Type 1 collaboration is where the researchers are conducting their action research as a unified team. The team shares the same theory of action and research questions, collects the same data, analyzes those data as a group, and produces a single report. An example might be a team of teachers at the same grade level investigating the impact of a new textbook adoption on student concept acquisition.

Type 2 collaboration is where the researchers share an interest in pursuing answers to the same question. For example, they might all be members of a language arts department trying to improve student voice in persuasive writing. Type 2 collaboration is a very common approach for teachers who are working together in a professional learning community. What makes Type 2 different from Type 1 is that in this case, while the members of the team are pursuing the same goal (enhanced voice), it is assumed that they hold different perspectives on the best way to accomplish their shared goal. Therefore, while they share the same vision and will use the same criteria and data sources to measure students' success, they likely will be attempting fundamentally different interventions. Elsewhere (Sagor, 2010), this was referred to as the *competing pilot projects model*. The wonderful thing about Type 2 collaboration is that colleagues are empowered to be creative in their pursuit of common goals, yet everyone is still able to learn from their teammates' unique experiences.

Type 3 collaboration operates much like an action research support group. Each participant is involved in a project of personal passionate concern. In all likelihood, he or she is the only one in the building pursuing action research on that particular topic. There is no question that one will find it invigorating and exciting to pursue an investigation into a project that they deeply care about. However, it can also be very lonely doing a project and having no one to discuss your ideas with. Finding a group of colleagues (perhaps classmates in a graduate class or colleagues working in different departments or at different grade levels) to meet with on a biweekly basis for the sole purpose of sharing what you are doing and what you are learning can prove incredibly reinforcing.

EDUCATIONAL LEADERSHIP

Opportunities for teacher leadership are expanding at an incredible rate (Reeves, 2008). Initiatives that once were routinely created and directed solely by administrators are now frequently collaborative ventures or even entirely managed by teacher leaders. In the revisions for this edition, we have attempted to provide examples of work at each of the four stages, with implementation techniques (where relevant) for both classroom teachers and school leaders. The reader will notice that the terms we are using are *leader* or *school leadership,* not school administrator. This choice in language was quite deliberate. Hopefully, the school administrators reading this book will find the leadership examples helpful and relevant to the action research they will be conducting on their administrative work. In fact, two of the cases that will be followed throughout the book are projects conducted by principals: Mr. Johnson, who is studying his leadership of the schoolwide effort improve the quantity, quality, and equity of student engagement, and Dr. Hernandez, who is studying her efforts to build a more collegial school. Mr. Johnson's and Dr. Hernandez's examples weren't included just for the administrators who might be reading this book. We believe that people serving on collaborative school leadership teams (made up of administrators and teachers), as well as teacher leaders, will find these same strategies particularly helpful when they are pursuing process or program targets.

In an effort to accommodate the diversity of our readers while we work our way through the four-stage process, we will draw our discussions, examples, and procedures from both classroom and leadership projects. Where necessary to maintain the flow of the text and/or maintain continuity and especially where there was only space for a single example, the default example will be a classroom application of the concept. However, when this needed to occur, we tried to follow the classroom example with a boxed comment explaining a leadership application and/or with supporting materials in Resource C. In Resource D, you will find a complete but abbreviated set of action research projects.

THE NEED FOR CREATIVE PROBLEM SOLVERS

While there may be increased acceptance of standards, professional educators are rightfully wary of standardization. We applaud this resistance to a one-size-fits-all approach to instruction. Sadly, there are still some policy makers who continue to argue for mandating all instructional and educational practices. As a school improvement strategy, educators are frequently told to implement "scientifically proven practices" and do so with "fidelity." Sadly, that approach is built on a myth—the myth being that one approach has ever or could ever be proven to work effectively for every student and every teacher in every classroom and every school. To understand the relevance of this issue, we find it helpful to use an analogy.

In all modern societies, there are legally binding construction standards. For purposes of safety and consumer protection, it is understood that all buildings, bridges, and infrastructures be built to withstand unforeseen threats, such as fires, floods, and earthquakes. Yet no one would ever suggest that there is only one appropriate design for each category of building or bridge. Not only would such a position produce an aesthetically appalling result, but it would result in the construction of many inappropriate projects. This is why our society needs architects. An architect is a professional who understands building standards and knows how to determine if a design meets those standards. But that's not all. More importantly, the architect is capable of creatively and artistically adapting everything that is known about civil engineering to the uniqueness of the site and the needs of the client.

We have begun thinking of the professional educator as an educational architect. While technical drawing is the major tool for the architect, action research is the essential tool for the educational architect. Our goal is to creatively design classroom interventions and school programs that will enable our students to demonstrate proficiency with standards. But just as with our peers in the construction business, that will take more than knowledge of the standards and how to assess them. This challenge calls for all of our creative insights in adapting what we have learned about the principles of teaching and learning to the unique characteristics of our current students, our classes, and our schools.

This book was written to serve as a guide for the next generation of educational architects. More than anything, we believe that the practice of education is a thoughtful and creative endeavor. The tool of action research is a flexible and pliable tool used toward that end. There is no one approach for engaging in this process; hence, this book is organized around the following four stages:

1. Clarifying vision and targets

2. Articulating theory

3. Implementing action and collecting data

4. Reflecting on data and planning informed action

Our principal reason for using this organizational strategy was to create a handbook that would provide a busy educator with an easy-to-follow template yet one that could be readily adapted to a variety of professional interests and foci. We hope we succeeded in accomplishing that goal.

TWO CATEGORIES OF ACTION RESEARCH

There are two principal categories of action research: *descriptive research*—studies whose purpose is to illuminate what is occurring in a particular setting—and *quasi-experimental research*—inquiries designed to test a hypothesis or examine a chosen innovation being implemented by the practitioner. This is another case where our goal was to be inclusive. We attempted to address both types of action research, as much as space permitted.

Considering all of the pressure today's educators face, it would be nice if one could call a time-out in order to get a definitive answer to each of her or his perplexing problems. But since that isn't possible, educators are frequently obliged to simply go with what seems best. As a result, when most educators first engage in action research, their goal is to determine if the actions they have decided to take (their hypotheses) are working as they had hoped, which explains why most action research ends up being quasi-experimental. For this reason, we will introduce each topic in terms of how it applies to quasi-experimental research and then follow that with examples of how this concept can be used with descriptive research, should the process be different.

Hopefully, conducting action research will help you better understand the efficacy of your practice as you document the impact of your work on the variety of learners with whom you work. Every day, you receive feedback through the dynamic relationship of teacher and learner, and that feedback fuels growth.

We, too, have a need to grow professionally and would very much appreciate your feedback on the effectiveness of this handbook. While writing it, we imagined ourselves interacting with each of you in a workshop setting. Now, as you explore the ideas in this book, we would love to know your reactions and hear about your experiences. Please write and share your ideas, your research, and your wisdom.

In closing, we want to extend to each of you our very best wishes. We hope you find action research to be as enriching as we have. We hope this book proves helpful as you explore and enrich your work and endeavor to enrich the lives of those you work with. But most of all, we hope your work provides you every ounce of joy, fulfillment, and satisfaction that is humanly possible. As you do your good work empowering the young, you enrich us all.

Publisher's Acknowledgments

Corwin gratefully acknowledges the contributions of the following reviewers:

Christopher J. Maglio
Professor of Education, Research Methods and Design
Truman State University
Kirksville, MO

Frankie Rabon
Certified Family Life Educator
Grambling State University
Bossier City, LA

Diane Smith
School Counselor
Smethport Area School District
Smethport, PA

Carter A. Winkle
Assistant Professor
Barry University (Adrian Dominican School of Education)
Miami Shores, FL

About the Authors

Richard D. Sagor recently retired from his position as professor and director of the Educational Leadership Program at Lewis & Clark College. In 1997, he founded ISIE (pronounced "I see"), the Institute for the Study of Inquiry in Education, to work with schools and educational organizations on the use of action research and data-based school improvement while he was a professor of educational leadership at Washington State University.

Prior to his work at the university level, Sagor had fourteen years of public school administrative experience, including service as an assistant superintendent, high school principal, instruction vice principal, disciplinary vice principal, and alternative school head teacher. He has taught the entire range of students, from the gifted to the learning disabled, in the areas of social studies, reading, and written composition.

Educated in the public schools of New York, Sagor received his BA from New York University and two MA degrees and a PhD in curriculum and instruction from the University of Oregon.

Beyond his work as a teacher and administrator, Dr. Sagor has had extensive international consulting experience. He served as a site visitor for the U.S. Department of Education's Secondary School Recognition Program and has worked with the Department of Defense's overseas schools, numerous state departments of education, as well as with over two hundred separate school districts across North America. His consulting has focused primarily on leadership development, the use of data with standards-based school improvement, collaborative action research, teacher motivation, and teaching at-risk youth.

His articles on school reform and action research have received awards from the National Association of Secondary School Principals and the Educational Press Association of America. Sagor's books include *The TQE Principal: A Transformed Leader; At-Risk Students: Reaching and Teaching Them; How To Conduct Collaborative Action Research; Local Control and Accountability: How to Get It, Keep It, and Improve School Performance; Guiding School Improvement With Action Research; Motivating Students and Teachers in an Era of Standards;* and *Collaborative Action Research for Professional Learning Communities.*

Dr. Sagor can be contacted at the Institute for the Study of Inquiry in Education, 16420 SE McGillivray, Suite 103–239, Vancouver, WA 98683, or by e-mail at rdsagor@isie.org.

xxii The Action Research Guidebook

Charlene Williams has more than twenty years of experience in education including multiple leadership roles in both public and private K–12 educational settings, as well as in higher education.

In recent years, her work has been focused on training and supporting teachers and school leaders in inquiry-based, culturally responsive strategies. She has lectured at several colleges and universities on topics ranging from mathematics: a social justice issue to transformational leadership.

Dr. Williams was recently appointed Assistant Superintendent for Educational Services of the Camas (WA) School District. Prior to assuming that position she worked in the Portland (OR) School District as Senior Director, Office of School Performance, where one of her most significant responsibilities was providing supervision and instructional leadership for a nine-school region from elementary to high school. In this capacity, Williams led school leaders and teachers in the use of the inquiry, data, and the action research process.

As a member of the district teacher evaluation team, Dr. Williams collaborated with classroom teachers and school leaders to create an innovative and culturally responsive teacher evaluation tool. She continues to build on this work, constantly exploring additional ways to embed culturally responsive inquiry into educator practice.

For many years Williams's professional focus has been developing and expanding the use of culturally responsive education. Her doctoral dissertation, *On me: How African American male students in an urban setting describe high teacher expectations*, combined her commitment to inquiry with her passion for culturally responsive teaching.

Her calling to the field of education is to ensure that all children, regardless of gender, ethnicity, or past educational experience, have the requisite skills to advance successfully along the education continuum and realize their highest aspirations. She is passionate about working with students who have not been successful in school and empowering their teachers with the tools, support, and motivation needed to make a significant, measurable difference.

Dr. Williams can be contacted at the Camas School District #117, Camas, WA, 98607, or by e-mail at Charlene.Williams@camas.wednet.edu or charlenedvw@hotmail.com .

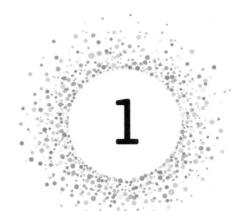

Introduction to Action Research

Action research: "A disciplined process of inquiry conducted by and for those taking the action. The primary reason for engaging in action research is to assist the actor in improving or refining his or her actions."

—Sagor (2000)

WHY CONDUCT ACTION RESEARCH?

Listening to politicians and policy makers, one might conclude that the consumers of education—parents, students, and their future employers—are those most passionate about school improvement. While the general public is clearly interested in school reform, no group of people are more emotional and passionate about promoting universal student success than classroom teachers. Most days, even the most celebrated teachers, who are teaching the highest-achieving students, leave their classrooms frustrated, feeling that despite their best efforts, each individual student didn't progress as far as he or she might. The ritual is replayed on a regular basis; exhausted teachers drive home every day wondering why things hadn't gone better and then hoping against hope that tomorrow will be a better day.

Let's begin by unpacking the concept of universal student success. The examples contained in this edition of *The Action Research Guidebook* were chosen to illuminate the challenges and opportunities today's educators face with a workforce that is largely drawn from the majority culture while the student body is rapidly getting more diverse racially, ethnically, and by educational need. Whatever instructional approach you ultimately choose to implement to assist your students, we want these pages to provide a real-time lens through which you can examine the alignment of your intent with its actual impact on your students. As pedagogy and policies adjust to meet the needs of twenty-first-century citizens, action research will offer an opportunity for you and your colleagues to examine which approaches are really working and for whom.

We've yet to meet the teacher who didn't enter the profession with a commitment to helping every one of his or her students prosper. Andy Hargreaves (1991) has insightfully pointed out that the greatest emotional turmoil faced by contemporary public school teachers is guilt. This guilt grows from an acceptance of the reality that they seem unable to generate the level of student success they desire. It is clear to anyone familiar with today's schools that this guilt syndrome, the debilitating experience of continually falling short of your own high expectations, isn't the result of a lack of commitment, caring, or intellect.

Several things conspire to keep educators in this chronic state of feeling that they are coming up short. One is the high expectations held by teachers, parents, and society. There is no question that the higher the bar, the greater the pressure. But no one who cares about youth would want the bar lowered. Nevertheless, while we pursue high expectations, we should acknowledge that the goal of universal student success, a dream held by most dedicated educators and an expectation now codified through state and federal regulations, has never been realized on a large scale. To our knowledge, in the history of humankind, no community has ever succeeded in getting *all* its children to high levels of performance on meaningful standards. However, that is our dream as well as the expectation of many other educators committed to equitable education. What this means for educators pursuing the simultaneous goals of equity and excellence is not only that we are pursuing lofty goals but that we are pushing ourselves to travel where no one has ever traveled before. For this reason, it isn't surprising that so many of our colleagues feel they have been abandoned in the wilderness without a guidebook, a map, or a recipe.

Besides having to deliver on their own and society's high expectations, there are three other significant factors that we believe contribute to chronic educator frustration:

- The complexity of teaching and learning
- The manner in which teacher work is organized
- The increasing diversity of student needs

The good news is that we can address all three of these factors while simultaneously pursuing the goal of universal student success.

THE COMPLEXITY OF ROUTINE INSTRUCTIONAL DECISIONS

Any problem we confront—be it personal, social, or scientific—can be expressed in the form of a mathematical equation. Arriving at a thoughtful solution requires considering all potential possibilities and probabilities. Every variable (factor) involved in the decision needs to be considered in light of (and multiplied by) each of the other variables. This is true for simple as well as complex problems. For example, even when dealing with something routine, such as deciding the best outfit to wear to work on Thursday, once we review the decision-making equation, we can easily see its complexity. The equation for choosing an outfit for Thursday might be illustrated as follows:

$$(A) \times (B) \times (C) \times (D) \times (E) = X$$

A = Shirt choices

B = Pants choices

C = Jacket/sweater choices

D = Sock choices

E = Shoe choices

The more complex problem, confronted at least twelve times per day by the typical elementary teacher and minimally five times daily by the typical secondary teacher, is determining the most appropriate answer to the question, What is the best strategy for teaching this content to this particular group of learners?

Coming up with a viable answer to that question requires the teacher's consideration of a multitude of variables. To illustrate, let's assume we are middle school math teachers preparing a lesson where we will be introducing the concept of signed numbers. The set of variables we must take into account begin with the relevant student affective factors. For example, we will need to consider how each one of the students feels about the teacher, about math, about himself as a math learner, about his peers in the class, and so forth. Then, we will need to multiply these variables by thirty (or the number of students in the class), since the goal is meeting each student's individual needs. If this sounds complex, just wait; this is only the beginning.

Of course, we must also take into account the unique cognitive characteristics of each learner. For example, what prerequisite skills does the student possess, or what skills is the student missing? Where is this student developmentally? What are her strongest learning styles? And what cultural and conceptual understandings is she bringing to the learning of this particular math concept?

That's a lot to take into account, but simply knowing the affective and cognitive characteristics of each one of our students is only one aspect of the equation. Because even if we understand each student perfectly, that still won't be enough to inform us on how we should teach the class. There are at least two other sets of factors that must be considered by a teacher when designing a lesson. As professionals, we will minimally want to consider the knowledge base on culturally responsive teaching and middle school pedagogy (methods of teaching) so we can choose the most appropriate strategy for our students. For example, we could elect to teach this particular content using direct instruction. Alternatively, we could use individually guided instruction, cooperative learning, demonstrations/ modeling, and so on. As complex as all this is, just considering these affective, cognitive, and pedagogical factors still won't be enough to solve this equation. For meaningful learning to occur, our lesson plans will need to be grounded in a thoughtful understanding of the discipline itself. Specifically, why are we teaching this particular piece of content (in this case, signed numbers)? How does this concept fit with the previously taught content, and how will it relate to the upcoming material? What are the specific skills we want our students to gain from the study of this material?

Without belaboring the statistical aspect of this decision-making equation, it should now be clear that each and every lesson-planning decision made by a professional educator requires the consideration and integration of hundreds of factors. In reality, the design of an appropriate lesson for a diverse class of public school students is one of the most complex tasks any contemporary professional might ever be asked to tackle alone.

The Way Teacher Work Is Organized

But the complexity of the decision making is only one part of the problem. After all, in many fields, being expected to creatively solve complex problems is not a source of frustration or dissatisfaction. In fact, for many professionals, active engagement in the problem-solving process is the very thing that makes their work fun and motivating. Even as complex as teaching is, we aren't the only practitioners that are expected to grapple with perplexing, mind-numbing problems on a daily basis. So why does the complexity of designing innovative solutions to persistent problems of student learning prove more frustrating for educators than for professionals in other fields?

To answer that question, we need to take a look at the second problematic issue: the work context for most teachers. Even when the issues that a professional must overcome are complex, if the working conditions are such that the practitioner believes she has a reasonable chance of prevailing, there will be justification for optimism. Unfortunately, the reverse is also true: If the conditions of the work are such that it is unreasonable for a practitioner to expect success, then pessimism, alienation, and burnout are to be expected.

In other fields where practitioners are expected to prevail over unique and complex problems, two types of assistance are usually provided: adequate planning time and a support staff. Unfortunately, most classroom teachers aren't provided this type of assistance. Typically, classroom teachers work in isolation and are provided with minimal planning time. These are critical working-condition issues that will need to be addressed. Hopefully, one day we will develop the political will to provide these resources for all classroom teachers. Realistically, however, this isn't likely to occur in the immediate future. On the positive side, there are things that can be done to address the conditions of work in the short run. This is where this book fits in.

Action research is a small idea. It involves examining data on one's work to help improve one's performance. Although there isn't consensus on a single set of processes or steps that constitute action research, as presented here, action research is a straightforward four-stage process. The four stages of the action research process are as follows:

1. Clarifying vision and targets
2. Articulating theory
3. Implementing action and collecting data
4. Reflecting on data and planning informed action

These four stages help bring to the surface the critical knowledge and insights needed to improve our practice and move us ever closer to the goal of universal student success. As with many simple ideas, the ramifications can be huge. The greatest virtue of action research is its potential for radically transforming some of the most critical working conditions of the classroom teacher, specifically those conditions that, when left unaddressed, have been shown to frustrate and burn out the best and brightest. The cultural norms and organizational practices that support professional inquiry have an impact on student performance (Reeves, 2010). In schools where the ethic of action research has been institutionalized, teachers routinely experience success, as demonstrated by continually improving levels of student performance and a reduction in achievement and opportunity gaps (Hattie, 2008; Little, 1982; Rosenholtz, 1989). Better yet, in these settings, teachers find their work becomes more satisfying, more energizing, and less guilt producing (Nir & Bogler, 2008).

In the chapters that follow, we will explore numerous strategies used by teachers and school leaders as they work though the four stages of the action research process. As you read through this text, you will encounter specific examples of teachers working through each of the four stages and have an opportunity to examine the strategies they are using. Each example will be followed by step-by-step instructions and sample materials for you to use or adapt for use with your own action research. As we wind our way through the four-stage process, we will continue to return to the issues of teacher working conditions (complexity of the challenges, limits on time and support, etc.) and discuss how incorporating the habits of action research into your work might help you improve the conditions of your own work.

The Increasing Diversity of Student Needs

It is clear that America has been and continues to evolve demographically. According to the U.S. Census, "By around 2020 more than half the nation's school children are expected to be part of a minority race or ethnic group" (U.S. Census Bureau, 2015). The fact that our schools and classrooms are increasingly populated with children from a myriad of backgrounds provides us with great opportunities. The mosaic of cultures that make up our classrooms has the potential to enrich the education of all our students. Being educated in a diverse community should enhance any young person's appreciation of art and culture; it will help them improve their ability to understand, empathize, and problem solve. And lastly, it will provide them with preparation and appreciation for living in a global society. But change in the racial and cultural composition of our schools is not the only area where we are seeing increased diversity. Like us, most educators welcome the move for greater heterogeneity in our classrooms. We enjoy having boys and girls learning together, and nearly everyone is in agreement that the movement to educate all young people with physical and/or learning challenges with their peers in the mainstream has provided benefits for everyone concerned.

Having schools and classrooms enriched by diversity is full of plusses for our students. Yet this same diversity presents challenges for educators. It requires us to question some of our long-held (and too often unchallenged) assumptions about how teaching and learning should be organized.

The most powerful of these "constraining myths" is what Richard calls "the myth of homogeneity" (Sagor & Rickey, 2012). The myth of homogeneity is predicated on the assumption that the prime organizing unit for schooling is the class rather than the individual student. Consequently, we attempt to make our schools large enough so that building administrators are able to create classes of students who are so alike in their learning needs that all a teacher will need to do is design and teach a lesson that is appropriate for that class. This seems so efficient. For example, all a fourth-grade teacher needs to do is teach the fourth-grade curriculum. The assumption being that all of her students will have already mastered the third-grade material, and they now need the skills she plans on teaching (i.e., what's contained in the fourth-grade curriculum). Yes, on the surface, it sounds rational and efficient. But as soon as teachers begin conducting action research in their classrooms and examining individual student data, they discover that all the fourth graders aren't alike, regardless of how well the administration may have crafted the classroom assignments. Even in the largest schools with the most sophisticated student assignment systems, teachers find they have children who still aren't proficient with the skills taught in third grade sitting next to others who may be ready to tackle some of the challenges that normally aren't even introduced until sixth grade.

When teachers begin collecting data from students on their students' classroom experiences and looking for patterns in those data, the myth of homogeneity is shattered, and there is no going back. Seeing your classroom as a collection of unique individual learners and not as a single unit creates a paradigm shift that can make teaching both more rewarding and more challenging. As we work our way through the four-step action research process, we will explore strategies that will help you respond to the particular learning needs of each of your students and empower them to make the most of their experience in your class. You will become better at personalizing your instruction, and as a result, students will feel better about themselves and more at home in your classroom.

KEY TERMS AND CONCEPTS

Action Research

At the start of this chapter, we offered a definition of action research that said action research was any investigation conducted *by the person or the people empowered to take action concerning their own actions, for the purpose of improving their future actions.* At this point, it would be helpful to expand on that definition so that we can clearly distinguish *action* research from other forms of scientific or educational research. The best way to decide if an inquiry qualifies as action research is to ask three questions regarding the proposed study. If the answer to all three questions is "yes," then the inquiry justifiably fits under an action research umbrella. If the answer to any of the questions is "no," then while it might be an area worth investigating, action research probably isn't the appropriate approach. The questions are as follows:

1. Is the Focus on Your Professional Action?

If you are studying your own work, then the answer to this question is clearly "yes." In addition, if you are studying an issue that you are considering making part of your work in the future, then the answer can also be "yes." According to Kemmis and McTaggart (1988), there are three types of action that can legitimately serve as foci for action research:

Research of Action (Past Action): In this case, the action being studied has been completed (such as an evaluation study).

Research in Action (Present Action): In this case, the action is underway (as in a monitoring study).

Research for Action (Future Action): In this case, the action will occur in the near future (for example, evaluating materials being considered for adoption).

2. Are You Empowered to Adjust Future Action Based on the Results?

This question pertains to your sphere of influence. Most teachers are free to adjust their instructional strategies as they deem appropriate. Therefore, a proposed investigation into a new instructional strategy probably merits a "yes" to this question. This is because most teacher-researchers are free to adjust their teaching based on the data they collect in their classroom. Likewise, the members of a school's improvement team who were tasked with investigating a schoolwide issue and have been empowered to propose changes for implementation in their building could answer this question with a "yes." If, however, you have reason to believe that circumstances will prevent you from implementing changes, regardless of the quality and quantity of the data you amass, then you will have to answer "no" to this question.

3. Is Improvement Possible?

Although we all know that research for its own sake is a worthy pursuit, the only justification for practicing K–12 educators to invest their finite time in research is if their particular inquiry holds promise for increasing the success of their teaching or the learning in their schools. If you hold serious doubts that performance can be improved in a particular area, then you would be wise to avoid action research concerning it. If you are reading this text, it is highly likely you are an educator in pursuit of universal student success who believes improvement for every child is possible.

To recap, an investigation qualifies as action research if it pertains to one's professional action, focuses on an aspect of one's work where one can exert a significant degree of control, and thoughtfully focuses on a performance where (with enough information) improvement could be expected to occur.

The Four Stages

As you pursue the action research process through its four sequential stages, you will find that each stage is designed to help you answer a key question.

Stage 1: Clarifying Vision and Targets

Key Question: What do I want to accomplish?

In Stage 1, action researchers clearly enunciate their goals, clarify each of the subskills or attributes that contribute to success for that goal, and identify specific criteria that can be used with validity and reliability to document changes in performance on that goal. Ways to accomplish the tasks of Stage 1 and answer its question are the focus of Chapters 2 and 3.

Stage 2: Articulating Theory

Key Question: What approach do I believe has the greatest potential for helping me to realize my goal(s)?

In this stage, the action researcher articulates a detailed rationale for proceeding in a particular fashion. Earlier, we talked about the many factors that need to be considered when making a lesson-planning decision. When there is no proven best way to accomplish a goal, professionals may elect to pursue alternative strategies that seem theoretically sound. It is in Stage 2 when the action researcher is engaged in a thoughtful, deliberative planning process—one that has him or her examining and incorporating all of the dynamic relationships and interactions he or she believes might exist between the relevant factors that influence success on the performance targets identified in Stage 1. We will work through several strategies designed to help you identify and articulate your theory of action and answer Stage 2's key question in Chapters 4 and 5.

Stage 3: Implementing Action and Collecting Data

Key Question: What data will I need to collect if I am to understand the effectiveness of my theory of action?

This is the portion of the action research process that takes place as we are doing our work—that is, while we are taking our professional action. It is here that we carry through on our theory of action while systematically compiling information (data) that will help us understand what is going on, both above and below the surface. It is at this stage where we determine what has been accomplished and the relationship between the actions we've taken and the results obtained. Our work on Stage 3 will begin in Chapter 6, where you will learn how to generate a set of research questions to guide your study. Then, in Chapter 7, you will develop a viable data collection plan designed to produce valid and reliable answers for your research questions.

Stage 4: Reflecting on the Data and Planning Informed Action

Key Question: Based on these data, how should I adjust my future actions (teaching)?

Stage 4 is where you complete your first lap around the action research cycle. It is here that action researchers are invited to return and revisit their original visions or targets (Stage 1), as well as their theories or best thinking on how to realize that vision (Stage 2). Then, based on data regarding the impact of specific actions (Stage 3) and an analysis of those data, action researchers can produce a revised theory of action, which will then become

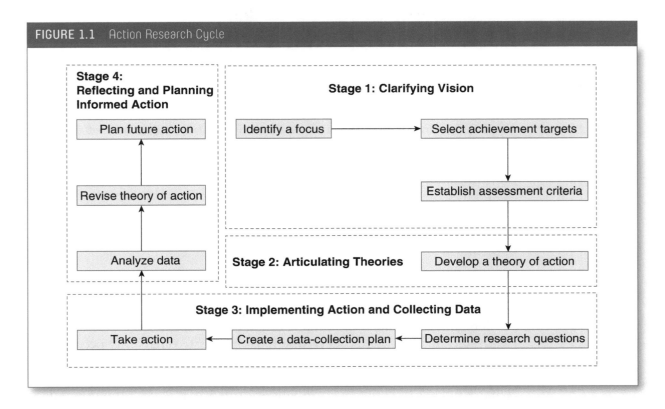

FIGURE 1.1   Action Research Cycle

the basis for their future action. Figure 1.1 illustrates the cyclical nature of the work accomplished through the four stages.

The Two Categories of Action Research

Action research, like most types of inquiry, is generally undertaken for one of two fundamental purposes:

1. To determine what is currently occurring or

2. To test a hypothesis (theory)

When researchers seek to understand what is occurring, they are engaging in what is called *descriptive research*. When the research is primarily concerned with testing a hypothesis, the inquiry is called *quasi-experimental research*. (The qualifier *quasi* is used here because in the social sciences, it is both ethically and practically impossible to implement a classic experimental design, since that would require a control group. Consequently, research that seeks to test a hypothesis without a control group is defined as quasi-experimental.)

Quasi-Experimental Research

As teachers, we are frequently involved in quasi-experimental research, although most of us haven't been in the habit of documenting our studies. Every day, teachers make use of the best approaches they know. Yet it is the very rare day when all of the students in a class accomplish everything they possibly could. More often than not, when we reflect on why a student or group of students hasn't succeeded, it triggers some creative thinking. We find ourselves asking, "What if . . . ?" When we are pondering the what-ifs, we are considering ideas or hypotheses that we might investigate. If we decide to attempt something new, we are saying that we believe this approach is likely to produce more superior outcomes than had been obtained before. When you decide to focus on the use of a new or modified approach, your research becomes a quasi-experimental study of the adequacy of that approach or, what is called in this text, your *theory of action*. Because of the dynamic and ever-changing nature of teaching, it shouldn't be surprising that this is the most common form of action research undertaken in schools.

Descriptive Research

There are many times when we find ourselves concerned about something occurring in our classrooms, with our kids, or in our schools. We know that we want to do something about the problem, but we don't feel we currently understand the issue in the context of our school or classroom well enough to design an effective strategy for improvement. When this occurs, our long-term goal is no different than that of educators who have decided to conduct quasi-experimental research. In both cases, the desire is to learn what we need to know to improve performance; it is only the immediate focus that is different. While the lens of the quasi-experimental researcher is trained on the efficacy of a particular approach (the theory of action) and its impact, the lens of the descriptive researcher is on the system or approach that is currently in place (the *operative* theory of action) and trying to understand its workings. Whatever the focus of your study, be it your theory or the operative theory, at Stage 4, all action researchers end up doing the same thing: They produce a plan for future action based on valid and reliable data regarding what has transpired. Figure 1.2 contrasts these two types of research across the four stages of the action research process.

It is worth noting that these two categories of research (quasi-experimental and descriptive) are not mutually exclusive. Frequently, they will even occur simultaneously.

In Chapters 7 and 8, we will explore an example of action research being conducted by a middle school principal in an urban school district in the Pacific Northwest, Mr. Johnson. He is implementing a theory of his own design. His theory of action involves, among other things, providing professional development for teachers on the use of specific strategies to increase overall student engagement, especially the engagement of males of color. The major thrust of his study will be quasi-experimental, as he wants to understand if and how his theory of action has succeeded in furthering the goal of increased student engagement across all categories of students. But at the same time, he will be conducting a second study within a study. This is because he is particularly concerned about the overrepresentation of students of color in disciplinary referrals. His two studies are related because he suspects that the increased disciplinary referrals result from an overall passive culture that has become pervasive in the school's classrooms and that results in significant disengagement of students of color.

FIGURE 1.2	Comparison of Four-Stage Action Research Process Between Quasi-Experimental and Descriptive Research	
Stage	**Quasi-Experimental Research**	**Descriptive Research**
1: Clarifying vision and targets	The researchers draw clear and robust pictures of the desired outcomes. An attempt is made to visualize and imagine success in as much detail as possible.	Same as quasi-experimental
	The researchers identify the subcomponents of their vision. For each critical component, they decide on criteria to assess changes occurring with that component.	
2: Articulating theory	The researchers consider their own experience as well as the experience of others attempting to realize the vision and its components.	The researchers consider their own experience as well as the experience of others attempting to realize the vision and its components.
	Based on this examination, the researchers develop a new theory of action that involves a modification of past practice and holds promise for improving performance.	After reflecting on personal experience and the experience of others, the researchers conclude that more information (on what is occurring and how things are working) would be helpful.
	The new theory of action becomes the focus of study.	The researchers clarify the operative theory of action (what is now being done), which becomes the focus of their study.
3: Implementing action, collecting data	The researchers examine the new theory of action and determine a set of questions that they need or want to have answered.	The researchers examine the operative theory of action, looking for aspects of the theory (strategies, materials, outcomes, and so on) whose effects need to be better understood.
	The researchers develop a viable plan for collecting the necessary data.	The researchers develop a viable plan for collecting the data needed to illuminate the implementation of the operative theory.
	The researchers implement the new theory of action and collect the data as outlined in their plan.	The researchers collect the data as indicated in their plan.
4: Reflecting on data, planning informed action	The researchers compile and summarize the data collected in Step 3 and generate a list of findings.	Same as quasi-experimental
	Using these findings, the researchers summarize any insights gained regarding the realization of the vision.	
	The researchers develop a revised theory of action, incorporating new and relevant insights.	
	The researchers make plans to implement the revised theory of action.	

In order to better understand this relationship, he will be examining the experience of a subgroup of students in three classrooms at the middle school. He hopes this descriptive action research study will help him and his faculty understand the range of experiences students of color tend to encounter within the school's instructional environment. Mr. Johnson's hope is that after gathering more data on these students' experiences, he will be better able to develop a theory of action on improving the level of engagement for all students, especially those students of color who now seem to be minimally engaged. Implementing the resulting theory of action should enable these students to achieve greater success at school. Testing that theory or other theories that emerge will then become the basis for quasi-experimental action research carried out by the faculty.

It should be noted that *descriptive* and *quasi-experimental* are not simply synonyms for *qualitative* and *quantitative* research. While qualitative research methods are used to paint a robust picture of a phenomenon, they are also frequently used by action researchers conducting quasi-experimental studies. For example, if we were trying to determine the success of a new reading program across a culturally diverse student body (a quasi-experimental study), we might well choose to use qualitative data drawn from student reading journals and observational notes to illuminate the phenomena under study. Likewise, a team conducting a descriptive study aimed at understanding the climate at their school might make use of a numerical survey in which students and teachers rate attributes of the school on a ten-point scale (a quantitative method). In reality, most action research studies end up making use of both qualitative and quantitative data collection methods.

UNIVERSAL STUDENT SUCCESS

As mentioned earlier, most teachers approach their work with very high expectations. The disparity we witness in opportunities and outcomes for various groups of students most often results from well-intentioned educators proceeding to action without a process for carefully examining and revising their practice. Most educators share the goal of having all students producing their very best work and becoming as skillful as possible. This is not unlike physicians approaching their work with the goal of curing *every* condition and helping *every* patient live a long and vigorous life.

Realistically, we may know that this can't and won't happen all at once. While there are numerous texts and training programs available to assist educators with shifting their paradigms related to the success of every child, action research provides a shift in practice that will accelerate the evolution of those paradigms. Rome wasn't built in a day, and all human illness will not be eradicated in one fell swoop. Likewise, figuring out how to assist all learners in realizing their potential will take some time. But as inquiring professionals, we want to be continuously advancing our wisdom on what will be required to realize a vision of universal success. In the next chapter, we begin working on Stage 1, where you will be asked to take stock of your personal vision of success. To accomplish this, you will articulate a picture of truly outstanding performance. That picture will be detailed enough to enable you to incrementally measure your success as you move ever closer to assisting each of your students in achieving proficiency. When we use the term *universal student success*, that is precisely what we mean. It is that promised land that we are constantly striving for, that wondrous time and place where all of us educators are in possession of all that we need to know to maximize the learning of all of our students.

With this as our goal, it is likely that our collective search for answers to the perplexing problems of teaching, learning, and school organization will keep us occupied for the rest of our careers. However, as long as we are purposefully engaged in the action research process and continue to learn our way forward along the road to universal student success, we can anticipate a career of repeated celebrations, times when we can stop and collectively acknowledge each and every breakthrough we are making along the way to the promised land.

2

Finding a Focus

Every educator and any parent with his or her eyes open can see how demanding teaching has become. There simply aren't enough hours in the day for teachers to accomplish all the things on their plates, much less attend to their families, their mental health, and the everyday chores of modern life. But even with all that is required of them, teachers habitually volunteer to abuse themselves, put in countless hours, and burn an infinite number of calories attempting to improve performance in the areas they feel are a priority. Consider, for example, the time spent by English teachers responding to individual pieces of student work or the time coaches invest analyzing film and preparing game plans for the next contest. The reality is when educators have reason to believe that their efforts will result in a payoff in student performance, they willingly and excitedly invest whatever it takes to make success a reality.

Action research has been proven to be a productive strategy for improving teaching and learning (Brown & Macatangay, 2002; Fishman, Marx, Best, & Tal, 2003; Hord, 1997; Joyce & Calhoun, 1996). Furthermore, educators have found conducting action research to be both enjoyable and rewarding (Caro-Bruce & Zeichner, 1998). While this is most often the case, these positive outcomes aren't guaranteed.

ZEROING IN ON YOUR PRIORITIES

Research has demonstrated that the intellectual and affective benefits of action research correspond directly to the focus of the research conducted (Sagor & Curley, 1991). If a teacher's action research addresses an issue of significant personal and professional importance, then, invariably, the time invested in conducting the research will be considered time well spent. However, if the issue under investigation turns out to be peripheral to the priority concerns of the action researcher, even the smallest investment of energy will be resented. This is completely logical. With time in short supply, any time spent on one endeavor is time not available for other things. Therefore, encouraging educators to pursue anything they lack passion for is encouraging them to invest in frustration and guilt.

For this reason, the selection of a focus for one's action research is a step that should never be taken lightly. Prematurely rushing to a research focus may be the single worst thing a prospective action researcher can do. While there is no one best way to choose a focus for inquiry, there are a number of strategies that have proven helpful. We will explore a few of these approaches as we get started on *Stage 1: Clarifying the Vision and Targets* of the action research process.

The remainder of this chapter will be devoted to five specific strategies that have assisted educational action researchers in identifying high-priority, meaningful topics for study. The strategies we will explore are *reflective writing, journaling, reflective interviewing, analytic discourse,* and *team reflection*. It is suggested that you begin by reading through the entire chapter and then decide which of these approaches, which combination of approaches, or what approach of your own design would work best for you; then, use that process to narrow your focus before proceeding to Chapter 3.

USING REFLECTIVE WRITING TO FIND A FOCUS

Most educators find their daily to-do list is huge. The have-tos are often-times so numerous that they frequently crowd out the want-tos. Worse, the absence of time for meaningful reflection often results in busy educators losing touch with their own priority want-tos. Occasionally, it has been such a long time since educators have had the luxury of pausing and reflecting on what really matters to them that matters of professional passion can no longer even be found on their to-do lists.

If you are to enjoy your work as an action researcher, you will be well served to call a time-out at this point precisely so you can reconnect with your professional priorities. While most everyone agrees with the need for and value of reflection, the pace of school life leaves little opportunity to engage in purposeful reflection. We have found that to overcome this situation, we must find a way to temporarily shut out all other distractions and create a time and space for the quality reflection needed for zeroing in on a meaningful topic(s) for action research.

Creating a time and space for private thought is the primary virtue of the *reflective writing* process. The cognitive process of composing our thoughts and producing a written narrative necessarily consumes all of one's available intellectual energy (even if just for a few minutes), and consequently, it provides us with the concentration necessary for reflecting on a potential action research focus.

While no one questions the writing process as a marvelous way to become focused, it is frequently difficult to overcome writer's block and get started. Many teachers who have used the writing process with their students have found an effective way of helping someone overcome negative inertia is through the use of prewriting exercises. It is not uncommon for teachers to invest several class periods just helping their students get ready to write. This isn't just a problem for novice writers. Many professional authors spend days, weeks, or even months reflecting and mentally working over an issue before they feel ready to approach the keyboard.

Since it can be difficult to get started with reflective writing and since time is usually in short supply, it is a good idea to create boundaries prior to starting the process. Boundaries help with concentration and jump-start one's writing. An effective way to create boundaries for reflective writing is through the use of a prompt. Any prompt that helps you focus on your professional priorities will work.

The prompts that we've found most helpful are ones that have us engaged in an imaginary conversation with a significant other. We suspect there are several reasons why imagination and fantasy are so helpful in stimulating our reflections. The most important is that sometimes, especially when we might be feeling depressed or worn down, we find ourselves losing confidence. But as long as we're breathing, we will never lose our innate human capacity to dream. There is, however, another, more important reason why the use of imagination and fantasy may prove productive for an action researcher. When we free ourselves to imagine and dream, we are no longer limited by the constraints of what is realistic; instead, we get a chance to dwell, at least momentarily, on the fantastic.

One writing prompt that we have found particularly helpful is the following:

Writing Prompt

Imagine it is the close of this school year. The year that just concluded has been, without a doubt, the most satisfying of your entire career. It has been so good that you are actually feeling depressed that you won't get a chance to return to school for nearly three months! You leave school on that last day positively glowing. You are practically walking two feet off of the ground, feeling terrific about your work, about the profession you are a part of, and about the impact your work is having on your students.

Returning home, you find yourself talking on the phone with an old college friend. Your friend asks how the year went. You reply that it was unequivocally the best school year ever, exceeding even your wildest expectations! Your friend then asks, what specifically did you and/or your students do and what was accomplished that made this such a wonderful year?

What do you hear yourself saying in return?

Write your answer in as much detail as possible. Write in the same conversational voice you would likely use with a friend. (When we avoid professional language and jargon, most of us tend to become more creative, and our ideas tend to flow more easily.)

In this example we will hear from Jose, a hypothetical middle school teacher, working in a culturally diverse school. While Jose is not a real person, the thoughts, feelings, and frustrations expressed in his narrative are drawn directly from what Charlene recently heard and observed while conducting research on the experience of African American students in an urban district.

Prompt Response

I will begin by providing some background: Each year, for most of my career, I have entered the classroom believing this year will be the year I make the difference that I entered education to make. However, while I do see some improvement in my practice and student outcomes, my students are not performing nearly at the level I believe they can. I find myself battling the voices of colleagues playing in my head—"These students are behind before they enter the door," or, "There is only so much we can do." Or I wonder, How much can I do?

I want to believe that I can eliminate achievement disparity, at least in my classroom, but I am stumped as to how to do it. I have attended numerous training sessions on equity and diversity, yet I am hesitant and uncertain about how to implement and put in practice what I've learned. And I haven't known what to do. Sometimes, I felt like a hypocrite telling students they can do anything, when the truth was they couldn't! I no longer wanted to be a part of saying these things to them without qualification; I believe it is disingenuous and a setup because they world they will be entering is not fair. In our society, it takes more than hard work and good intentions, especially if you are not white and male. The students I have been most concerned about, mostly students of color, are not reading or writing at or near grade level and are performing well below most of their white peers. Their mathematics performance is often worse. The pressure of implementing the adopted curriculum and following the pacing guide has the effect of stifling practices I would have liked to try for fear of not covering the curriculum and being criticized by the administration. As a result, I have likely awarded inflated grades and justified them on account of effort because I know the students are trying hard. But in the end, I realize this is not reflective of their learning, nor is it what they deserve. Worse, my previous grading practices may have served to perpetuate or even exacerbate the gap. Since I had been investigating culturally responsive teaching techniques, I had encountered various schools of thought but was not certain where to start. Truly, I felt overwhelmed.

Last summer, not knowing what else to do, I attended training where the presenters encouraged us to use action research, along with the implementation of the best culturally relevant practices. The emphasis was on learning how we could know if what we were doing was working for the students we serve. I was inspired by the structure of the process and wanted to see if it could help me become more strategic and intentional with my teaching. To that end, I decided that this year, I would focus on providing higher-level questioning and ensuring equitable response opportunities for all of my students. The research I read said student descriptions and reports on their response opportunities in class frequently reflected the racial and gender bias (often unconscious) of their teacher. I took particular note of the finding that most males of color felt excluded from participation or reported that when the teacher called on them, they were asked embarrassingly low-level questions. Meanwhile, girls and white males were called on more frequently and asked more intellectually demanding questions. As I reflected on my past teaching, I could not be sure that I wasn't contributing to or reinforcing this same pattern with my students.

This year, I was determined to become skilled with culturally responsive strategies and practices. Specifically, I made a commitment that prior to each class, I would thoughtfully prepare questions and strategically choose discussion strategies

(Continued)

(Continued)

designed to increase engagement. Prior to each class, I envisioned who should be asked what question and the processes I could use to manage the flow of discussion. I then purposefully choose processes that would direct the flow of discussion in a manner that would ensure an equitable distribution of participation and access to challenging content. This planning process forced me to regularly consider each student's depth of knowledge of a given topic. I also realized I would need to establish a process for monitoring each individual student during classroom discussions to be sure that all the students felt included and challenged. Lastly, I decided I would hold frequent quick classroom meetings to assess how well my strategy was working and to be sure that all of the students felt heard and respected during our class discussions.

Well, after the first few weeks of school, my students were starting to warm up to active participation in class discussions. I began to see some patterns. For example, I noticed some students participated better when I posed questions through cold calling while others preferred advance warning and a chance to prepare. I also noticed that some males of color enjoyed the open debate style of banter while others shied away from such discussions. It was now time for my first class meeting and a chance to see how things were going from the student perspective.

In that meeting, the students shared their likes and dislikes, and I made adjustments based on their feedback. I am excited about the way they responded, and clearly, we are growing and learning together. My check-ins with the males of color in my class during individual conferences were particularly helpful in alerting me to the strategies that were not working for them. I am finding I am now more mindful of their needs. The best part is that I am seeing a pronounced increase in the frequency and depth of their responses to my questions.

This year was amazing. While I clearly made mistakes along the way, I learned from them, and I have high expectations for continued improvement next year thanks to my students, who are also my teachers. My focus on response opportunities has fostered higher-quality work with all of my students, and at least in my classroom, race and gender no longer predict student engagement or student success. And the best part is that I feel I'm becoming more effective by using culturally responsive practices in my classroom.

Notice that this teacher truly let his imagination flow. He didn't get bogged down in educational lingo or shorthand; instead, he simply fantasized what heaven might look and feel like for him. In his case, heaven was having a classroom with high engagement, where race and gender were no longer determinants of success. Later, you may want to try your hand with this same prompt. The Reflective Writing Worksheet (Figure 2.1) has been provided for your use when drafting your vision of the promised land.

Most state laws or district evaluation policies require educators to set goals at the start of each school year. While on the surface, these policies appear rational, rarely do they result in the development of meaningful goals that hold emotional significance for the authors. This often happens because the drafting of those goals occurs devoid of meaningful reflection. In all likelihood, the narrative you wrote (or will write) using Figure 2.1 will bring to the surface goals that matter more to you personally and professionally than the often perfunctory goals that you are required to generate as part of the evaluation process. Hopefully, your narrative

FIGURE 2.1   Reflective Writing Worksheet

Imagine it is the end of the next school year. The past year has been, without a doubt, the most satisfying of your entire career. You left school glowing with good feelings about your work, your profession, and about the impact your work is having on students.

A close friend has just asked you how your year went, and you reply that it was the best ever. When your friend asks you to share what specifically occurred that made you feel this way, what do you reply?

_____

_____

_____

_____

_____

_____

_____

_____

_____

_____

_____

_____

_____

_____

_____

_____

_____

_____

_____

_____

_____

_____

_____

_____

_____

_____

brought to life those things that *you* would really love to see accomplished. Jose's narrative certainly did. It contained a vision that, if realized, will undoubtedly make him a very happy and fulfilled educator.

While written narratives are helpful in illuminating an overall focus, they are often too general. One way to sharpen your focus and gain the precision that will be needed for your action research is to systematically dissect your reflective writing. This is done by looking at the big picture contained in the narrative (reflective writing) and then identifying the specific outcomes/accomplishments that contributed to the realization of the overall vision. From this point on, we will refer to these specific outcomes as your *priority achievement targets*. The range of potential achievement targets is quite broad. However, we have found that priority achievement targets inevitably fit into one of three categories:

1. Performance targets

2. Process targets

3. Program targets

Performance targets relate to what students are expected to gain from our actions. There are many synonyms for performance targets; sometimes, they are called content standards, essential learning, curriculum goals, and so on. A well-stated performance target can help us focus on what students should know and should be able to do and/or choose to do, and they may even cause us to look for changes in how students should feel if our instruction is successful. There are four major categories of performance targets:

1. *Cognitive:* What students know

2. *Demonstrative:* What students can do

3. *Behavioral:* What they choose to do

4. *Affective:* How they feel about themselves and the situation they are in

Process targets relate to techniques or strategies that we want to become part of our teaching or professional repertoire. While performance targets refer to what students can do (or will be able to do better), process targets focus on specific improvements that we would like to see in ourselves (such as our teaching skills, communication skills, and leadership skills). For example, we might want to improve our ability to conduct classroom discussions or become better at modeling problem-solving strategies.

Program targets focus on outcomes for an entire classroom or school as an organization. In many ways, program targets are similar to performance targets, but with program targets, we are primarily concerned with the impact on the group or the organization, as opposed to the impact on any one individual participant. For example, a program target might refer to the impact a new initiative will have on school climate, faculty morale, or parental involvement.

The Target Identification Form (Figure 2.2) is designed to help you identify your priority achievement targets through a review of your reflective narrative. Use this form to locate and synthesize the specific

---

FIGURE 2.2   Target Identification Form

Reread your reflective writing or your journal or review your interview, asking the following questions (write your responses under each one):

What specific accomplishments were made by the people whose work you are facilitating (such as taking greater personal responsibility, more precision in their writing, improved thinking skills)? These are *performance targets*.

_____

_____

_____

_____

_____

_____

_____

What specific changes did you observe in your teaching or leadership behavior (more use of project-based learning, improved questioning skills, more personalized instruction, more interactive faculty meetings)? These are *process targets.*

_____

_____

_____

_____

_____

_____

_____

What specific changes did you observe in your classroom or school (greater sense of community, higher levels of on-task behavior, less misbehavior)? These are *program targets.*

_____

_____

_____

_____

_____

_____

_____

_____

FIGURE 2.3 Jose's Priority Achievement Targets

- Improved scores for all students on assignments and assessments (performance target)
- Improvement in conceptual understanding of level of questioning in multiple contexts and formats (performance target)
- Increase in the quantity and quality of student responses to rigorous questions (performance target)
- Improved question and discussion techniques (process target)
- Effective tracking of response opportunities (process target)
- Development of the skills required for facilitating rather than directing learning (process target)
- Improved student participation, self-esteem, and attitude as a result of working response opportunities into the curriculum (program target)

---

targets (components or outcomes) that, when taken together, contributed to your imaginary most satisfying year. To illustrate, the priority achievement targets that contributed to Jose's "great year" are shown in Figure 2.3.

PERFORMANCE, PROCESS, AND PROGRAM TARGETS AND ACTION RESEARCH BY SCHOOL LEADERS

The same three categories of targets (performance, process, and program) are applicable when, rather than being classroom based, a school leader or teams of leaders are carrying out the action research. For example, a principal, concerned about becoming a better instructional leader, might choose to pursue the *performance target* of providing high-quality formative feedback to the teachers she supervises. Or if the leader's goal were to improve the quality of collaboration at the school, and she felt this could be advanced through changes in the way faculty meetings are conducted, she might find herself pursuing the *process target* of facilitating faculty meetings with greater amounts of engagement. Likewise, a school leader might want to investigate a *program target*, such as an initiative to make literacy development the central focus of the school.

Charlene was responsible for supervising all of the principals in one region of the Portland (Oregon) School District. Last summer, she decided to use the reflective writing process to help sharpen her vision and develop her personal goals for the school improvement efforts she was going to be facilitating with the principals in her region. Reprinted below is the reflective writing she authored in response to a prompt similar to the one used by Jose.

I can't believe it. This has been a year of tremendous success. Instead of the usual incremental progress, initiative fatigue, and dueling between administration and teachers over which instructional approach will be most effective, principals in my region are elated that alas, the work of transforming their seemingly eternally labeled "low-performing schools" are finally bearing fruit. Teachers and their building leaders now have a shared vision of student success and are in agreement on methods to effectively target instructional strategies. Further, they are becoming quite effective at crafting promising theories of action based on data and research. No longer are teacher teams simply passing blame among each other, their students, the community, the district, the union, and so on. Now they are focused, using evidence and working from a well-informed and articulated plan of action to accelerate the outcomes they desire. They can identify specific approaches and strategies with confidence that they have the power to affect improvement for their lowest performing students. My principals entered the summer with shoulders and heads up with confidence, instead of the weight of blame and helplessness for outcomes over which they previously felt little or no control. Now their leadership is focused and deliberate and is inspiring teachers to take risks to transform their practice. Principals have made their thinking transparent by co-constructing theories of action with teachers and staff, and as a result, morale is at an all-time high.

Testimonials of student success fill PLC and staff meetings with examples of how action research provided them with the tools they needed to bridge the gap between their professional development in culturally responsive practices and the realities of their classrooms. My conversations with principals are now more robust and revolve around data and the evidence the principals are using to foster a culture of inquiry and improvement in their buildings. The path for improvement is now clearly visible throughout these schools.

I saw these principals modeling reflective practice. They were deeply engaged with their teachers in action research to assess the effectiveness of their efforts to improve instruction at their schools. To accomplish this, each leader identified strategies for implementation that she believed would have high impact on student outcomes and devised ways to regularly assess the effectiveness of the implementation. Specifically, these building leaders targeted culturally responsive practices that are known to improve outcomes for all students and create excellence and equity in achievement. In areas where they fell short, they knew exactly where to adjust their focus and the approaches they wanted to try to address and monitor student success. Not only were these principals excited, but they were able to provide multiple sources of data to back up their assertions. These included anecdotes, surveys, and classroom assessment data, along with scores on agreed-upon rubrics collected during regular cycles of classroom visits. Numerous tales of teams of teachers using this data to inform cycles of instructional improvement have been heard in all of the schools, and these buildings are now buzzing with talk of open, data-driven practices.

I should take a moment to describe what I have termed a "coalition of the willing." I recall a discussion with a teacher who joined a cohort of teachers I organized to track the impact of high-leverage lesson design and instructional strategies. These teachers met monthly over the course of the year on a volunteer basis. I wanted to create a coalition of the willing in order to test my theory of action that teachers who had experienced success with this work would serve as the greatest evangelists for change. The approach the teachers used did not require a scripted curriculum but rather was a strengths-based intentional approach that required the type of cognitive demands students generally only encounter in a TAG classroom. I recall after one particular session, I was pulled aside by a frustrated teacher, who, after discussing her concerns with her PLC, made this statement: "I totally get that we need to have high expectations for students, but those questions are geared toward TAG students." She was taken aback by our vision and the level of instruction that was being promoted for all students. This made sense since she had never

FIGURE 2.4   Charlene's Great Year: Priority Achievement Targets

- Improved reading scores for students in the cluster (performance target)
- Conceptual understanding and implementation of the action research cycle to monitor impact of instructional practices (performance target)
- Create effective "coalitions of the willing" in each school
- Increase in the quality of principal plans in response to student performance (performance target)
- Improved process for monitoring the effectiveness of instructional practices (process target)
- Effective tracking and use of student data to inform practice (process target)
- Increased job satisfaction (program target)

taught or had experience with students in her classroom performing consistently at that level. As the year went on, teachers in her building continued to demonstrate alternative ways of successfully teaching the curriculum, and after reviewing evidence of student work, this teacher had an aha moment. The same teacher was now seeing how she could make her own practice more transparent, and she learned several concrete strategies designed by her colleagues and used in their classrooms to promote a higher level of cognitive rigor. Later in the year, on a return visit to the school, this same teacher pulled me aside to show me student work that reflected a level of reasoning she never believed possible from her students. My experience with this teacher affirmed and clarified my belief that by providing a space through action research where teachers could experience success, we could create the paradigm shift my schools needed to alter practices and improve student achievement.

The Target Identification Form we designed (Figure 2.2) should prove helpful while isolating a focus for most action research. We created a slightly modified version of this form specifically for those in leadership positions. That form can be found in Resource C (Exhibit 1). Figure 2.4 presents the targets that Charlene surfaced after completion of her reflective writing.

Once you have identified your priority achievement targets, you are getting closer to isolating a focus for your action research. All that needs to happen now is for you to preface each of your bulleted targets with the phrase "Investigating how to produce . . . ," and you will have a list of potentially meaningful foci for action research. What makes these targets good topics for action research is that they focus on the three essentials:

1. Your actions

2. Improving performance

3. An issue of significant concern for *you*

USING A JOURNAL TO IDENTIFY ACTION RESEARCH FOCI

The use of a journal to find an action research focus has many of the same virtues as reflective writing. The major difference is that journaling spreads reflections over a period of time. What is so good about extending the time frame for reflection is that it allows us to observe patterns and trends in our thinking concerns and passions.

Some educators are already in the journaling habit. However, for many, keeping a journal is not part of their daily routine and probably isn't very likely to become so in the future. This is another instance when establishing boundaries is helpful for structuring our work. If the discipline of journal writing isn't part of your nature, this is another occasion when boundary setting can limit the time needed for this exercise while not reducing its value.

Boundaries or guidelines that we have found useful when using a journal to pinpoint an action research focus include the following:

- Two weeks (maximum) of daily journal entries
- Approximately ten minutes of writing per day (fifteen-minute maximum)
- Respond to the same prompt each day

When using journal writing to find a research focus, it is wise to make use of a consistent prompt. Writing to the same topic each day creates boundaries and makes it much easier to analyze your reflections once you are finished. One versatile and productive prompt we have used appears in the boxed text.

Writing Prompt

What occurred in class today that that seemed significant to me?
Significance means what *went exceptionally well*, what *went worse than expected*, what *surprised* you, and *what questions* did you end the day with?

The following is a hypothetical journal entry from a fifth-grade teacher, written during the first two weeks of school.

Journal Entry

As promised, I held a class meeting to see how things were going with classroom discussions. I am always inspired by the honesty and transparency of my students, but sometimes, their unfiltered candor can leave me a little bristly. But as I think about it, they are right. I tried to capture exact comments as reminders for planning and future discussions. I can't forget Shaune's comment, "I like how you are trying to get everyone to participate, but sometimes, you still talk a little too much." And Marcus was spot on when he said, "It would be nice if we could lead some of the discussions and select some of the topics." I realize I will have to give them some parameters to make sure we get close to covering what we need to. I was surprised at Jermaine's observation about my inconsistent use of the sticks-of-justice technique. He said, "We really like the sticks of justice, but sometimes, you don't use all the sticks, and then, some of us never get called on. That made me mad last year because I feel like my name never got called, at least most of the time." And then, there was this comment from Rachel, often my worst critic, which showed me she has caught on. She said, "At least you are now asking us what we think. Thanks. It's like you are really trying to be fair."

This is one of Charlene's journal entries written after an early fall meeting with one of the principals she is working with on school improvement:

> ## Journal Entry
>
> *Wow! Franklin really does seem to have a clear vision of academic excellence and the great complexity of transforming a struggling school. But it is so global that I'm afraid this could be tough to manage if I don't help him narrow his focus. He admits he can see how a large number of factors impact student success, but it is difficult for him to figure out where the best leverage points are to change what he calls "the culture of student disengagement," at least as he defines it. He essentially listed everything in the school as a contributing factor. . . . I love how he thinks, and I admire how focused and committed he is to creating a school culture supportive of good instruction. Even though I came prepared with questions, I found I had to craft very specific questions to help keep him focused and guide him along as he zeroed in on the issue. I also realized I will need to be more vigilant about helping him stay on topic. Bottom line is that if I want him to be clear and focused, I need to make sure I model that every way I can.*

Journaling is an especially good way to isolate a topic for collaborative or team action research. When using journaling for this purpose, every member of the team should write daily entries in response to the same prompt over the agreed period of time. Later, the entire team will look for patterns in the issues and concerns that surfaced across the reflections of the team members.

What we like most about the journal process is how much material it produces in so little time. After a mere two weeks, you will produce ten separate journal entries. Now consider this: If you were planning on conducting action research collaboratively (for example, with nine other teachers from your school), just two weeks of journaling (ten to fifteen minutes a day) would yield one hundred real-time teacher reflections.

In Chapter 7, journaling will be revisited as a data collection strategy. Perhaps you can already see what a powerful data-gathering instrument a journal can be. One hundred individual journal entries generated by people working on a regular basis with the students attending a single school, each one focused on classroom issues that are significant to them, would constitute a gold mine of data. And collecting all that treasure would take merely ten minutes per day.

Returning to our original purpose, which was using journals to identify a focus for research, your ten entries may appear, on the surface, to be creating too much material. However, once you spend a little bit of time analyzing the entries, you will easily be able to spot an issue or a few select issues with personal meaning that will be worth spending your time researching.

If you choose to use the journaling strategy, you will likely want to create forms similar to the Action Research Journal pages shown in Figure 2.5 as a method to capture the journal entries that you and any other members of your action research team generate.

FIGURE 2.5 Action Research Journal

Date: _____

Make ten copies of this sheet for your daily journal entries. Beginning on the agreed-on start date, keep a journal for ten consecutive days. Do your writing after the school day has ended and when you have fifteen minutes of uninterrupted quiet time.

Be sure to place the date on the top of the page, and write in response to the prompt decided on (for instance, *What went well, what went poorly, what surprised me, and what questions did I end today with?*).

_____

_____

_____

_____

_____

_____

_____

_____

_____

_____

_____

_____

_____

_____

_____

_____

_____

_____

_____

_____

_____

_____

_____

FIGURE 2.6 Journal Analysis Form

Read through your ten journal entries in chronological order, with a pad of paper by your side. Whenever you come upon something that concerned you, pleased you, surprised you, or raised a question for you, write it down. If you see a reference to the same concern, satisfying experience, surprise, or question on another day, put a check mark by that item on your list.

Now prioritize the items on your list in descending order of how many times each showed up during your two weeks of journaling.

_____
_____
_____
_____
_____
_____
_____

For each item, ask the following questions:

1. Does this item have an impact on a performance outcome that matters to me? (Keep in mind an outcome can be academic, behavioral, or affective.) List the items that you responded to with a *yes:*

_____
_____
_____
_____
_____
_____
_____

2. For each item listed in #1 (above), ask yourself, Do I understand this issue or phenomenon as well as I'd like to? List the items that you responded to with a *no:*

_____
_____
_____
_____
_____
_____
_____
_____

The items listed above may be good candidates for action research foci.

Once you have collected all of your journal entries, it is time to look for patterns. The questions found on the Journal Analysis Form (Figure 2.6) should help you identify recurrent themes that surfaced during the two-week writing period. Now, use the same process that was used with the narrative visions: Preface each of your items with the phrase "Investigating how to produce . . . " You now have a list of personally meaningful foci for action research.

REFLECTIVE INTERVIEWS

Another approach for identifying a meaningful focus is the reflective interview, a process where we make use of the ear of a colleague as we verbally articulate our thinking on an issue or concern. Most often, the reflective interview is carried out in pairs. Participants take turns discussing a matter of personal concern regarding their work. Each person has a predetermined amount of time to talk about his or her issue. We like to allocate fifteen minutes per participant. This way, in a scheduled forty-five-minute meeting, each person can have a full fifteen minutes for his or her issue, with another fifteen minutes available for clarification and summarizing.

Reflective interviews give the action researchers a chance to hear their own ideas as they are spoken and as they are heard through the schooled ear of a colleague. It is important to understand that the reflective interview *is not a discussion*. If someone were to track the talking with a stopwatch during a reflective interview, the interviewee would be seen using at least 90 percent of the allocated airtime. The only occasion when an interviewer should be talking is when he or she is confused and needs clarification or if the interviewee seems to have run out of things to say. In such a case, the job of the interviewer is to say something to get the interviewee started again, for example, by probing with questions such as these:

- Has this concerned you for a long time?
- What other things have you tried?
- What would you like to do about this?

Figure 2.7 shows an example of a meeting agenda designed for paired reflective interviewing.

To recap, the purpose of the reflective interview is the same as with reflective writing and journaling: to clarify a focus for research that is

1. of significant personal professional concern,

2. within the researcher's personal sphere of influence, and

3. in an area where improvement is possible.

Frequently, the single act of conducting a reflective interview, followed by filling out the Target Identification Form (Figure 2.2), is all that is required to identify a focus for research. Other times, it is helpful to follow the reflective interview with a few minutes of reflective writing, using a

---

FIGURE 2.7   Reflective Interview Meeting Agenda

0:00–0:15

Interview 1

The first person takes fifteen minutes to talk about a work issue. The issue discussed must meet the following criteria:

- It is a matter of significant interest (something one is excited or concerned about).
- Performance in this area can be influenced by the work of the interviewee.
- Significant improvement could potentially be made in this area.

0:15–0:17

The interviewer takes two minutes to summarize what was heard. The interviewer prefaces the comments with, "I understood you to say . . ."

0:17–0:22

The interviewee and interviewer clarify their understanding of the interviewee's issue.

0:23–0:38

Interview 2

The second person takes fifteen minutes to talk about a work issue. The issue discussed must meet the following criteria:

- It is a matter of significant interest (something one is excited or concerned about).
- Performance in this area can be influenced by the work of the interviewee.
- Significant improvement in this area could potentially be made.

0:38–0:40

The interviewer takes two minutes to summarize what was heard. The interviewer prefaces the comments with, "I understood you to say . . ."

0:40–0:45

The interviewee and interviewer clarify their understanding of the interviewee's issue.

---

prompt like the one in Figure 2.1 and then proceeding to fill out the Target Identification Form (Figure 2.2).

REFLECTIVE INTERVIEWING AND THE PROBLEM OF ISOLATION

One of the negative by-products of working in a contemporary school is how lonely the work can become. This seems counterintuitive to most noneducators. They wonder, "How could anyone be lonely working all day in a building with all those kids and all those other teachers?" Of course, the people asking that question have never worked in an environment where they weren't even free to leave their workstation for a simple trip to the restroom without worrying that they might be abrogating their responsibilities. The sad reality is that many teachers and school leaders go for weeks and months without the simple luxury of fifteen minutes to speak their mind and reflect on pressing issues in the presence of a caring and knowledgeable colleague. One of the particular virtues for the busy educator of the reflective interview process is that in addition to helping us isolate a focus for our research, it creates islands of adult support in what often becomes a lonely workplace.

ANALYTIC DISCOURSE

The analytic discourse is a close cousin of the reflective interview. However, in this case, a panel of three to six colleagues conducts the interview, all of whom share an interest in or concern about the same general topic. This is a popular strategy for collaborative action research conducted by a department, grade level, or PLC team.

An analytic discourse generally follows the following format:

1. *Presentation of Issue.* The action researcher takes five minutes to outline his or her area of interest.

2. *Clarifying Questions.* Each panel member gets to ask for clarification of anything that is not clear.

3. *Probing Questions.* Panel members ask questions designed to push the researcher to explore and enunciate a deeper understanding of the area of concern. The types of questions asked can include things such as, *What do you think explains this? What things have been tried to address this in the past, here or elsewhere? What would you like to see happen?*

When conducting an analytic discourse, three ground rules must be followed by the interview panel. These rules are designed to ensure that the researcher/interviewee arrives at a deeper personal understanding of the issue. The ground rules are as follows:

1. *Questions only; no comments* (The goal is clarifying the researcher/ interviewee's understanding of the issue.)

2. *No critical comments* (The purpose is not to debate but to enhance understanding.)

3. *No suggestions* (It is the job of the researcher/interviewee to make all proposals.)

At the conclusion of an analytic discourse, use the Target Identification Form (Figure 2.2) to fine-tune a potential focus or foci for action research.

TEAM REFLECTION

Many times, a work group (a PLC team, a grade level, a department, or a cross-district group) will want to work together on a collaborative action research project. One good strategy for finding a meaningful group topic combines the attributes of the reflective writing process and the reflective interview. The focus form (Figure 2.8) is a worksheet that has been designed for use by grade-level, departmental, or PLC teams when selecting a focus for their collaborative action research.

FIGURE 2.8   Collaborative AR Group Focus Worksheet

Group: _____

Purpose: Conducting action research collaboratively has proven to be both rewarding and productive for teachers, if the focus for the research meets four conditions: it is sharply focused, pertains to the realization of a shared vision, focuses on an area where improvement could and should be made, and is situated within the group's sphere of influence. Using this form will help your group find a meaningful focus for group work.

Instructions: Find a time and place where you can allocate fifteen uninterrupted minutes for writing and reflecting on the work your group will be engaging in next year. Check the time and begin responding to the four questions on these sheets. Stick with the task until the full fifteen minutes are up. If your thinking stalls, continue to reflect on the issues, as new thoughts and ideas will likely emerge if you give it time. If you need more space, write on the back of these sheets or add paper as necessary—the more elaboration the better! After fifteen minutes of reflection and writing, your work is done.

Here are the questions:

1. What are the priority issues, projects, and programs that we should be working on collaboratively next year?

_____
_____
_____
_____
_____

2. Which of the listed issues, projects, or programs is the highest priority to you? Why? (Please expand your answer as much as possible.)

_____
_____
_____
_____
_____

3. If the group succeeded with this endeavor beyond our wildest expectations, what would the results look like? (Please be as specific as possible.)

_____
_____
_____
_____
_____

4. In the past what factors, issues, or obstacles have interfered with our achieving this extraordinary level of success (#3, above)?

_____
_____
_____
_____
_____

The process begins with each person separately spending fifteen minutes answering the four questions on the focus form. After everyone has had a chance to do their own reflective writing, a one-hour team meeting is called. The first half of the meeting is spent with random pairs conducting reflective interviews built on the material they wrote on the focus form (Figure 2.8). Once every person has had a chance to verbally discuss his or her ideas with a peer, the entire group convenes and compiles any common issues, ideas, and targets that were identified in the multiple paired reflective interviews. Achievement targets that surfaced repeatedly in separate interviews become potential foci for a group (collaborative) action research project.

There is no one technique to choose a focus for action research. Any one of the strategies discussed in this chapter or a combination of them should help an individual educator or team select a direction for research that will prove worthy of his, her, or their time. Whatever approach you decide to use, it is imperative to *stop before proceeding any further* to ask yourself or your team this question about the action research focus that has emerged: Is this topic really worth an investment of my or our precious time and energy? Put another way, you could ask yourself,

> If I/we invest time in learning how I/we can improve my/our professional action in pursuit of success on this target or these targets, and what I/we learn enables me/us to be more successful, will this time have been well spent?

If you can answer that question with an emphatic "yes," you are ready to proceed.

3

Refining the Focus

Recreational travel to exotic and infrequently visited destinations can be exhilarating. The anticipation that builds for months before your departure can be nearly as much fun as the trip itself. While there is no question that planning a trip takes significant time, planning is frequently the single most important thing one can do to guarantee that the trip will end up a success.

One of the aspects of pretravel planning that makes it so much fun is that there are few, if any, constraints on our imaginations. As we envision what it will be like to go where we have never gone before, we are free to fantasize what the trip might become. Because we are open to every possibility and potentiality, we can approach our adventure with both excitement and optimism. In our day-to-day lives, we often find ourselves overwhelmed by what feels like an endless set of roadblocks lying between our goals and our current situation. Yet when anticipating a new adventure, anything seems possible.

At this point in the action research process, you are in a similar position to a traveler who has just chosen a destination. In Chapter 2, when you identified potential research foci, you were, in effect, selecting the part of the world you plan to visit.

However, as any seasoned traveler knows, choosing a destination is just the beginning. The savvy traveler doesn't stop there. Part of the ritual, as well as the fun, of trip preparation is pouring over maps, reading guidebooks, and speaking with others who've traveled to the same or similar places. It is those inquiries that help the traveler identify the cities, the sites, and the attractions he or she plans to visit and the experiences he or she hopes to enjoy along the way. In Chapter 2, with the identification of your priority achievement targets, you identified some specific destinations and sites you want to be sure not to miss on your upcoming trip.

VISUALIZING SUCCESS

As you daydreamed about your trip (through the reflective writing and/or reflective interviewing processes), you began visualizing what a perfect excursion might look like. For the educator conducting action research, this amounts to imagining all of the aspects of teaching, learning, and program performance one would witness when all of one's priority achievement targets were met by all of one's students in an exemplary manner.

In the last chapter, we discussed how our goals could be categorized as performance, process, or program targets. If your action research will be focused on achieving a performance target, you probably have already started thinking about what you believe outstanding performance would look like when achieved. For example, if we chose to focus on improving our students' writing, we would need to visualize what a truly outstanding piece of expository student writing should read like. Or if our goal was enhancing student engagement, we might be asking what would we see in the behavior of a deeply and meaningfully engaged student.

If an action researcher is focused on achieving success with a process target, she or he will want to envision how things ought to be working when and if the processes have been fully implemented and are working perfectly. For example, if we desire to improve our skills in leading class discussions, we would try to visualize what our classes would be like once productive and engaging discussions had become the norm in our classrooms.

And when the focus is on a program target, the action researcher will want to envision all of the attributes of a truly outstanding program. For example, if we wanted to create a positive school climate, we would be asking ourselves what one would see in a school where the climate was maximally inclusive and supportive of child development.

Why Is Having a Clear Vision So Necessary?

It has been said, "If you don't know where you're going, any road will get you there." That is more than a clever play on words. When people are unsure of their destinations, they tend to take wrong turns, extend their trips with unnecessary detours, and potentially end up where they hadn't intended to go. In our classrooms and schools, this could mean using inappropriate strategies, going off on tangents, and coming to the end of the year and realizing that our students are still lacking the skills we had hoped and intended for them to gain. Nothing feels worse for an educator. When this happens, we feel a sense of loss. This is because at school, time inevitably marches on. Opportunities rarely exist for going back and giving things a second try. This very real risk of losing our direction and thereby failing to reach our desired destination should motivate us to be disciplined and deliberative when planning our action research—that is, our planned exploration of a not-yet-visited destination.

Dedicated teachers don't need to be encouraged to plan. In fact, it is insulting to infer that teachers don't consistently engage in meaningful planning. When our students aren't performing at the level we want (such as all students failing to produce excellent work), it doesn't mean we didn't plan; nor does it mean we didn't follow our plans. Furthermore, it is likely our plans were grounded in the best information we had available, and we implemented our plans with all the energy and enthusiasm we could muster. Simply beseeching educators to plan "more" or "better" is like trying to squeeze blood from a turnip. If we are already doing the best we know how, and we are working as hard as we can, then what we are currently getting is, in all likelihood, the best that can be expected—at least without a significant change in our approach.

CONDUCTING AN INSTRUCTIONAL POSTMORTEM

Let's return to the phrase, "If you don't know where you're going, any road will get you there," and think of a lesson, unit, or class you recently taught. Now cast yourself in a new role. You have now become your own personal teaching coach.

After a performance or a match, coaches often conduct postmortems on the recently completed action. They review everything that occurred (even reviewing video of the event when available), trying to learn as much as they can from what went according to the plan as well as what went wrong. Good coaches are particularly concerned about identifying the shortcomings so they can avoid repeating them the next time. Now we'd like you to conduct an *instructional postmortem* on a class you recently taught, but do so in your new role as your teaching coach. Begin with an examination of the outcomes obtained, where your students ended up after instruction, or, if your action research will be focused on the achievement of process or program targets, where you and/or your program ended up. For an athletic coach, these outcomes are the equivalent of the final score.

Following the travel metaphor, the first question your teaching coach should ask you to reflect on is,

> What road or roads did you travel on your way to where you ended up? Or in other words, How did you get here?

This is a critical question since it is logical to assume that if you take that same road again, it will lead you to the same destination. If we want to end up at a different and better place, it will, therefore, be necessary for us to travel on a different route. The instructional postmortem is a process of reflection that helps us learn from our past experience so we can avoid repeating past mistakes.

A golfer trying to understand what led to his final score will mentally replay every hole, trying to recall each and every shot. When we do this in our role as teaching coach, we try to review every lesson we taught, every strategy we used, and each assignment we made. Frequently, we begin this process by thinking of a particular student, a student whose performance we wish to understand better. Most often, when we've done this, we find we are reflecting on a student whose final performance was a disappointment to us. Consequently, when thinking through each instructional activity engaged in by this student, we aren't thinking of what we had hoped would occur (hit the green with my second shot and then two putt for par) but instead what actually transpired (three balls hit into the woods, landed in a sand trap, and then four putted for a quadruple bogey). The Instructional Postmortem Form (Figure 3.1) is designed to help guide you in reviewing a student's experience with a recently taught unit of instruction.

FIGURE 3.1   Instructional Postmortem Form

Briefly describe the lesson or instruction unit:

_____

_____

_____

_____

_____

_____

_____

State the skill or outcome that you had expected students to gain from this instruction:

_____

_____

_____

_____

_____

_____

_____

List the significant characteristics of a learner whose experience you will be tracing (such as English language learner, precocious, cooperative, disruptive, gifted, and so on):

_____

_____

_____

_____

_____

_____

_____

Describe the performance of this student following instruction:

_____

_____

_____

_____

_____

_____

_____

_____

(Continued)

FIGURE 3.1   (Continued)

Using the table provided, list in sequence all the significant instructional activities and the facilitation you provided during this unit or lesson and what the learner produced (grades, scores, products) or what you recall the learner doing in response to the activity:

Date	Activity	Performance, Comment

Use additional space if necessary.

TAKING STOCK OF ONE'S
RECENT LEADERSHIP EXPERIENCE

Frequently, school leaders find it helpful to deconstruct what transpired with an initiative they recently lead in much the same way that teachers deconstruct a lesson or unit they have just finished (the instructional postmortem). You can find a modified version of the Instructional Postmortem Form (Figure 3.1) called the Post Hoc Analysis of Leadership Form in Resource C, Exhibit 2. This form was created for use by school leaders wishing to conduct a disciplined review of their past leadership actions to understand how these were experienced by individual staff members or by their teams.

Once we have reviewed the road traveled to get to our current destination, our next step will be comparing our experience with that of others.

COMPARING YOUR EXPERIENCE
WITH THE EXPERIENCE OF OTHERS

Suppose you have spent the last three years saving for a European vacation. This promises to be a once-in-a-lifetime experience. You have arranged to spend as much time in Europe as possible, but alas, the time available will be far less than you had hoped. Considering the expense involved, as well as your time constraints, you are motivated to do whatever planning is necessary to provide the best possible travel experience.

You have good reason to minimize mistakes and missteps, such as wasting time at attractions with little to offer, and you are, no doubt, motivated to get the most out of each venue. Going into an adventure blindly could make sense—it might even make a trip more exciting—providing one had unlimited time and money. But given your parameters, you likely want to engage in serious and focused planning. For most of us, this begins with research. Experienced travelers seek out the insights of others, people who have taken similar trips. They want to learn from the successes, what was enjoyed most, as well as from the mistakes, the places to avoid. When collecting this information, the wise traveler has good reason to consider where the advice is coming from. When weighing others' opinions, it is always essential to consider the source. This caution is absolutely critical for our work as action researchers because "considering the source" will ensure that we are taking into account those variables that pertain to context—for example, any unique aspects of the setting and the students, the teachers, and community. Action researchers concerned about increasing excellence and equity will want to take special note of the cultural diversity and gender of the population reported on in any study. When it comes to making decisions that will guide teaching and learning, understanding the context frequently can be the most important factor and, often to our peril, the one most frequently overlooked. We know this intuitively, but when adopting school programs that were developed elsewhere, decision makers often fail to take this factor into account.

Often, the people who develop and market commercially available instructional materials operate as though the nature of the specific teaching and learning context where the materials will eventually be used is irrelevant. They presume that what was successful in one setting will inevitably work in any other setting. While this may be a good marketing strategy, this posture denies what everyone who has managed a school or classroom knows through experience: No two students, no two teachers, and no two classes can ever be exactly alike.

Gathering Insights From Colleagues

There are two main places where travelers go for information prior to embarking on their journeys. If they know people who have recently made a similar trip, they often contact them to hear about their experiences. Similarly, when we are about to engage in action research, if we know of teachers who have been having success in our focus area, we would be wise to talk to them and hear about their experience. The eight questions in the Colleague Interview Guide (Figure 3.2) should prove helpful when you ask professional colleagues about their experiences working in your focus area.

Many travelers also find it helpful to consult guidebooks written and published by reputable authorities. As mentioned above, when consulting authorities, it is essential to consider the source. One way travelers do this is by paying attention to the publication date of the travel guides they are consulting. This way, they can be sure they are using the most current information. Ultimately, these two sources of data (fellow travelers and reputable authorities) are invaluable when planning an itinerary. While it was reasonable to rely on intuition and personal passion at the start, when you were selecting the destination (the focus for either action research or exotic travel), it is hard to overstate the prudence of consulting experts before purchasing or adopting an expensive program or locking in a non-refundable plane ticket.

For action researchers, the equivalent of consulting travel guides is conducting a review of the literature.

The Literature Review

While the phrase *literature review* is clear and descriptive, it frequently carries negative connotations for individual teachers and teams of educators who are preparing to conduct action research. Every educator has experience conducting searches of the literature. For many folks, this last occurred when completing the requirements for a college degree. While some of us may have found our time in the library to be stimulating, many others will remember this aspect of the research process as unpleasant, unproductive, and time consuming.

It is an understandable fear of the time involved that keeps many of us from going to the library and conducting a literature review prior to teaching a new unit, adopting a new program, or introducing a new concept. This is understandable yet terribly unfortunate. We omit this step to save time. But as a consequence, we often find ourselves going over terrain where others have gone before, yet we do so without the benefit of their counsel. Later, if we encounter problems that could have been avoided with a little helpful advice, we find ourselves frustrated that we wasted our finite time and energy.

FIGURE 3.2 Colleague Interview Guide

The following questions can help you assess the applicability of an instructional process or program. Prior to conducting the first interview, ask yourself Questions 1 to 4 regarding your school or classroom. At the start of the interview, share a summary of your answers with the person or persons being interviewed.

Date: _____ Program, site: _____

Person(s) interviewed: _____

_____

_____

Your Setting	Interviewee's Setting
1. Why are you interested in the use of this program or process?	1. Why did you develop or introduce this program or process?
2. In what ways, if any, are those who will be affected by this prgram unique or unusual?	2. In what ways, if any, are those who will be affected by this program unique or unusual?
3. What are the characteristics of the staff members who would be working with this program or process (such as certification, teaching assignment, other responsibilities)?	3. What are the characteristics of the staff members who have been working with this program or process (certification, teaching assignment, other responsibilities)?
4. What resources will be available to support the use of this program or process?	4. What resources are used to support the use of this program or process?

(Continued)

FIGURE 3.2   (Continued)

Your Setting	Interviewee's Setting
	5. What specific outcomes do you attribute to the use of this program or process?
	6. In your opinion, what other factors contributed to the achievement of those outcomes?
	7. What problems did you encounter when developing or introducing this program or process?
	8. What else do you think a teacher or a school should know before implementing this program or process?

We are reminded of a commercial for automobile oil filters that aired several years ago. The company's goal was to encourage consumers to invest a few dollars in their product and use it as part of routine auto maintenance. They sold this concept by contrasting the comparatively minor cost of an oil filter with the far larger cost of a complete engine rebuild. The company's commercial had a mechanic reciting their slogan, "You can pay me now or pay me later!" At this point you may be saying, "Enough already! I don't need to be lectured on the value of standing on others' shoulders, but I simply don't have the time to conduct a lit review."

Fortunately, the Internet has made examining the professional knowledge base far easier than many of us recall from college, and continuous advances in search engine technology are making it more efficient every day. The Literature Review Planning Form (Figure 3.3) was designed to help you structure and organize a literature review online.

Tips for Conducting Online Research

When using the Internet for your review of research, it is especially important to consider the source. The best method we've found to do this is to follow these two steps when you encounter a report or article on a promising practice:

1. Look in the article for the identity of a school or district that is currently using the approach. If it is asserted that this is a promising practice, but you cannot find evidence of its use anywhere, this should raise a caution.

2. If an implementing school or district is identified, contact teachers or others at the site, by phone or e-mail, who are currently using the program or practice or who have recently used it. Ask them about their experience while taking notes using the Colleague Interview Guide (Figure 3.2). When conducting your phone interview, pay particular attention to gleaning everything you can about the context of the implementation site to determine how similar or different it is from your own school or classroom.

On occasion, after a literature review or an examination of the commercially available materials, we will identify a comprehensive program that appears to be a good fit for our needs. When this happens, we instinctively recognize that the most efficient thing to do is to *adopt and implement* the program as it was designed and packaged. This is another occasion where the travel metaphor may prove helpful.

Adopting Commercial Programs

Many times, vacationers will sign up for an all-inclusive package tour. This is a sensible thing to do, especially if the tour includes your priority destinations, and you know other people who have taken and enjoyed that same tour. This is frequently the wisest, safest, and most economical strategy to follow. As individual classroom teachers or as a faculty team, this would be analogous to identifying an approach that we know other

FIGURE 3.3   Literature Review Planning Form

Review the area you've selected as the focus for your action research and the achievement targets you hope to impact through your work. Then answer the following questions:

1. List all the priority achievement targets you hope to see impacted by your actions.

_____

_____

_____

_____

_____

2. List every strategy you are aware of that educators have used in their efforts to improve performance on the achievement targets listed.

_____

_____

_____

_____

_____

3. Go over your answers to Questions 1 and 2, highlighting every key word.

4. Do an Internet search following these steps:

    a. Place the keywords in order of importance.

    b. Do a search using all of your key words.

    c. Repeat the search, dropping the least important key word.

    d. Repeat the process, dropping a key word each time, until you feel you have acquired enough information.

Note: If you are unhappy with the results obtained, repeat the process using a different search engine.

5. Review the material from your search using the following table to record the strategies that have been reported as successful, noting the context and impact:

Strategy	Impact	Context (Student and School)

6. Reorder the data from the table in order of the similarity of the reported context to your own school or classroom:

Strategy	Impact

teachers in similar contexts have used and obtained the results we would like to obtain and did so with students similar to our own. Adopting such an approach or program often makes a great deal of sense.

The logic of this explains why the adoption of commercially available programs is, far and away, the most widely used approach to educational program improvement. Finding what has worked for others in similar situations and then using it ourselves prevents us from having to reinvent the wheel. But while the decision to purchase someone else's theory of action may be a wise initial course of action, it does not relieve us of the need to determine whether the program we have adopted actually turned out to be a good fit for us in our context through our own action research. In Chapter 4, we will discuss a suggested process to use when conducting action research on any commercially available programs you have adopted or will be adopting.

Tip on Adopting a Commercial Program

If, after conducting a review of the pertinent literature, you haven't identified ideas, programs, or strategies that you feel are superior to what you have been doing, it might indicate that you would be better served by first conducting a descriptive study on your current program in an attempt to understand what is currently going right and wrong before rushing ahead to introduce a new innovation.

An investigation of what is occurring now may help you identify specific aspects of your program that need to be modified to foster further improvement in performance on your priority achievement targets. Either way, you are encouraged to wait before deciding whether or not your research will be *quasi-experimental* or *descriptive* until after completing your work on *Stage 2: Articulating Your Theory* (see Chapters 4 and 5). Frequently, the activities you will engage in during the theory articulation stage will result in the generation of an innovative strategy that you will be excited to try out and investigate.

This is a good time to pause and review where we are with the action research process. By now, you should have selected a focus area. You have visualized what excellence looks like, and you have identified a set of critical subelements (priority achievement targets) that, when taken together, you believe constitute excellent performance in that focus area. Lastly, you have reviewed the literature and considered the experience of others who have pursued improvement in your focus area. This brings us to the final aspects of our work in *Stage 1: Clarifying Vision and Targets*—establishing clear and unambiguous criteria for use when determining if we are, in fact, producing the desired improvements with our achievement targets.

DEVELOPING CRITERIA TO MEASURE CHANGES WITH PRIORITY ACHIEVEMENT TARGETS

Earlier, you identified areas of student or program performance, called priority achievement targets. The targets spelled out specifically what you hoped to see improved. Once again, it is worth emphasizing how wide a range of achievement targets can be pursued through action research. It was also stated that achievement targets could be divided into three categories: performance, process, and program. Those three categories cover a great deal of territory. Examples of the types of foci that come under each of these categories are listed in the box that follows.

Achievement Targets Foci

Performance targets can include foci such as

- Changes in student academic performance, for example:
  - Improved computation skills
  - Improved inferential comprehension
  - Expanded variety of voices in writing

- Changes in student behavior, for example:
  - Increased attention to high-quality finished products
  - Increased on-task behavior
  - Enhanced cooperation and collaboration

- Changes in student attitude/affect, for example:
  - Enthusiasm for learning
  - Appreciation of art
  - Willingness to engage in long-range planning

Process targets can include foci such as

- Changes we would like to see in our teaching skills and methods, for example:
  - Leading more invigorating discussions
  - Providing clearer explanations for complex topics
  - Providing timely feedback to students

- Changes in school procedures, for example:
  - Adult–student rapport
  - School rules
  - Parent involvement

Program targets include foci such as

- Changes in curriculum, for example:
  - Making the content more relevant for the students
  - Integrating concepts across disciplines
  - Incorporating more creative problem-solving opportunities

- Changes in offerings, for example:
  - Elective programs
  - Required classes and experiences
  - Co-curricular programs

Occasionally, educational action researchers feel they should restrict the focus of their inquiries to a limited and specific range of targets. That is unfortunate for a number of reasons. When we place arbitrary limits on the focus of our research, we risk working on issues that might be relatively low on our professional priority list. When this happens, our work may, in fact, produce a positive change but also produce an unintended side effect. If our finite energy was expended doing action research on a low-priority issue, we will likely be reluctant to engage in this work in the future. This is a reasonable decision, since the time and energy we spent conducting the research was time that could otherwise have been invested in pursuits that might have proven more personally and professionally rewarding.

When we limit our focus to low-priority objectives, it most often happens for one of two reasons. The first is because of a faulty premise that educators should only concern themselves with goals that are cognitive and academic—a stance reinforced by much contemporary political rhetoric. This is a misguided notion for several reasons. There isn't a parent or student who doesn't expect more from education than mere facts and isolated skills. Furthermore, that isn't why most of us went into education. If all we wanted to accomplish was the transmission of bits of information, we should have become computer programmers, not teachers. As was mentioned earlier and cannot be emphasized enough, an action researcher's focus should be his or her area of passion. For that reason, it is once again appropriate to pause and ask yourself,

> What matters so much to me that were I to spend my valuable time pursuing improvement with it, I would deem my time well spent?

If your answer includes such issues as student motivation, behavior, attitudes, or affective outcomes, then those are perfectly legitimate foci for your action research.

There is a second reason why action researchers occasionally avoid the pursuit of high-priority yet nonacademic achievement targets: the concern that many priority nonacademic targets, even those with great transcendent value, cannot be effectively assessed. This is incorrect. Any target that can be articulated can be assessed and with a high degree of validity and reliability.

CREATING PERFORMANCE RATING SCALES

Every car comes equipped with a tool for measuring its progress. This instrument is called an odometer. The tool most frequently used by educational action researchers for monitoring progress when pursuing long-term or complex achievement targets is the performance rating scale. In recent years, educators started using the term *rubric* as a synonym for the performance rating scale. Before we leave Stage 1, it is a good idea for you to develop performance rating scales to measure growth on each of your priority achievement targets.

A relatively easy strategy for constructing a performance rating scale for use with action research is to follow these three sequential steps:

1. Visualize excellent achievement.

2. Identify the essential component traits.

3. Create performance continua for each trait.

Step 1: Visualizing Excellent Achievement

At the start of this chapter, we discussed the importance of holding a clear vision of success. Now, as we are shifting our attention to measurement, it is a good time to return to that concept. For each of the priority achievement targets that you want to see improved through your work, you should ask yourself this question:

> If performance on this target were precisely as I'd like it to be, what would it look like?

To illustrate, let's take the case of Dr. Hernandez, a high school principal who is interested in helping her school become a more collegial workplace, in order to combat what she describes as a culture of low expectations. Her philosophy is that "culture trumps strategy." Teachers at her school have participated in multiple professional development activities aimed at improving student achievement, yet student performance continues to vary widely across classrooms, and there continues to be a large achievement gap between advantaged and disadvantaged students. To help the faculty improve student performance, achieve greater consistency between classrooms, and reduce achievement gaps, she concluded it would be a good idea to encourage greater collaboration.

Dr. Hernandez might summarize her vision as follows:

> I want to see a collegial workplace that is supportive of continuous progress toward universal excellence in student performance. I envision a professional work environment that is supportive of the needs of faculty and results in high levels of staff morale.
>
> I want all of our teachers to feel they are part of a supportive faculty team so that whenever a student or program issue arises, we are able to apply creative problem solving in an effective and timely fashion. Then, as our collegiality increases, I see a tighter and tighter alignment of curriculum, instruction, and assessment.

For a classroom example of visioning, we'll consider Mr. Collins, a fourth-grade teacher who hopes to see his students become highly proficient readers. He might describe his vision this way:

> I want to see my students become skillful readers who love reading. For me, it isn't enough for them to simply gain the skills to comprehend grade-level material; I also want them to be able to read between the lines. Of course, I want them to understand what the author is saying, but I also want them to gain insights into the author's point of view. I want them to see themselves in the curriculum and find the material as relevant and engaging as possible. I want them to appreciate the versatility of the English language by understanding a variety of techniques that successful authors use to convey meaning and tone. In so doing, each student will feel validated by a curriculum that reflects him or her and the assets he or she brings to the classroom as a reader.

Both principal and teacher have expressed detailed visions, which helped them clarify their targets. The principal is working on a *program* target, the development of a more collegial school, while the teacher is in pursuit of a *performance* target, the creation of skillful readers.

Step 2: Identifying Traits

Frequently, significant targets such as these are made up of components (subskills) that we will refer to as *traits*. A trait is a specific quality that is characteristic of a performance, process, or program that is critical for hitting the achievement target.

In the case of the collegial school, we can identify the component traits by carefully reading through the principal's statement. We noted the following traits as characteristic of the school Dr. Hernandez envisioned:

- Universal excellence in student performance
- Excellent staff morale
- A collaborative team culture
- Staff as skilled problem solvers
- Alignment of curriculum, instruction, and assessment

Mr. Collins's goal of producing more skillful readers also contained several components:

- Ability to use grade-level material
- Enjoyment of reading
- Literal comprehension skills
- Inferential comprehension skills
- Find relevance and validation in the curriculum

In Chapter 7, when our focus shifts to the design of a comprehensive data collection plan, we will examine how action researchers can make use of performance rating scales as instruments for data collection. However, at this point, the rating scales we develop will serve two other immediate and important functions:

1. Help us to further clarify the priority achievement targets we are pursuing

2. Provide us with confidence that we can effectively document changes in performance on our priority achievement targets

Step 3: Creating Continua

Performance rating scales with an odd number of columns (scores) are highly recommended for action research purposes since they enable us to identify a clear midpoint. We operationally define the midpoint on a performance rating scale as "good performance" or "meeting expectations." Good performance, or a score "right in the middle," is where we would like all of our students to be; functionally, it might be understood to mean "at grade level."

You can practice building a performance rating scale by using the Rating-Scale Worksheet (Figure 3.4). Construction of the rating scale begins by listing the components (the traits) of your priority achievement target in the extreme left column (one per row). Then, in the middle column, in bulleted form, write your description of what would constitute *a good level of performance* for each trait. Mr. Collins, who is working on improving his students' reading proficiency, might have put these items in the middle column (3) for the trait of inferential comprehension:

1. The student can correctly state the main idea.

2. The student can articulate the author's thesis and back up the thesis statement with multiple details from the text.

Now ask, What would be the *minimum performance* one might observe that could still be called a demonstration of the trait? This is a level of performance that constitutes any sign of movement in the right direction, the tiniest baby step along the road to proficiency. For inferential comprehension, this could be something like, "being capable of making a reasoned guess at the author's main idea." In the column labeled *Emerging*, to the left of the middle column, write down those observable behaviors that you felt would constitute a minimum observable performance on each trait. (Note: For both statistical and motivational purposes, the furthest left-hand column must be for something accomplished, albeit minimal, and not used for failure or rank incompetence.)

Lastly, ask what *a truly outstanding example of performance* on this trait looks like. Here, you are being asked to envision performance that is near perfection. For inferential comprehension, Mr. Collins might list the following items:

1. The student can accurately retell and support the author's thesis with multiple details from the text.

2. The student can draw logical inferences about the author's point of view.

3. The student can persuasively support those inferences by referencing specific rhetorical techniques, language usage, and vocabulary employed by the author.

Figure 3.5 reflects Mr. Collins's rating scale partially filled in for the trait of inferential comprehension. Now, using copies of the rating-scale worksheet provided (Figure 3.4), build a five-point rating scale that you believe illustrates a continuum of performance for each of your priority achievement targets.

RATING SCALES AND PROGRAM ACTION RESEARCH

Often, people think of rating scales or rubrics as devices to be used exclusively for assessment of student performance. This is unfortunate, as the rating scale is a wonderful way to articulate a shared vision of program

FIGURE 3.4 Rating-Scale Worksheet

Trait	Emerging (1)	Basic (2)	Developing (3)	Proficient (4)	Fluent (5)

FIGURE 3.5   Rating Scale of Reading Proficiency

Trait	Emerging (1)	Basic (2)	Developing (3)	Proficient (4)	Fluent (5)
1. Ability to read grade-level material					
2. Enjoyment of reading					
3. Literal comprehension					
4. Inferential comprehension	After reading a grade-level appropriate essay, the student can make a reasonable guess at the author's main idea.	After reading a grade-level appropriate essay, the student can accurately retell the author's thesis.	After reading a grade-level appropriate essay, the student can accurately retell and support the author's thesis with multiple details from the text.	After reading a grade-level appropriate essay, the student can accurately retell and support the author's thesis with multiple details from the text and can draw logical inferences about the author's point of view.	After reading a grade-level appropriate essay, the student can accurately retell and support the author's thesis with multiple details from the text, can draw logical inferences about the author's point of view, and can persuasively support those inferences by referencing specific rhetorical techniques, language usage, and vocabulary used by the author.

Source: Adapted from Sagor (2000).

excellence and can prove to be a wonderful monitoring device when facilitating school or program improvement initiatives. In Resource C (Exhibit 3), you will find a copy of a rating scale Dr. Hernandez might have used to articulate a vision of performance with the program goal of faculty collegiality.

Tip on Rating Scale

The longer term the achievement target, the more columns you may find you will need for your rating scale. That is fine. However, be sure that the distinction between the performances that make up each step on the rating scale are clear, distinct from each other, and unambiguous.

THE SPECIAL PROBLEM OF LONG-RANGE GOALS

Both of the targets discussed in the previous section—building a collegial faculty and developing skillful readers—are significant goals. In all likelihood, it will take these educators considerable time to move performance to the top of the scale. Nevertheless, it is reasonable for a fourth-grade teacher or a principal to expect some improvement on these types of targets during the course of his or her initial research.

There are targets, be they academic or nonacademic, that educational action researchers often shy away from simply because they take so long to complete, and people are often impatient and want to see quick results. The long-term nature of the targets makes them appear nearly impossible to monitor in the short term. For example, it is common for educators to value long-term targets for their students, such as

- developing lifelong learning skills,
- preparing for success in college or careers, and
- developing integrity.

Because it takes many years of concentrated effort to get students to success on those targets, many action researchers will elect to avoid them. That is unfortunate because in this era of high-stakes testing, if we don't deliberately focus on something and measure our progress toward its attainment, it is unlikely to receive the attention it deserves.

To understand the challenge of assessing progress on long-term targets, we use the work of the U.S. space agency, NASA, as an analogy. As part of its interplanetary studies, NASA sent several *Cassini* probes to make flybys of Saturn and Jupiter and relay data on those planets back to Earth.

These were long-range projects in two ways. First, it took years to develop the technologies needed to design spacecraft capable of performing these missions. Furthermore, once the probes were launched, it took several years to reach Saturn and Jupiter. Clearly, it would have been folly for NASA to bypass these projects simply because they were so long term. After all, interplanetary studies are at the very core of its mission. But it would be equally wrong for NASA to have proceeded with such ambitious projects without a strategy to monitor short-term progress.

Consequently, the two key assessment questions for NASA became these:

1. How do we determine if our research and development efforts are proceeding on schedule?

2. Once a spacecraft has been launched, how can we determine if the spacecraft is on course to pass by Saturn and Jupiter as scheduled, although several years hence?

The issues those questions present for rocket scientists (aerospace action researchers) are not conceptually different from the ones confronting educational action researchers pursuing long-term learning or program goals. Keep in mind, it could be twenty-five years before anyone will know with certainty if any particular student has, in fact, become a lifelong learner. Likewise, character traits are not acquired overnight. The challenge for NASA and the educator is one and the same: creating systems that reliably assess incremental advances on targets that may not be fully realized for years to come.

ASSESSING RATE OF GROWTH

It usually isn't enough to simply know that progress is being made. Steady progress could be occurring but at such slow rates as to be functionally ineffective. Consequently, when working with long-range goals, the question that demands an answer is whether the rate of progress is satisfactory. When it comes to the achievement of academic objectives, most educators are familiar with the concept of *rate of growth*. In the common school vernacular, when a student continues to perform *at grade level*, we classify his or her rate of growth as appropriate. This translates to achieving *one year's growth in one year's time*.

When working on a five-year project, the appropriate rate of growth is progress at a rate that will result in completion of the project in sixty months' time. For every NASA mission, there is an expectation of when the launch should occur. Therefore, the acceptable rate of progress is one that will have everything in place and ready to go on or before the projected launch date.

In 2001, as part of the No Child Left Behind Act, the U.S. government codified what was deemed to be an acceptable rate of growth for students. That law required schools to demonstrate that individual students, groups of students, and entire student bodies achieved what was called *adequate yearly progress* (AYP). The procedures for accomplishing this involved the use of annually administered tests designed to determine if the progress made by students during the past year was at a rate sufficient to get them to the targets on time. This annual monitoring system, even when accurate, was far from helpful for classroom teachers. The results of spring testing came too late for any teacher to make instructional modifications for a student or class. In reality, this information was about as helpful for a classroom teacher as receiving feedback on the efficacy of a 365-day weight loss program by weighing yourself just once and doing so at the end of the year.

DETERMINING ADEQUATE YEARLY PROGRESS IN REAL TIME

Let's assume we are teachers who are deeply committed to helping each of our students make adequate yearly progress. And let's assume we've developed a very clear vision regarding the target performance that we are after. In most cases, this would be the skills that the Common Core standards presume our students will possess by the end of the year. Lastly, let's assume we are unwilling to wait until June to determine if our hypothesis on the best way to prepare our students worked as well as we had hoped (helping them progress at a rate of "one year's growth in one year's time").

In all likelihood, the type of rating scale discussed earlier in this chapter won't be satisfactory. As good as a five-, seven-, or nine-point rating scale may be, it's not likely to be sensitive enough to detect minor incremental developments. Using such a scale would be like assessing a weight reduction program by weighing yourself every morning but doing so with an industrial scale that reports weight in twenty-pound increments. While it might be a great scale, it won't provide you with feedback that is either sensitive or precise enough to meet your monitoring needs.

Figure 3.6 is a visual from NASA that illustrates the trajectory of a *Cassini* spacecraft as it completes its seven-year mission. By knowing the launch date and the current position of the spacecraft, the aerospace action researchers were able to use this diagram throughout the mission to determine if the vehicle was, in fact, proceeding appropriately—achieving its AYP.

Let's now look at an academic example (see Figure 3.7). In this case, we will assume the goal is to have our students prepared to successfully take Advanced Placement calculus upon the completion of eleventh grade. Let's also assume that at least some students entering kindergarten in our district aren't yet even able to identify numerals correctly. Figure 3.7 illustrates the slope of the growth that will need to be demonstrated by a student entering school with zero math knowledge if she is to stay on track to meet the goal of succeeding in AP calculus as a high school senior.

As teachers in pursuit of long-term objectives, we will need to monitor our students' rates of growth by plotting their performance as they move up the grades. Then, a quick look at a longitudinal graph will tell us if the slope of progress reflects a rate of growth that is

1. right on target (at AYP), enabling the student to take calculus as a senior;

2. faster than expected, which would enable the student to take calculus earlier (faster than AYP); or

3. below the expectation (slower than AYP) and not ready for calculus as a senior.

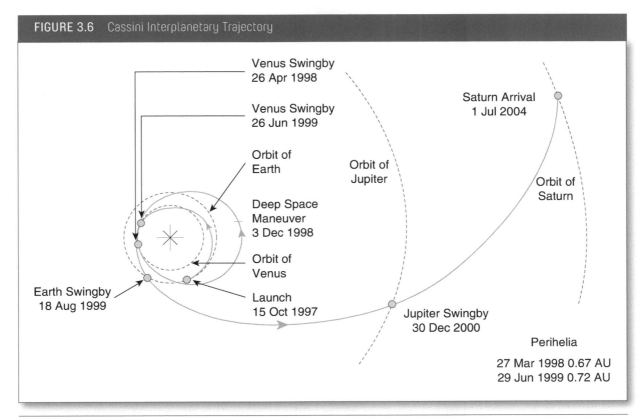

FIGURE 3.6 Cassini Interplanetary Trajectory

Source: http://saturn.jpl.nasa.gov

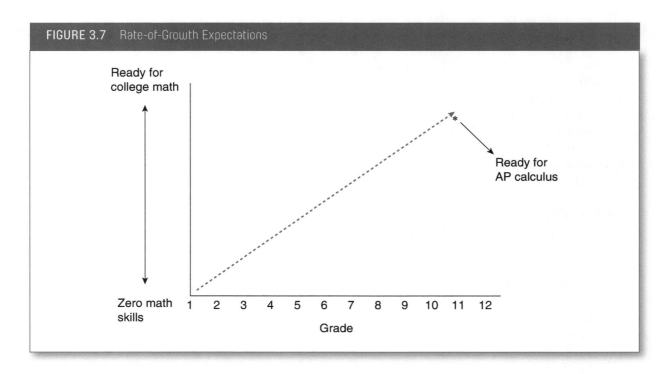

FIGURE 3.7 Rate-of-Growth Expectations

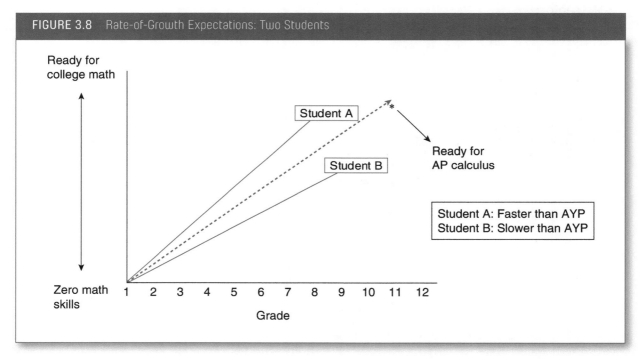

FIGURE 3.8 Rate-of-Growth Expectations: Two Students

Figure 3.8 indicates the rate of growth of two students: one who is performing at a rate faster than AYP and one at a rate slower than AYP.

PRODUCING YOUR OWN RATE-OF-GROWTH CHARTS

There are seven steps you can follow to produce a rate-of-growth chart that can be used to track progress toward any long-term target. By using this strategy, you can meaningfully trace the efficacy of your work on a target, even when the ultimate success may not be fully determined for several years to come.

Step 1. When pursuing a long-range, multiyear target, the first step is to place in sequence a list of the skills, backed up by an example of the type of work that is expected of students upon entrance into each grade, for that particular achievement target.

Step 2. Examine the list of skills to determine if it is logical, has any obvious gaps, and seems achievable.

Step 3. Now, take a look at examples of on-target work for a student entering the grade you will be teaching and on-target work for a student exiting your grade. Ask yourself or your team to brainstorm every single little baby step of a subskill that must be attained to move from the entry piece of work to the exit piece. Come up with as many subskills as possible.

Step 4. Make any necessary adjustments to the sequence of skills on your list until you believe it is as accurate and inclusive as possible. It's okay if some of the subskills on your list aren't sequential in nature, but to the best extent possible, place them in the order they should be mastered.

Step 5. Now, divide the list by the number of weeks in the school year (usually thirty-six). Let's assume that you identified seventy-two separate subskills. In such a case, you would be able to say that a student who is acquiring skills at the rate of two per week is making AYP.

Step 6. Maintain a running record of each student's acquisition of the identified subskills. Periodically make a line graph from your running records to illustrate which students are demonstrating proficiency at an adequate pace, which are proceeding slower than a rate of "one year's growth in one year's time," and which are showing a rate of progress that is exceeding expectations. Note: This is valuable material to share at parent conferences.

Step 7. (Note: This step can only be done on a schoolwide or systemwide basis.) Place the listings of subskills on a continuum across all the grades served in your school. Then, conduct an entry assessment for each child, either at the beginning of the school year or when he or she enters your room. Make plans to conduct an exit assessment of each student as well. With this type of assessment, you will be able to determine the rate of progress for each of the children during the time each of them spent in your school or class.

Keep in mind that what is considered AYP for any particular student is a value judgment. If we are teaching remedial students, and we hold high aspirations for each one of them, our goal would likely be to produce a rate of growth significantly in excess of one year's growth in one year's time, since that is what will be required for them to catch up with their peers. This is especially true for historically underserved and otherwise disadvantaged students, disproportionately affecting students of color and students from low socioeconomic backgrounds. But regardless of how AYP is defined, a rate-of-growth chart will enable you to monitor and adjust in a timely fashion without having to wait for a year-end test or perhaps several years for evidence of achievement of a long-term goal.

ASCERTAINING RATE OF GROWTH IN LEADERSHIP PROJECTS

The importance of monitoring the adequacy of the rate of progress of an initiative is especially important for those engaged in school leadership. As was the case with the example of NASA's *Cassini* mission, whenever we are managing a long-term improvement effort, we have a continuing need to know if we are on schedule, falling behind, or if we are likely to meet our goals ahead of time.

There is a basic strategy school leaders can follow to track the rate of progress on their initiatives that is functionally similar to the rate-of-growth charting discussed for tracking student progress. The steps for following this process are detailed in Resource C (Exhibit 4). However, when leaders want to monitor the rate of progress of an initiative they are facilitating, it is best for them to have completed their *Stage 2: Theory Development* work before conducting this analysis. For this reason, leaders may wish to defer their work on rate-of-growth charting until after completing Chapter 5.

End of Stage 1

We have now finished our exploration of the first stage of the action research process, clarifying the vision and targets. To recap, at this point you have selected a focus for your research that relates to an area

- that you care deeply about,
- where performance could be improved, and
- where the actions needed to make changes in performance are within your sphere of authority.

In addition, you have identified a set of specific priority achievement targets where you hope to see demonstrable improvement. By now, you should have consulted the literature and considered the experience of others who have worked at achieving success in the same focus area. Lastly, after reflecting on each of the traits or components of your target, you have identified a range of observable performance and a pace of development that you feel constitutes AYP.

You have now teased out and achieved some degree of precision on where you want to go, and you have sketched out a mechanism to measure your progress as you travel to the desired destination. You have closed your eyes and visualized the promised land as well as the mileposts you expect to pass along the way.

This brings us to the threshold of *Stage 2: Articulating a Theory of Action*. This is where you will engage in the rigorous but fun work of figuring out what route has the greatest potential for getting you closer to your vision.

4

Articulating a
Theory of Action

In Stage 1 of the action research process, you identified your priority achievement targets and reflected on what you believed would constitute appropriate growth on those targets. You are now ready for the second stage of the action research process: articulating a theory of action. When choosing to become action researchers, *action* became more than just our first name. Our passion for providing the very best professional *action* is the rationale for making investments of our finite time and energy in this work. The products you've produced up to this point are very important; in fact, the work you have already completed in Stage 1 (Chapters 1–3) will prove essential to your ultimate success. However, it is here, at Stage 2, that the really creative intellectual work begins. While doing the work of theory development, you will be crafting original strategies and designing innovative techniques with promise for producing superior outcomes and better performance than you have been able to achieve in the past.

Action research, often referred to by other terms, is a key component of the systems approach to continuous improvement pioneered by W. Edwards Deming (1986/2000). Deming famously asserted that 95 percent of organizational performance could be attributed to the tactics, strategies, and processes used to accomplish the organization's work. Over the years, a great deal of research has shown support for that perspective. It is now clear that organizational success is not evidence of the inherent goodness or badness of the personnel working for the organization. Outstanding organizational performance is not a reflection of *who* is doing the work, but rather, it is a reflection of how things are being done (Deming, 1986/2000; Senge, 1990). Consequently, when an improvement in performance occurs, significant credit belongs to the theory of action that was implemented by those carrying out the work. When we find ourselves disappointed in an individual student, group, or program performance, it doesn't mean we and our colleagues are bad people or less-than-competent professionals. Rather, disappointing performance is an indication that our actions and the particular theory or theories that informed those actions weren't adequate to the challenges we were confronting. Consequently, it is those actions that will need to be changed if we are to expect better results in the future.

Action research is an empowering strategy. Exercising control over the theory of action that informs our work is the most powerful thing we can do as professionals. That being said, the idea of having educational practitioners assuming responsibility for the critique of their own practices and the design of innovative solutions for their own problems, while at the heart of the action research process, still generates more than a little controversy. The two criticisms most often voiced against empowering educators with this authority are the following:

1. Full-time educators aren't capable of focusing on theory development and program design while, at the same time, attending to their other responsibilities.

2. An adequate professional knowledge base already exists, and educators should simply be expected to implement those "proven" practices with fidelity in their schools and classrooms (Century, Freeman, Rudnick, & Leslie, 2008; Los Angeles Unified School District, 2010; O'Donnell, 2006).

IF NOT US, WHO?

The first argument—that practicing educators aren't the ones who should be doing this work—flies in the face of a reality that educators face on a daily basis. All professional work is complex. And education is arguably the most complex, with hundreds of variables influencing each instructional decision (see the discussion in Chapter 1). Due to the complexity involved in professional decision making, the development and maintenance of each discipline's knowledge base has always been considered the responsibility of the profession itself. In most professions, the people who are taking the action are expected to be the ones designing the innovations, conducting the research, and consequently producing the evolving body of professional knowledge. This makes sense. After all, who is in a better position to identify the problems, understand the context, and integrate new insights into prevailing routines than those working on the frontlines?

Richard has two dogs that he loves dearly. Every time he takes one of his retrievers to the vet, he is literally betting their lives on the soundness of the treatment protocol that his veterinarian prescribes. On these occasions, Richard is comforted by the knowledge that it was veterinarians who conducted the research that will inform the decisions his vet makes when treating his dogs.

When tasks are simple and straightforward, there is a certain efficiency to separating responsibility for the design and approval of the task from the actual conduct of the work. This is why supervisors are generally hired to monitor and direct blue-collar work. However, when the work is complex, when it requires an understanding of nuance and idiosyncratic behavior and calls for constant monitoring by a trained eye, followed by continual adjustments in the theory of action, then that work needs to be informed by the insights of those taking the action: the practitioners themselves.

AN ADEQUATE KNOWLEDGE BASE ALREADY EXISTS

The second criticism leveled at educators conducting research on their own practice is a bit bizarre. For quite a while, the stated goal of educational policy throughout most of North America has been to get every student to a high level of performance on a set of meaningful standards. If a knowledge base currently exists that documents and shows how to accomplish this, why has this research been so widely ignored? We are aware of no reported evidence documenting the success of any city, state, or country in getting all of their students to high levels of performance on meaningful objectives. So unless there has been a worldwide and intergenerational conspiracy to deny the children of the world access to a good education, it would appear that the answers on how to accomplish universal student success have eluded the best and brightest throughout history. From this, we can conclude that the current educational knowledge base is inadequate to guide us to our achievement target of universal student success.

So to paraphrase the words of the Hebrew sage, Hillel,

If not us, who?

If not here, where?

If not now, when?

GOING BEYOND PROVEN PRACTICES: BUILDING A THEORY OF ACTION

In Chapter 3's discussion of the literature review, a careful reader may have noticed that we avoided using a catchphrase that has become part of the school improvement vernacular: *scientifically proven practice*. It is a term that rolls nicely and easily off of the tongue. The words *scientifically proven* deliver a good public relations punch, but shopping for and adopting those proven practices is a strategy that doesn't work nearly as well as the terminology might suggest.

Obviously, there is nothing wrong with making use of successful strategies. When a practice has been shown to work in a context similar to your own and the results obtained match your expectations, then adopting that practice for your school or classroom makes perfect sense.

External Pressure and Proven Practices

In a desire to encourage educators to make use of the best available practices, many government agencies and publicly supported programs now mandate the use of what have been labeled scientifically proven practices. On the surface, policies like these seem quite rational. After all, if a strategy has been scientifically proven to be effective, we ought to employ it whenever and wherever appropriate. To ignore a proven practice would constitute educational malpractice since it would mean denying a student a clearly beneficial educational experience. In other aspects of our lives, it is easy to think of acknowledged proven practices that people are always wise to follow, such as these:

- File your taxes on or before April 15.
- While arguing a case in court, show respect for the presiding judge.
- Avoid contact with other people when you have a contagious disease.

Obviously, failing to adopt these proven practices would be irresponsible. In fact, not doing so could put you and/or others at risk.

But what of these so-called proven practices in teaching and learning? Repeatedly, we hear of programs that were proven to be successful. Furthermore, when we examine data on these programs, we might frequently encounter impressive statistics, such as the following:

- With this program, attendance improved for three out of four students.
- While using this program, 75 percent of the students posted gains in comprehension.

It is only right that we are impressed with reported gains such as those. But simply adopting and faithfully implementing programs, even ones with such positive results, won't, in the long run, prove that satisfying for most educators. This is because in the opinion of most dedicated teachers, a 75 to 80 percent success rate simply isn't even close to adequate. While at first blush, those statistics might have sounded impressive, stated in another way, those same data say the following:

- Under this program, 25 percent of the students' attendance declined or showed no improvement.
- While using this program, one out of four students showed virtually no growth in reading comprehension.

Logically, a faithfully adopted program can only be expected to work as well for adopters as it did where it was first proven successful. Therefore, the teacher or faculty adopting programs like those cited above should expect to leave school every day knowing that 25 percent of their students likely won't be prospering. Few dedicated teachers will find this an inviting prospect. Simply adopting a program that hasn't produced universal student success elsewhere and then considering your school improvement work to be complete means accepting an intolerable degree of failure as inevitable. Having to go along with such an assumption is both emotionally and morally untenable for most of us.

This is not an argument against using or even adopting practices that have worked with many students. However, it does alert us to a set of critical questions that should be raised whenever a review of research or a reconsideration of a school policy directs us to implement a "scientifically" proven practice.

The first question we should be asking is, *With whom has this practice been proven successful?* As professionals concerned with promoting equity and excellence, we need to know about the characteristics of the students who prospered, as well as the characteristics of those who didn't. Were there patterns of performance that might help us to predict success or failure for our students? For example, did boys and girls succeed equally well, or did they fail in equal proportions? Was this program successful with gifted students? How about kids with dyslexia or other learning challenges? Was the student performance obtained reflective of ethnic or cultural differences among the students?

If a proposed or adopted program appears to have been beneficial for all categories of students in your class, then by all means, you ought to use it. However, if there is a type of student for whom the program was not successful in the past, and you have that type of student in your class or classes, then you may just have identified an excellent focus for your action research. Specifically, this recognition might motivate you to investigate this question:

> What *alterations*, *modifications*, or *alternatives* could I make to this program that will make it more likely that all of my students will succeed, especially those students who haven't shown success with this program in the past?

This question highlights the challenge for any inquiring educator who is hoping to isolate techniques with promise to increase the percentage of students and expand the category of students experiencing success. When working toward achievement of the twin goals of excellence and equity, all of our instructional strategies must be designed with the expectation that they will succeed with the full diversity of our student body. There is no escaping the truth of the saying, "If we keep doing what we've been doing, we will keep getting what we've been getting."

As this text is being updated, the United States is in transition from the No Child Left Behind Act (2001) to the Every Student Succeeds Act (2016). Both of these laws provide a clear window into current educational policy. Though varied in their accountability structures, both acts give voice to an ideal that hopefully every educator, parent, or policy maker shares: Every child, irrespective of her or his status or family background, deserves and should be expected to perform at the highest level possible.

Since continuing to get what we've been getting won't meet our own high expectations, and it will likely place our school outside of compliance with federal and state education regulations, we would be wise to turn that old saying around and restate it in reverse.

> If we want to get *more than* we've been getting, then we must figure out how to *do things differently* than we've been doing them in the past.

While this doesn't mean you will forever be engaged in conducting full-blown action research projects, it does mean that if you are seeking universal student success, then you will need to be involved with the four stages of the action research process—*envisioning success, clarifying a theory to get you there, collecting data while implementing your theory,* and *reflecting on the results obtained*—for as long as you are working in education.

One of the benefits of using the best practices developed by others is that it often helps us construct boundaries around our inquiries. When we build a revised theory of action on top of an existing theory of action (one that has already succeeded with a significant number of students), we aren't committing ourselves to solving the entire riddle all by ourselves, and we aren't starting from scratch.

Whether we are building on a strong program that has been implemented elsewhere or creating a brand new program, being *innovative* in the development of a theory of action isn't a choice; it is essential. Since we recognize that things now must be done differently than before, creativity will be required for us to figure out what needs to be changed. If the theory of action we are developing is to succeed, it will need to take into account three factors:

1. What is known about the context where it will be implemented?

2. What has been reported in the professional knowledge base?

3. What have we come to understand through the wisdom of practice: our own professional experience?

TWO KINDS OF VARIABLES

In Chapter 3, you established success criteria and created rating scales for measuring changes in performance on your priority achievement targets. Researchers refer to a phenomenon they are trying to improve or change as their *dependent variable*. The word *dependent* is used because the researcher is positing that changes in performance will be *dependent* on something specific occurring. When doing action research, it is suggested that you consider the term priority achievement target as being synonymous with dependent variable. For example, if we desire to lose weight, our achievement target (dependent variable) is our weight. The criteria we would establish to determine change on this target would be our weight in pounds and ounces, as measured on our bathroom scales. Since we believe that changes in our body weight are dependent on our choices regarding behavior and diet, our weight is the dependent variable in our search for lighter selves.

The other important category of variables for researchers concerns the phenomena the researcher believes might influence changes in the dependent variable. These phenomena are called the *independent variables*. The term *independent* is used because the person carrying out the research is free to adjust or change the independent variables however he or she thinks best. Later, the researcher will be able to determine if those adjustments were worthwhile by looking for corresponding changes in the dependent variable. The independent variables that we might choose to adjust in our investigation of weight loss are our specific behavioral choices (our diet and exercise regime). This relationship is illustrated in the following table.

Choice of Independent Variables =		*Change* in the Dependent Variable
(our actions)	→	(achievement target)

The rating scales you have already developed will be used in your action research to measure changes in your dependent variables, your achievement targets. From this point on, we will use the terms *achievement target* and *dependent variable* interchangeably. In the first two chapters, we concentrated on the dependent variables: your priority achievement targets. Now, we will shift our focus and begin the process of identifying the critical independent variables: those things that you believe hold the greatest potential for producing the changes you desire to see on your priority achievement targets.

CREATING MILEPOSTS ON THE ROUTE TO MASTERY

As we worked our way through Stage 1, we broke down our global visions into smaller component parts that we called achievement targets. We moved from a general improvement focus to a defined vision of success by articulating specific priority achievement targets. Then, we broke down those achievement targets into subcomponents (traits) that could be effectively assessed. Now, as we develop a theory of action, we will engage in a similar sequential process but do so in reverse order. In constructing your theory of action, you will build a comprehensive theory by starting with the component parts (like pieces of a puzzle), and then, you will systematically arrange them to illustrate the big picture.

Discerning the components of your target (the traits) was important because performance on the target was defined as the sum of performance on its constituent traits. Likewise, when you have completed your theory of action, you will see that the efficacy of your comprehensive theory is the sum of a defined set of strategies and actions—the independent variables.

INFERRING INDEPENDENT VARIABLES

The first step in the process of building your theory will be to combine what you already understand from personal experience with what you've gathered from your review of the literature. The process begins by generating a list containing all of the key factors (independent variables) you think need to be addressed through your actions if significant improvement is to occur on the identified achievement target.

Now, let's put ourselves in the position of Mr. Johnson, the principal whose goal was providing leadership for the schoolwide effort to increase student engagement. Reflecting on the key variables that he felt he could affect as the school's principal, he might have generated a list like the following:

- Co-construct a research-based definition of student engagement with teachers.
- Provide faculty with training on ways to increase student engagement.
- Create space for teachers to observe each other's classrooms with a focus on student engagement.
- Increase my presence in classrooms, and provide positive and constructive feedback to teachers regarding student engagement.
- Find exemplars of student engagement, and encourage sharing of ideas and strategies.

The identification of critical independent variables is an important step for action researchers like Mr. Johnson. However, regardless of the quality of the list he generates, the list he produces is unlikely to contain enough specificity to provide him with adequate direction for planning his work each day toward the achievement of his desired result. In addition, the list he created wasn't prioritized, nor did it provide any insight into how those five separate actions would influence or interact with each other. Consequently, Mr. Johnson would have a hard time articulating a reasoned and coherent strategy for hitting his target (universally high student engagement) without first thinking through the answers to two additional questions:

- What is the relative importance of the identified independent variables?
- How do the identified independent variables relate to and interact with each other?

In this and the next chapter, we will examine two strategies that, when taken together, will allow you to respond to both of those questions. The first is a technique called the *priority pie*. The second technique, *the graphic reconstruction*, will be our focus in Chapter 5.

USING THE PRIORITY PIE TO IDENTIFY, CLARIFY, AND WEIGH INDEPENDENT VARIABLES

Decades of educational research have clearly established the relationship between time and learning. Both the allocation of time and the time spent on task have been shown to be key correlates of learning (Aronson, Zimmerman, & Carlos, 1998; Stanley, Spradlin, & Plucker, 2007). Time is, without a doubt, the most valuable resource under our control. And since class time is a zero-sum commodity, the decisions we make on how to spend this scarce resource are crucial. It isn't an overstatement to assert that in large measure, our effectiveness in hitting our targets is determined by the wisdom of our choices regarding the allocation and expenditure of the time and energy available to us. The priority pie is a simple strategy, one that will help you determine how you could most effectively allocate this critical resource.

The priority pie process has four steps:

1. Brainstorming
2. Summarizing
3. Evaluating
4. Graphing

Let's now follow two action researchers, both from AR academy, as they work their way through the theory-building process. One is Mr. Johnson, who is trying to increase student engagement in his school. For the second project, we'll look at the work of Ms. Montgomery, a middle school teacher at AR Academy who wants to hone her questioning and discussion techniques to both minimize and eliminate any potential bias students may be experiencing and help each child to maximize success with the response opportunities they are provided.

Step 1: Brainstorming the Critical Independent Variables

If we are to succeed in improving performance on our priority achievement targets, we will need to identify and attend to *each key independent variable*. This process of identification must occur consciously and deliberately because should an essential variable be overlooked, it could have a significant impact on our ultimate success. Therefore, the first step is thinking through and answering the following question:

> What are the issues, factors, programs, and processes that *must* be addressed to achieve success with this target? (Success, in this instance, means everyone or every system performing at or above expectations.) If you prepared a rating scale for your priority achievement target in Chapter 3, then success should be defined as everyone or every system performing at the top level on the rating scale.

As you recall, the middle school principal, Mr. Johnson, had five items on his list of dependent variables. They were as follows:

- Co-construct a research-based definition of student engagement with teachers.
- Provide faculty with training on ways to increase student engagement.
- Create space for teachers to observe each other's classrooms with a focus on student engagement.
- Increase my presence in classrooms, and provide positive and constructive feedback to teachers regarding student engagement.
- Find exemplars of student engagement, and encourage sharing of ideas and strategies.

Ms. Montgomery, the middle school teacher wishing to create more equitable response opportunities for her students and thereby enhance their engagement, generated the following list of independent variables:

- Explicit teaching of strategies for students to engage in class discussion
- Safe environment
- Time to think and reflect
- Time allotted for classroom discussion
- Tracking who is speaking and how often
- Tracking levels of questions
- Discussion structures and techniques
- Variety of questions used
- Use of sentence stems to assist students who are shy or feel insecure

Step 2: Summarizing the Independent Variables

Once action researchers feel confident that they have identified the key independent variables, they are ready to begin articulating an emerging theory of action. At this stage, Mr. Johnson could summarize his emerging theory as follows:

In order to increase student engagement in my school, I need to work with the teachers to co-create a shared understanding of what student engagement means. I need to ensure that teachers are provided with the necessary training and support to utilize a variety of engagement strategies. Also, in order to promote sharing of best practices for engagement, I will need to create space for faculty to collaborate and visit each other's classrooms. Since teachers, like students, love exemplars, I will provide them with models from as many sources as possible. And finally, I will conduct frequent mini–classroom observations and provide the faculty with data and feedback specific to our implementation of engagement strategies at the individual and school level.

Ms. Montgomery might articulate her theory as follows:

For my students to actively participate in class discussions at high levels, I need to explicitly teach my expectations for classroom discussions. I also need to make sure that the students have a proper amount of think time to process information and prepare their thoughts. Since response opportunities are an important component of displaying my expectations to a student, I will need to find ways to track and monitor the frequency and level of questions posed to all students in all subgroups. I will be intentional about planning my questions ahead of time, considering each student to ensure equitable participation. To build support for this process, I must become a learner with my students, checking in with the class and each individual student to see how I am doing.

Since time and energy are limited, both of these action researchers will soon realize they will need to apportion their limited time among each of the proposed actions (independent variables) referenced in their emerging theories. This brings them and us to Step 3.

Step 3: Conducting an Intuitive Regression Analysis

The next step in the priority pie process is determining the appropriate amount of attention to be paid to each identified factor. Determining the relative importance of each item (independent variable) on our lists is a judgment call, one that the action researcher will ultimately have to make for himself or herself. But it will be an informed judgment based on a combination of the review of the literature, past experience, and intuition.

One strategy to determine the relative importance of the independent variables is to divide the time and energy available to be expended across the list of factors, based on the perceived importance of each factor to the realization of the whole—that is, excellent performance (as illustrated by a top score on the performance rating scale) on the achievement target. This can be accomplished using the Intuitive Regression Analysis Worksheet, as shown in Figure 4.1. When using this worksheet, each item brainstormed in Step 1 is assigned a percentage based on how critical the researcher feels that item is to the achievement of the whole. There is no limit to the percentage that can be assigned to any one item; however, the total must equal 100 percent.

FIGURE 4.1 Intuitive Regression Analysis Worksheet

Using the following form, make a judgment regarding the relative importance of each of the factors that you had identified as critical to success on this achievement target. Use a separate form for each target being pursued.

Achievement Target: _____

List each factor deemed critical to fostering success with this achievement target	Importance of this factor (%)
	Total: 100%

FIGURE 4.2   Mr. Johnson's Priority Pie on Leadership for the Student Engagement Initiative

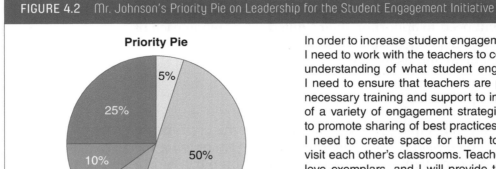

Priority Pie

- 5%
- 25%
- 10%
- 10%
- 50%

☐ Co-construct definition
☐ Training and support/exemplars
☐ Providing and collecting feedback
☐ Peer observations and feedback
☐ Increased administrator observations

In order to increase student engagement in my school, I need to work with the teachers to co-create a shared understanding of what student engagement means. I need to ensure that teachers are provided with the necessary training and support to implement the use of a variety of engagement strategies. Also, in order to promote sharing of best practices for engagement, I need to create space for them to collaborate and visit each other's classrooms. Teachers, like students, love exemplars, and I will provide them with models from as many sources as possible. And finally, I will conduct frequent mini–classroom observations and provide teachers with data and feedback specific to our implementation of engagement strategies at the individual and school level.

FIGURE 4.3   Ms. Montgomery's Priority Pie on Enhancing Class Discussions and Response Opportunities

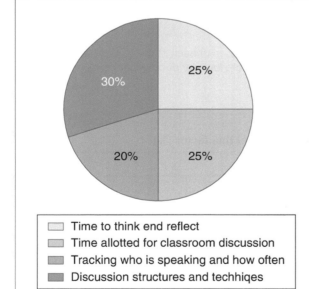

- 30%
- 25%
- 20%
- 25%

☐ Time to think end reflect
☐ Time allotted for classroom discussion
☐ Tracking who is speaking and how often
☐ Discussion structures and techhiqes

For my students to actively participate in class discussions at high levels, I will need to make sure that the students have a proper amount of think time to process information and prepare their thoughts (25%). Since response opportunities are an important component of displaying my expectations to a student, I must track who is speaking and how often (20%). In addition I will need to be intentional about the discussion structures and techniques to be utilized (30%). Last, I need to design my lessons in all subjects to provide adequate time for class discussions (25%).

Step 4: Graphically Displaying the Emerging Theory

Once you have completed your analysis using the Intuitive Regression Analysis Worksheet, you should be able to draw your emergent theory as a pie chart and write a summary paragraph explaining the reasoning behind your proposed allocation of resources. Above, Figures 4.2 and 4.3 show Mr. Johnson's and Ms. Montgomery's graphs and narratives, respectively.

Drawing the priority pie forces us to do the hard intellectual work of determining what we believe to be of critical importance, and it also causes us to reflect on the relative importance of each piece of the puzzle. As important as this is, it still lacks the detail and precision necessary to provide adequate direction to our work. There are still several other crucial things that will need to be considered before we will be able to confidently declare our theory of action to be complete and proceed with its implementation. Even the best priority pie can't provide the clarity and direction needed to proceed to the action phase. If we want to be confident of the potential of our "theory" to produce universal success, we will still need to incorporate the following into our theory development:

- What specific actions are necessary to accomplish each slice of the priority pie?
- Who is involved in each of these actions?
- When should these actions occur?
- Will multiple actions need to occur simultaneously?
- Is there a sequence of events that must be followed?
- If problems are encountered, what types of remedial steps should be taken?

When conducting a scientific experiment, as well as all other forms of exploration, it is necessary that the explorer work from as detailed a plan of action as possible. The process of clearly and unambiguously articulating one's plan of action serves several purposes:

- A detailed plan provides guidance and direction for the work.
- When and if success is achieved, the plan provides a road map that others can use as they attempt to reach the same destination.
- When and if the results don't come out as expected, the plan can be meticulously retraced to find out where problems were encountered.

USING THE PRIORITY PIE WITH DESCRIPTIVE RESEARCH

When conducting *descriptive* action research, it is no less important to have clarity on the theories of action that are being observed and documented. The essential difference is that with descriptive research, the purpose of the theory of action is to clarify your understanding of the way things are currently being done—*the operant theory*—rather than to articulate a proposed original theory of action.

It is hard to imagine any action being taken in the schoolhouse that isn't being taken for a reason. But oftentimes, things have been done a certain way for so long that it has been years since anyone paused to consider and reflect on the underlying rationale. To make these implicit theories of action explicit, action researchers who are conducting descriptive research should go through the same four-step "priority pie" process but do so in a slightly different manner.

Step 1: Brainstorming the Critical Independent Variables

Generate a list of independent variables by responding to the following question:

> What issues, factors, programs, and processes are currently consuming most of our time and energy relating to this target?

Step 2: Summarizing the Independent Variables

Explain, with a brief narrative statement, the main actions (see Step 1) that are currently being taken in pursuit of the target.

Step 3: Conducting an Intuitive Regression Analysis

Ask how time is currently being spent. Look over the list of independent variables (Step 1) and the narrative statement (Step 2) for each target being investigated. Estimate the approximate percentage of the available time and energy that *is currently being devoted to* each variable. The total must equal 100 percent.

Step 4: Graphically Displaying the Operant Theory

Draw the information from Step 3 in the form of a pie chart, and do your best to explain the percentages. When doing so, be careful to avoid using interpretive language. Rather than saying, "We are spending an enormous amount of time on *x*," or, "We are overly emphasizing the use of worksheets instead of teacher-generated examples," try to say things like, "We are spending 75 percent of our time on *x*," or, "Of the assignments used, 80 percent involve publisher-supplied worksheets while less than 10 percent are teacher-developed assignments."

Occasionally, someone anticipates that he or she will be doing descriptive research, but then, as the researcher makes the operant theory explicit, he or she becomes so uncomfortable with the current state of affairs that he or she decides that a better theory must exist or could easily be created. When this occurs, it is wise to go back and see if another priority pie can be created, one that will illustrate an improved and novel theory. To do this, it is suggested that you use the Intuitive Regression Analysis Worksheet (Figure 4.1).

Whether you are doing descriptive or quasi-experimental research, you will now need to use a second visual technique called the *graphic reconstruction* to provide the detailed action planning and clarification needed for a full articulation of your emerging theory of action. In Chapter 5, we will explore the creation and use of this essential research and planning tool.

5

Drawing a Theory
of Action

L et's expand upon the travel metaphor. As action researchers, we are traveling to distant lands, and in a larger sense, we are planning on exploring territory where, in all likelihood, no one has gone before, at least not successfully. This is not an exaggeration, nor is it self-congratulatory.

Clearly, if what you are hoping to accomplish had already been accomplished in a setting like yours, had been documented, and was well understood, it would be a waste of your time and energy to further document its effectiveness. In all probability, you are already using the best strategies and following the most promising practices known to you and your colleagues. In addition, you wouldn't be experimenting with something new or reexamining your current work were you not at least somewhat dissatisfied with the results you have been obtaining from your current practices. Perhaps, through your review of the literature (see Chapter 3), you have become inspired by the ideas and experiences of others. That inspiration may have led you to reconsider your current practice, and consequently, you may have decided to focus your action research on finding out if these promising ideas will succeed with your students and your classes. But even when you are going to attempt to replicate results produced elsewhere, you will still be venturing into unexplored territory because even if the promising practice had been well documented, it could not possibly have been attempted in the precise manner you will be implementing it, in the precise context where you will be using it, or with students identical to yours.

In Chapter 4, the priority pie was used to help you identify some of the specific categories of action that you (or the program developer) thought should be addressed. You identified these by combining what you had learned from the wisdom of your practice with the experience of others, and you created a prioritized list of independent variables. In all likelihood, the list of variables you ended up with (your slices of pie) didn't depart radically from your current menu of action. Perhaps you added a slice or changed your views on the relative importance of a particular category of action. Nevertheless, regardless of how deeply you believe in the narrative statement you wrote to explain your pie, that statement alone won't be enough to convince you (or your students, their parents, or your colleagues) that you have discovered the "silver bullet"—that wondrous approach that holds promise to succeed where all others have failed. This brings us to the need for detailing a clear and comprehensive theory of action—what we call an *implementation road map*. Geographic maps are used to illuminate the relationships among landforms. The maps we will be drawing have a slightly different purpose; they will illustrate the relationships between and among actions and variables.

WHY A MAP?

The map is the lifeline of the explorer. The route an explorer sets out to follow is informed by the best maps of others and the most detailed descriptions of the terrain ahead that could be gleaned from people with direct knowledge of the territory. On returning from their journeys, explorers share what they have learned by modifying and adjusting the best previous maps, augmented with their new knowledge. This is precisely what you will be doing. We begin by developing an initial road map informed by a combination of our experience and the experience of others. The map we prepare will then become our guide as we travel to places where we haven't ventured before. To the degree that our maps are clear and appear accurate, containing what researchers call *face validity*, the greater the chance we will be able to approach our adventure with confidence and purpose.

EUROPEAN EXPLORERS AS ACTION RESEARCHERS

Many years ago, Richard was assigned to teach the world history class that was required of all ninth-grade students in his high school. To this day, he can still remember students entering his class with a distinct lack of enthusiasm. Students had been warned by friends who had taken this required class in previous years that they were in for a long semester of memorizing boring, uninteresting, and unrelated facts. Richard realized pretty instantly that given that expectation, not much valuable learning was likely to occur. Furthermore, he was pretty certain it would prove to be a long, unpleasant, and unfulfilling slog for him if the curriculum required him to push this material down the students' throats.

That unpleasant realization was what inspired him to begin teaching history as if it were a mystery novel—the type of mystery where the author starts on the first page by telling you the end of the story (whodunit) and then spends the rest of the novel taking you on an adventure figuring out just how the detectives broke the case and solved the crime. One of the techniques Richard employed was posting historical world maps around his classroom in sequential order. The date the map was produced was printed prominently underneath each map. The mystery question at the heart of Richard's world history class was for the students to figure out and explain their understanding of the events that occurred between the dates the two different maps were created, which then explain the evolving views on the layout of our world.

Figure 5.1 was one of the maps Richard had displayed in his room. It was produced in 1489 by Henricus Martellus. It was the most accurate and detailed pre-Columbian world map Richard could locate. The next map on his classroom wall was the one shown in Figure 5.2. This map was the work of Englishman John Speed and was produced in 1627, at the tail end of the so-called "Great Age of Discovery." One of the mystery questions Richard posed to his students was, What caused the European cartographers view of our Earth to change so dramatically over this period, a mere 138 years? That particular question or puzzle was posed when Richard introduced what would become the unit on "The Great Age of Discovery." For our purposes here, it isn't important to dwell any further on the details of Richard's class or this particular unit beyond saying that one of his primary goals for this unit (as with all of his social studies classes) was to help students learn how to separate fact from myth and propaganda.

Needless to say, in the case of America's best-known explorer of this period, Christopher Columbus, there was a great deal to unpack: facts, distortions, myths, admirable accomplishments, and much shameful behavior. Among the many myths that surround Columbus were that he "discovered" America; that at the time of his voyages, most people

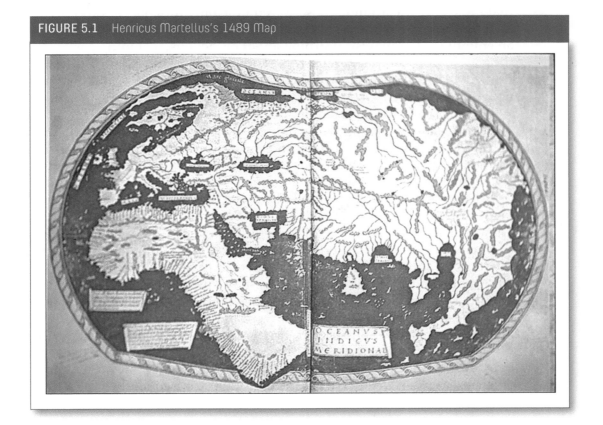

FIGURE 5.1   Henricus Martellus's 1489 Map

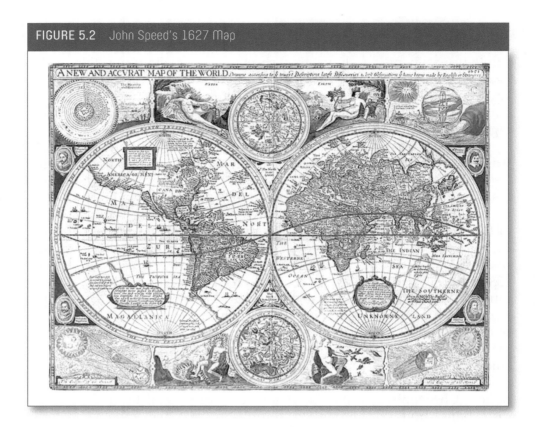

FIGURE 5.2 John Speed's 1627 Map

understood the Earth to be flat; and that Columbus's voyages "proved" that the world was round. Those weren't the only misconceptions uncovered by Richard's students; they discovered Columbus was anything but an enlightened humanist. Learning about his actions, including enslaving the native populations he encountered and subjecting them to extreme brutality and violence, pretty much ended his hero status for these young people.

Putting aside for the moment the reprehensible behavior of many of the European explorers, the explosion in geographic knowledge that occurred in Europe between 1450 and 1650 as a result of the age of discovery offered a rich opportunity for Richard's students to observe an actual example of the action research and inquiry process at work.

Richard's students discovered that at the time Columbus was promoting his first voyage, most knowledgeable European cartographers already knew the Earth was round. Furthermore, they even had a pretty good idea of its circumference based on celestial projection and mathematical computation. In addition, his students discovered that Ferdinand and Isabella were motivated primarily by self-interest, not the pursuit of discovery for its own sake. Having had their appetites whet by the reports of Marco Polo, these two Spanish monarchs were mostly driven by greed—their lust for inexpensive spices, gold, and wealth. Simply put, they knew it was extremely expensive, as well as dangerous, to import goods via the long, arduous overland route from Asia. They longed for a shorter, more efficient sea route to the riches Asia offered. Consequently, when they decided to invest in Columbus's first voyage, they were investing in a theory of action that already seemed well thought out and made considerable sense.

You can see a visual representation of what must have been Columbus's theory of action in Henricus Martellus's map (Figure 5.1). Some historians actually contend that Columbus had this map with him during his first voyage. Briefly summarized as a narrative statement, Columbus's theory of action might have read as follows:

> Since the Earth is round, if I sail due west from Spain and continue for approximately 4,000 miles, I will reach the east coast of Cathay. This sea route, if proven navigable, will provide merchants with a far less expensive mechanism for importing goods from Asia.

As "action researchers," Columbus and his benefactors could now articulate this theory of action verbally, as well as illustrate it visually, with a map such as the one developed by Martellus three years before Columbus set sail.

OK, enough with fifteenth-century action researchers. It's now time for us to shift our focus to your work and for you to prepare a detailed map of the journey you will be proposing for your exploration of a new world of excellence in student performance.

BUILDING A GRAPHIC RECONSTRUCTION

In Chapter 4, we looked at a priority pie prepared by a middle school teacher, Ms. Montgomery, to illustrate her view of the salience of the key independent variables that she theorized needed to be addressed if she was to substantially improve her ability to provide equitable response opportunities through effective questioning and discussion techniques. To recap, these were the variables that Ms. Montgomery believed would significantly influence the quality of discussions and improve student responses in her classroom:

- Time to think and reflect
- Time allocated for classroom discussion
- Tracking who is speaking and how often
- A variety of discussion structures and techniques

Now, it's time to consider some additional questions, ones that might have been raised yet probably could not have been adequately answered through the priority pie process. For example, Ms. Montgomery might have questions regarding the *sequence* of her actions.

- How often and when should she expect students to respond during the course of a lesson?
- When and how will she decide to probe "low-expectancy" students?
- When and how often should technology be used to enhance student response opportunities?

There could also be questions regarding *instructional strategies*.

- How should she share her intention around response opportunities in class?
- How would she like her students to identify their preferred response opportunities?
- How and when should she provide her students with feedback on participation?

It is likely that she has many other questions about her emerging theory. For example,

- Who should be responsible for what?
  - Should she assume the role of facilitator of all student discussions to ensure equity?
  - Should she teach the students how to facilitate conversations and monitor responses?
  - How will she assist students not accustomed to this level of participation and accountability?

While the priority pie was valuable in identifying the areas where Ms. Montgomery needed to focus her energy, it couldn't provide her with adequate guidance on how to respond to these or perhaps other relevant procedural questions.

Whether your study is designed to be a quasi-experimental inquiry or a descriptive study, it is important that you go through a deliberate process designed to flesh out and clarify in detail the full theory of action that will be examined by your research, whether it is one you invented or one that is already in operation elsewhere.

GRAPHIC RECONSTRUCTIONS FOR QUASI-EXPERIMENTAL RESEARCH

When we are undertaking quasi-experimental research, it is essential for us to carefully articulate precisely what it is we are attempting and why we have chosen to do so in this particular way. According to our revisionist view of history, Christopher Columbus qualifies as a quasi-experimental action researcher because he was testing out a promising new theory of action. In our work as quasi-experimental researchers, we also need to spell out our proposed actions for a number of reasons:

1. *To provide guidance to others who may follow us.* In Columbus's case, this would include future seafarers and explorers.

2. *To provide insights into the experimental process.* In Columbus's case, these insights would assist him in his future work as an explorer.

3. *To make our program clear to stakeholders.* In Columbus's case, this would be necessary to keep his benefactors happy and to keep his explorations funded.

To Provide Guidance to Others

When we engage in experimental or quasi-experimental research, we are, of course, hoping to find evidence that supports our hypotheses regarding the specific activities and interventions we are attempting and their relationships to changes in performance on our achievement targets. Should we be successful and the data that emerge confirm our hypotheses, it is to be expected that others will want to try to replicate our results. If those following in our footsteps are to have confidence in their ability to replicate our results, they will need to clearly understand the specific steps, actions, and procedures we followed to get the results we obtained.

To Provide Insights Into the Process

Even the most well-thought-out interventions rarely work precisely as they were designed. Occasionally, this means that the theory of action was fatally flawed. More likely, it was because one or two relatively minor aspects of the plan didn't end up functioning as anticipated. Unless each and every aspect of a plan has been clearly documented beforehand, it will be impossible for anyone to determine where exactly the breakdown or breakdowns occurred. This is no small problem. In schools, this is often seen when adopted programs are evaluated, deemed ineffective, and tossed out. When these decisions repeatedly occur without critical reflection on the actual reasons for the lack of success (the source of the breakdown), it can seriously erode staff commitment to the entire process of innovation.

If you are using an adopted program, in all likelihood, it arrived in a neat package, without an explicit theory of action delineated by the developer or publisher. Furthermore, the district's justification for implementing the program was probably stated in educational shorthand, perhaps simply mentioning the name of the author or publisher. For example,

> After reviewing the available materials, we decided to teach reading using the Sagor-Williams reading program.

Such a theory could be depicted like this:

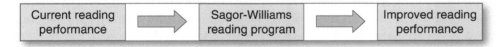

Then, if after implementation, performance didn't measure up to the district's expectations, one would expect to hear the assertion, "The Sagor-Williams program didn't work." As a result of this finding, the program would be abandoned, another one would be adopted, and the cycle would continue. Occasionally, throwing away complete programs that didn't live up to expectations is warranted; but often, it is not. Frequently, the program that was adopted was fundamentally sound. In all likelihood, the problem was simply that a few specific aspects of the program were inadequate for meeting the needs of the district's students. Certainly, it would be more efficient, as well as more intellectually honest, to isolate the specific flawed parts of the program so they could be modified, adjusted, or supplemented, rather than to throw out the baby with the bathwater and start all over again.

However, if the interventions implemented are viewed as mysterious black boxes, when legitimate concerns arise, it becomes impossible to determine which features of the operant theory need to be modified to fix the problem. When the process of adopt, evaluate, replace, adopt, evaluate, replace repeats itself over and over, it produces a syndrome of revolving-door programs that can lead a faculty to cynicism and defeatism. We can all agree that those two attitudes are antithetical to a productive school culture.

The same thing applies to our action research. More likely than not, our well-conceived theories of action will be fundamentally sound. Yet we still might not obtain the results we had hoped for. However, if we have a good implementation road map, it will be relatively easy for us to conduct a focused academic postmortem on our actions and use that information to understand precisely where things went awry.

To Make the Program Clear to Stakeholders

When students, faculty, and families clearly understand the programs they are involved with and can see the rationale for the tasks they are being asked to complete, they are more likely to cooperate and put forth their best efforts. Conversely, when people feel they are being asked to do something new and out of the ordinary and aren't provided with any explanation as to its rationale, they can be expected to rebel or give the program something less than their best efforts. For this reason, we have made it our habit to share our graphic reconstructions and to explain our theories of action on the first day of class or at the launch of any new program we're facilitating. Figure 5.3 is a copy of a poster that Richard prominently posted in the classroom on the first night for a graduate class he was teaching on action research.

GRAPHIC RECONSTRUCTIONS WITH DESCRIPTIVE RESEARCH

When engaging in descriptive research, our purpose is to develop a deeper and more profound understanding of what is actually going on here and now. If we are to succeed with this research, we need to be sure that we are looking under the right rocks and in the right places to collect the necessary data. The best way to do this is to invest some time at the outset to reflect on the rationale behind each of the significant actions (the operant theory) that are currently taking place and use the results of that reflection to focus our data collection. Frequently, a careful review of the teacher's manual or curriculum guide is the best place to start. Those documents likely detail the specific actions the program developers *expect* to occur.

Why Is It Important to Plan Visually?

When explaining something familiar, we often take intellectual shortcuts without even noticing them. For example, when outstanding teachers are

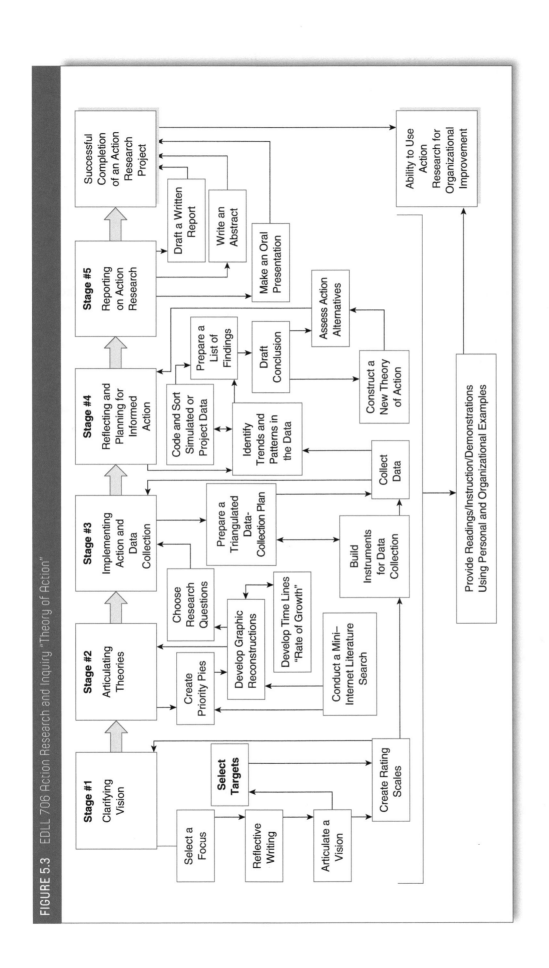

FIGURE 5.3 EDLL 706 Action Research and Inquiry "Theory of Action"

Stage #1 Clarifying Vision

Stage #2 Articulating Theories

Stage #3 Implementing Action and Data Collection

Stage #4 Reflecting and Planning for Informed Action

Stage #5 Reporting on Action Research

Successful Completion of an Action Research Project

Select a Focus

Reflective Writing

Articulate a Vision

Select Targets

Create Rating Scales

Create Priority Pies

Develop Graphic Reconstructions

Develop Time Lines "Rate of Growth"

Conduct a Mini–Internet Literature Search

Choose Research Questions

Prepare a Triangulated Data-Collection Plan

Build Instruments for Data Collection

Collect Data

Code and Sort Simulated or Project Data

Identify Trends and Patterns in the Data

Prepare a List of Findings

Draft Conclusion

Assess Action Alternatives

Construct a New Theory of Action

Draft a Written Report

Write an Abstract

Make an Oral Presentation

Ability to Use Action Research for Organizational Improvement

Provide Readings/Instruction/Demonstrations Using Personal and Organizational Examples asked to explain precisely what they do to produce the results they are obtaining, they are often at a loss to explain their accomplishments. It isn't rare to hear an excellent teacher explain her success by saying, "This is just how my students perform." Of course, this is an inadequate explanation. Without question, there are specific actions this teacher engages in on a regular basis that lead to positive results, but those actions have become so second nature that the teacher might not even recognize them as relevant.

Graphic reconstructions help us to flesh out and examine the details of our theories of action through the use of visualizations and pictures, as opposed to words. The graphic reconstruction is a flow chart, a web that illustrates the dynamic relationships that exist between the various components of a theory of action.

Figure 5.4 shows the graphic reconstruction produced by Mr. Johnson, the principal at AR Academy, illustrating his theory for leading his faculty in promoting quality equitable student engagement. Figure 5.5 reflects Ms. Montgomery's theory on enhancing the response opportunities provided to her students through effective questioning and improved discussions in her classroom.

There is no single way to build a graphic reconstruction, and there is no single format that will be effective in illustrating all of our theories. However, we suggest that when you create your first graphic reconstruction, you follow this five-step process. These five sequential steps were designed to help you produce a visual road map for whatever theory of action you wish to investigate.

1. Brainstorm variables, actions, and ideas.

2. Group and sort variables, actions, and ideas.

3. Put the parts into a logical sequence.

4. Proof the road map.

5. Review your final product.

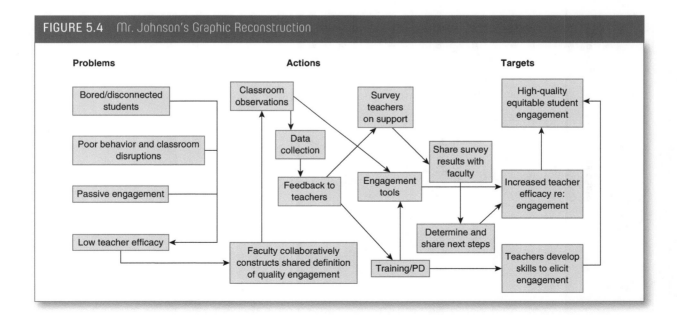

FIGURE 5.4   Mr. Johnson's Graphic Reconstruction

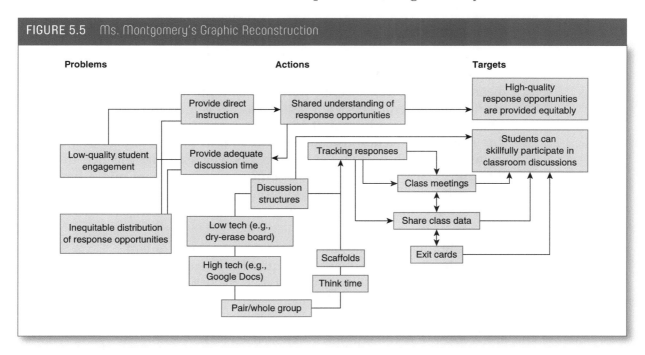

FIGURE 5.5 Ms. Montgomery's Graphic Reconstruction

To demonstrate the use of these five steps, we will return to the AR Academy, and this time, we will follow the work of the fifth-grade PLC team that is collaboratively working on increasing equitable student engagement. The team will be building a graphic reconstruction to clarify its theory for achieving success on their priority program target: an increase in high-quality equitable student engagement. Figure 5.6 shows the priority pie and narrative created earlier by the PLC team at the AR Academy.

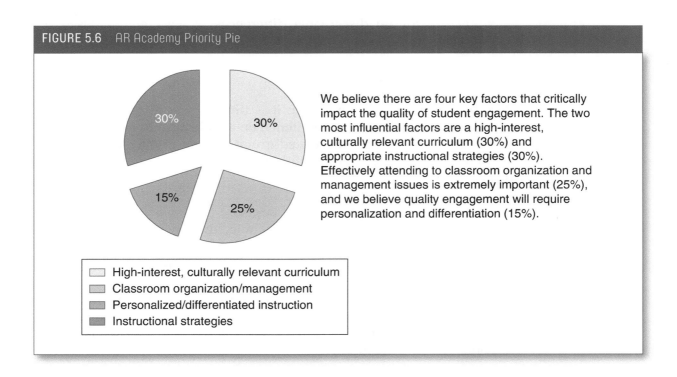

FIGURE 5.6 AR Academy Priority Pie

We believe there are four key factors that critically impact the quality of student engagement. The two most influential factors are a high-interest, culturally relevant curriculum (30%) and appropriate instructional strategies (30%). Effectively attending to classroom organization and management issues is extremely important (25%), and we believe quality engagement will require personalization and differentiation (15%).

- High-interest, culturally relevant curriculum
- Classroom organization/management
- Personalized/differentiated instruction
- Instructional strategies

Step 1: Brainstorm Variables, Actions, and Ideas

Using a pad of sticky notes, the action researchers brainstorm every factor, issue, phenomenon, program, and practice that they believe might have a bearing on the target being pursued. This includes ideas that surfaced during their literature review, as well as items that showed up as separate slices of their priority pie. It is always important to be expansive when brainstorming. Action researchers are wise to include things they've discovered through personal experience, as well as things gleaned from the literature. Here are examples of some of the items that might have surfaced during brainstorming by the fifth-grade PLC team regarding enhancing equitable student engagement.

- Students are disconnected and bored with content
- Increasing the quality and quantity of student-generated questions
- Students not always represented in curriculum or their representation is deficit based
- Student disruptions
- Teach effective note-taking
- Use of culturally relevant strategies to engage students
- Question and discussion strategies
- Role of technology
- Use of novel, controversial, and interesting facts to stimulate interest
- Thinking about and reflecting on content
- Student confidence and/or competence in use of academic language or content
- Student enthusiasm
- Testing effectiveness of engagement strategies
- Student-mediated dialogue
- Accounting for engagement in different contexts
- Connecting engagement to learning outcomes
- Desire for no discernable differences in engagement based on racial, linguistic, or other indicators

Step 2: Group and Sort the Variables, Actions, and Ideas

Once brainstorming is completed, it is time to spread the sticky notes (containing all the brainstormed items) on a table or onto a piece of chart paper and cluster them into related groups. Some of the categories that action researchers often find helpful for initially sorting our brainstormed ideas are

- problems, interventions, and targets;
- things that occur prior to teaching, during teaching, and after teaching; and
- teacher actions, student actions, rules, and requirements.

Keep in mind there is no one approach for categorizing the items that surfaced during brainstorming. Therefore, you should feel comfortable playing around with different categories until you find ones that best help you organize your ideas.

The PLC team working on enhancing equitable student engagement decided to sort their items as *problems*, *interventions*, and *targets*.

Problems

- Students disconnected and bored with content
- Students not always represented in curriculum or representation is deficit based
- Student disruptions

Interventions

- Teach effective note-taking
- Use of culturally relevant strategies to engage students
- Question and discussion strategies
- Use technology strategically to enhance engagement
- Use of novel, controversial, and interesting facts to stimulate interest
- Thinking about and reflecting on content
- Testing effectiveness of engagement strategies
- Accounting for engagement in different contexts
- Connecting engagement to learning outcomes

Targets

- Student confidence and/or competence in use of academic language or content
- Student enthusiasm
- Increase in quality and quantity of student-generated questions
- Student-mediated dialogue
- No discernable differences in engagement based on racial, linguistic, or other indicators

Step 3: Putting the Items in Sequence

In this step, the sticky notes are arranged on a large sheet of poster paper or a sheet of chart paper to illustrate all of the key presumed relationships. When doing quasi-experimental research, we generally format our graphics this way: On the left-hand side, we group the items that describe the current situation or the problem our actions are designed to address. In the case of the student engagement project, the left side of the graphic would look like Figure 5.7.

Then, on the right-hand side, we place our vision of success, or the promised land we are trying to reach. Here, we place descriptions of performance on the target that is at or above expected proficiency (the top score on the rating scales that were developed in Chapter 2). When those sticky notes are added to the student engagement graphic, it will appear like Figure 5.8.

The last step is to arrange all of the other items (that is, the variables or actions) in a manner that reflects the most logical and direct route that the action researcher sees the program or the learners traveling to get from the current situation to the target. Once the interventions have been added to

FIGURE 5.7 AR Academy PLC Engagement Project-Problems

Too many students are
Bored
Disconnected
Passively engaged
Disruptive

FIGURE 5.8 AR Academy Engagement Project-Vision

We would like all students
To be interested in course content
To see themselves in and make relevant connections to the curriculum
To actively track, respond, and probe each other's thinking
To lean into learning

the student engagement graphic, the complete road map might look like the example in Figure 5.9.

With quasi-experimental studies, researchers frequently assume that there is a defined sequence of actions, and there are causal relationships between certain actions. For this reason, it is often helpful to use lines or directional arrows to illustrate the way the different elements of the theory build upon or interact with each other. However, change doesn't always happen in a linear fashion. Particularly when working with early learners, instructional activities may be cyclical and repeated in a regular pattern. For this reason, it is up to the researcher to determine if causal or sequential relationships should be indicated on the graphic or not.

The formatting of a graphic reconstruction for a descriptive study will often be idiosyncratic. It is, however, important that with a graphic reconstruction that will be providing direction to a descriptive study, we identify each of the key phenomena that the researcher deems relevant to performance on the achievement target being studied and that one could expect to be observed in the environment under study. Therefore, it is critically important for descriptive researchers to identify these items at this point, since this information will be needed for the design of your data collection plan.

Tip on Drawing Graphic Reconstructions for Descriptive Research

The locations where items are placed on a graphic reconstruction for descriptive research can be important, as they will help inform the researcher regarding when and where to look for data. Beyond that, however, determining the possible or probable relationships between items or variables is not as critical with a descriptive study.

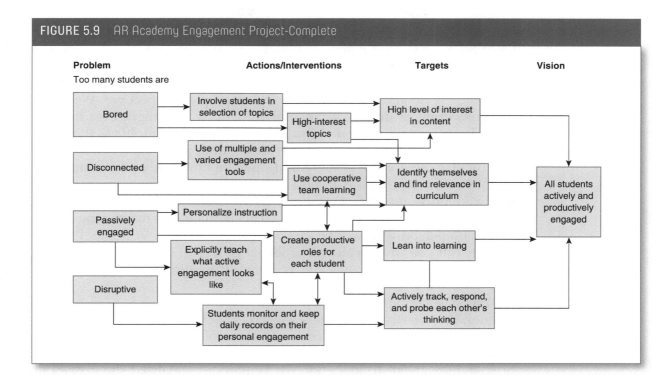

FIGURE 5.9 AR Academy Engagement Project-Complete

This part of the process is complete when the researchers are able to step back and look at their graphic reconstruction and agree that it clearly and unambiguously illustrates their "current" understanding of the dynamics of the issue being studied, including all of the independent variables (the actions to be taken) and the dependent variable (the achievement target being pursued).

When we think we have arrived at this point, we imagine ourselves explaining our graphics to three audiences: our students, their parents, and an imaginary colleague who is new to our faculty. If our graphic is complete and clear, when accompanied by a brief five-minute verbal explanation, our students should be able to understand what we are planning and will be able to demonstrate that understanding to us by restating our theory in their own words. Likewise, if after a five-minute explanation at an open house, the parents understand what we have planned and feel capable of explaining it to another parent, we would feel confident that our graphic had successfully communicated our theory. Lastly, if an educator who is new to our team could understand the program we have planned from our overview and would feel comfortable going ahead and implementing it, then we would feel we had illustrated our ideas with clarity. But if the graphic plus a short explanation didn't succeed in clarifying what was planned and the rationale behind our actions, then we would need to assume that our theory of action was still too abstract or overly general. If, in our imaginary presentations, the degree of clarity we were hoping for was not achieved, then it means we need to continue to refine our road map until it effectively communicates our intentions.

Step 4: Proofing the Graphic

Once Step 3 has been completed, and we are confident that the graphic reconstruction does, in fact, successfully communicate our ideas, it is time for us to examine it for possible flaws or omissions. We conduct this examination by reviewing our theory through multiple perspectives. We begin by considering as diverse a range of students as we might ever have in class. Then, we take several mental walks though our graphic as though it were a walking trail. Each time we walk the trail, we imagine ourselves as a particular category of student and imagine how one of these students might be experiencing the proposed program. As we take these walks, we try to identify any places where students such as these would likely encounter problems or lose their way. This is analogous to drawing a map to assist a person who will be making a first visit to your home. Prior to sending out your map, you will probably go over it one last time, looking for places where someone who is unfamiliar with your neighborhood might make a wrong turn.

When Ms. Montgomery shared her graphic (Figure 5.5) with her colleagues, they observed that there was no explicit reference to high-quality response opportunities. They observed that most of the graphic seemed to focus on the quantity, without attention to the quality of questions posed or responses given. To that end, Ms. Montgomery realized she needed to find a way to ensure that the response opportunities she was providing were of high quality. Additionally, upon reviewing her road map, she recognized that she would benefit from regular peer and student feedback.

When problems like these arise when you are proofing your graphic reconstruction, you should reflect on the following question:

> How could this theory of action be modified to make universal success more likely?

After spending some time reflecting and deliberating on that question, it is time for the action researcher(s) to work those modifications into the theory. Figure 5.10 is Ms. Montgomery's theory of action after proofing.

PROOFING A THEORY OF ACTION FOR LEADERSHIP PROJECTS

Often, when school leaders are planning an initiative that involves other members of the professional staff, we subconsciously assume that our colleagues are similar to ourselves in both motivation and temperament. We tend to assume they share our concerns, are motivated by the same things, and share our understanding of the issue at hand. This is analogous to teachers planning their lessons under the false assumption that all students share the same learning style. In many ways, our colleagues can be as diverse as the students in our classes. Therefore, a program implementation strategy that, on the surface, may appear perfect might look so only because of how well it suits our own personality and perspective. For this reason, the act of proofing the initial graphic reconstruction of an initiative we are leading, by walking through it in the shoes of different members of

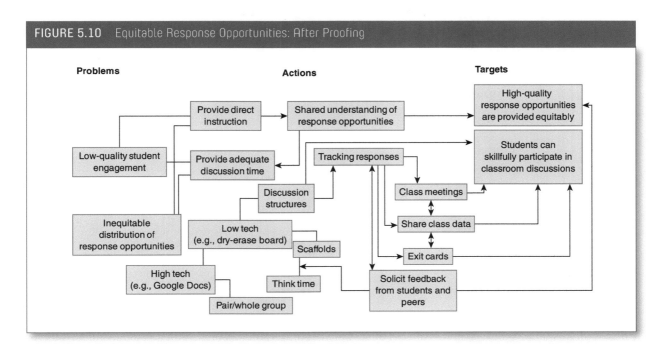

FIGURE 5.10 Equitable Response Opportunities: After Proofing

the faculty or staff, particularly ones who hold different perspectives and philosophies than our own, will alert us to issues that, left unaddressed, can cause an otherwise well-intentioned project to unravel.

Step 5: Finalizing the Graphic

For quasi-experimental research, the graphic reconstruction can be considered complete once the researchers can say with a degree of confidence, "We truly expect that every participant will experience success if this theory of action is implemented as displayed."

For descriptive research, the graphic can be considered complete when the researchers can say, "We truly believe that once we come to understand the manner in which all of the variables displayed on this graphic interact with each other, we will understand why performance is as it is."

Tip on Creating Graphic Reconstructions for Descriptive Research

When doing descriptive research on a commercially produced program or the implementation of an adopted program, it is a good idea to follow the steps provided in this chapter to construct a graphic reconstruction of the theory of action *as you currently understand it*. Then, prior to commencing your study, it is suggested that you ask the developers of the program or their representatives to take a critical look at your graphic and provide you with feedback. Even if you have made a conscious choice to exclude some elements of the theory as the authors or developers originally conceived it, understanding and acknowledging those differences in theoretical perspective will prove helpful later when you are engaged in data analysis.

When you have finished the creation of a graphic reconstruction that fully reflects your understanding of the issue under study, it is time to give yourself a deserved pat on the back. You have now completed *Stage 2: Articulating Your Theory*, and you are almost ready to move to the exciting implementation phase—the action part of the action research process.

6

Determining the
Research Questions

Having completed a graphic reconstruction that clearly communicates your best and most current thinking on how to achieve success with your priority achievement targets, you have completed the second of the four stages of the action research process.

You have now arrived at the *action* portion of action research. This is where you will be *implementing* and simultaneously *exploring* your theory of action. Two things will occur while you engage in your work during Stage 3:

1. Your theory of action will be implemented.

2. Data will be collected in response to a meaningful set of research questions.

The nature of your research questions will influence both the types of data to be collected as well as the methods used to collect those data. This makes it extremely important that care and thought be used in choosing the questions that will guide your inquiry. Just as it was important to choose a focus that was high on your personal priority list (Chapter 2), selecting the questions that will guide your inquiry must also be grounded in professional self-interest: A good action research question is one that leads to greater understanding of something you or you and your colleagues very much *need* or *want* to understand more deeply or learn more about.

In this chapter, we will examine two alternative approaches to the selection of research questions. The first approach involves the use of a set of generic action research questions that can effectively be applied to almost any issue you might choose to study. The data produced in response to these three questions will generally provide the information and insights sought by most action researchers conducting either quasi-experimental or descriptive studies. The second approach has you following a systematic process for analyzing your theory of action in order to tease out a set of context-specific questions designed to surface information you will find personally and professionally meaningful.

THREE GENERIC ACTION RESEARCH QUESTIONS

The range and scope of questions an action researcher might wish to pursue is unlimited. Nevertheless, here are three particular questions that, when effectively investigated, will provide valuable professional insight for any project:

1. What did we actually *do*? (This question focuses on *action*.)

2. What *changes* occurred regarding performance on the priority achievement targets? (This question focuses on *change*.)

3. What were the *relationships*, if any, between the actions taken and any noted changes in performance? (This question focuses on *relationships*.)

We refer to the three generic action research questions by the acronym ACR, which refers to their foci: *A* for action, *C* for change, and *R* for relationships. Let's examine the ACR questions, one at a time, to see if you feel they have the potential to surface the answers and insights *you and your colleagues want and need* to understand better.

ACR Question 1: What Did I or We Actually Do?

On the surface, this question seems so mundane that it is often overlooked, and the novice action researcher occasionally fails to collect the data needed to provide an adequate answer. Not knowing the answer to this question can create significant problems during the final and perhaps most consequential stage of the action research process (reflection and action planning). The rationale for probing and answering this question can be found in Newton's third law of motion:

For every action, there is an equal or opposite reaction.

Whatever is going on in our schools or classrooms was influenced by an earlier action or, more realistically, by a collection of actions. Knowing what factors precipitated an occurrence allows us to predict, with varying degrees of confidence, what might happen in the future. However, if we are unclear about the precipitating actions, our ability to predict an event or replicate results can be very difficult. This is not just an abstract or theoretical issue. It is a matter of real consequence.

In Chapter 5, we discussed the recurring problem of discontinuing fundamentally sound programs because of an initial failure to produce anticipated results. These premature abandonments of fundamentally sound programs spring from a set of understandable circumstances. Individual teachers, schools, and districts adopt programs because they believe those programs hold promise for improving student performance. Then, after a year or two of implementation, the programs are frequently deemed failures and are discontinued. The justification for ending the programs is simple and straightforward: After implementation, the anticipated outcomes weren't realized. Such decisions seem perfectly reasonable but only if one assumes the adopted program had been, in fact, fully implemented and implemented appropriately. Unfortunately, just because a program was adopted or was attempted doesn't necessarily mean it was implemented as intended or in accordance with the developer's theory of action.

This lesson was driven home to Richard a few years ago when a team of elementary school teachers attended an action research training program he was facilitating. Their superintendent asked them to investigate the effectiveness of a very expensive and complex literacy program that had been adopted in their district three years earlier. The program had been brought in with much fanfare and with high expectations for spurring improvement in the district's reading performance. The program included texts, videos, workbooks, and a host of other supplemental materials. While expensive, the program appeared to be well worth the money, considering its promise for improving reading scores. However, after three years of use, there was no evidence of gains in student performance on the state reading exam. It was no surprise that this team came to the action research training with a specific research question in hand. They wanted to know if the district's adopted program was worth the investment. As much as it had cost to purchase all of the program materials, the superintendent was willing to admit the error, move on, and try another approach were it determined that the adoption was, indeed, a mistake.

As part of their data collection plan, these teacher researchers decided to collect and analyze teacher-provided *curriculum maps* (Jacobs, 1997; Hale, 2008). The data collection process they utilized required every elementary teacher to keep records regarding those portions of the program they had been using, as well as the amount of time they were devoting to the various program components. When these implementation data were laid out on a chart, the team noticed something immediately.

Apparently, throughout all three elementary schools in the district, the teachers had been idiosyncratically selecting which program components to use and, even more importantly, which components to ignore, based on personal bias or taste. Many teachers omitted entire portions of the program while others gave some components minimal attention and spent considerable time with the parts they felt were useful. There were no discernable patterns of use, even across the same grade level and in the same school. As a consequence, in a typical class, a teacher would find he had students with considerable experience with certain portions of the program sitting right next to classmates who never even encountered those aspects of the same reading program. Once these data were analyzed, it became clear that no teacher in the district was able to fairly assume that any two of his or her students had experienced the same scope and sequence as they moved up through the grades.

When the superintendent asked the research team to report what they learned from their study, he expected one of two answers to his original question regarding the reading program's effectiveness:

1. The program was shown to be a worthy one and had, in reality, succeeded in improving student reading performance.

2. The program had not delivered on its promise for improving reading performance and should be abandoned.

But the research team determined that the data wouldn't support either of those conclusions and reported something quite different. Based on their data, *few, if any, students had actually experienced the program as it was intended.* Therefore, they told the superintendent that from the evidence collected, they were unable to evaluate the program's effectiveness (the adequacy of the program's *theory of action*) because in reality, that theory had never been completely implemented.

As this case demonstrated, neglecting to collect data which document what was actually implemented can prove costly in dollars, time, and missed opportunities.

In Chapters 4 and 5, we made our theories of action explicit by producing detailed graphic reconstructions and creating estimates of the amount of time and energy needed to realize success (our priority pies). Now that we have arrived at *Stage 3: Implementing Action and Collecting Data*, we will begin assembling the necessary data that allow us to draw conclusions about the adequacy of these estimates. To do this, we will need to document all of the critical actions that we took and the essential things that were experienced by our students. Fortunately, gathering these data is relatively easy.

Teachers develop and keep track of nearly everything they intend to teach and what they expect their students to experience in class. Our weekly lesson plans are repositories for all these data. However, a record of lesson plans (handwritten or electronic) alone is rarely adequate to provide accurate documentation for answering ACR Question 1. Using ourselves as examples, it was the very rare week when the activities we anticipated doing and consequently wrote up in our lesson plans on Sunday night actually matched what we taught and what our students experienced during the ensuing week. We make no apologies for this. Like most teachers, we willingly and readily adjusted our plans based on circumstances and student needs. We felt comfortable adding additional time for work on skills that students were having difficulty with, and neither of us felt guilty about omitting planned activities that later seemed redundant and appeared to be a waste of time. So although our weekly plans were written with sincerity and represented what we once thought we would do, they wouldn't provide an accurate record of what had actually transpired in our classrooms. This problem can be easily remedied. All that is required is allocating five minutes after class ends each Friday afternoon for going over the past week's plans and adjusting them to reflect what actually transpired. Figure 6.1 is an illustration of a week's lesson plans annotated by the teacher to reflect what actually happened.

By engaging in this one simple additional piece of record keeping, any of us can end each school year with a complete record of the actions that

FIGURE 6.1 Lesson Plan for Week of October 15

Subject: Government

Section: Sixth Period

Monday	Tuesday	Wednesday	Thursday	Friday
• Write in current events journals (ten minutes). • Discuss initiative petition process. • Review arguments pro and con in voters' pamphlets. • Discuss initiatives #118, #217, and #482. • Homework: Read essay, "Direct versus Representative Democracy."	• Pop quiz on homework. • Class debate: Be it resolved that representative student government should be abolished. • Random assignment to teams, draw debaters from hat. Twenty minutes preparation. • Twenty-minute debate. • Homework: Reflection worksheet.	• Film: *The Founding Fathers: Why a Republic?*	• Direct democracy scavenger hunt. • In cooperative learning teams, allow twenty minutes to find direct democracy events in past two months from classroom media and Internet. • Compile team lists and submit by end of period.	• Write in current events journals (ten minutes). • Team presentations, ten minutes per team. • Work on problem-based learning proposals.
Changes	**Changes**	**Changes**	**Changes**	**Changes**
• Didn't discuss initiative #482.	• Didn't do debate. • Didn't assign homework.	• Didn't show film. • Held twenty-minute debate (originally planned for Tuesday). • Homework: Reflection sheet.	• None.	• None.

occurred on each of the 180 school days in our classrooms. Furthermore, by correlating these data with student attendance records, we can create an accurate report on what specific learning activities were experienced by any one of our individual students. Later, should we find ourselves pleased with the learning that occurred, we will be able to track the precise instructional activities that corresponded with the successful learning. Conversely, if we find ourselves disappointed with student performance, we will be in possession of an accurate record of which events coincided with the less-than-stellar results.

An additional record-keeping device that we have found helpful is the Time Priority Tracking Form (Figure 6.2). On this form, we write in each category of action that appeared on our priority pie (see Chapter 4). Then, each Friday afternoon, after reviewing our weekly activities, we can record the approximate amount of time devoted that week to each of those categories of action. Later, when analyzing these data, we are able to note how closely the percentage of time actually spent compared to what we had once thought would be necessary.

ACR Question 2: What Changes Occurred Regarding Performance on the Achievement Targets?

If you were pleased with the rating scales and rate-of-growth charts you created in Chapter 3, you will probably want to use them to monitor ongoing changes in performance with your priority achievement targets. Even if you were delighted with the measuring tools you produced, you should still be suspicious of drawing conclusions regarding student performance using any single source of data. Putting that much weight on any single set of data is equivalent to a prosecutor, responsible for proving a case beyond a reasonable doubt, betting everything on the testimony of a single witness. Most trial lawyers would never rest a case after only one witness's testimony, regardless of how honorable and credible that witness might seem. This is because they know that a jury, which might be convinced of the integrity of the witness, could still have justifiable concerns about the possibility that the witness was confused or otherwise mistaken. This is why lawyers always seek to find and present corroborating testimony. That is also a good approach for an action researcher. When we assemble data to answer *ACR Question 2: What Changes Occurred Regarding Performance on the Achievement Targets?*, it behooves us to look for multiple *separate* and *independent* sources of information on changes in performance on each achievement target under study.

Fortunately, locating multiple sources of data on student or school performance isn't overly problematic. For example, if we want to know if our students have learned the proper use of writing conventions, we might assess this by having them edit a sample piece of work where they will be required to identify and correct common convention errors. However, if later, we want to make assertions about their competence, we will need to corroborate those results with other sources of data. In all likelihood, the data required to do this already exist and are present in our classrooms; therefore, additional testing or data collection often is not necessary. For instance, we could validate our initial findings with items found in the students' writing portfolios, where we could observe if they

FIGURE 6.2 Time Priority Tracking Form

Date: _____

Class: _____

Focus Area (from priority pie)	Approximate Class Time Spent (in minutes)	Comment

have been using conventions correctly in their own writing. This process of using corroborating evidence to establish validity and reliability is what researchers call *triangulation*. In the next chapter (Chapter 7), you will receive guidance on developing a full-blown, triangulated data collection plan to answer your research questions.

ACR Question 3: What Were the Relationships, if Any, Between the Actions Taken and the Changes in Performance?

Just because we can unequivocally report what we did and what our students experienced (ACR Question 1) and can establish with confidence what the students achieved (ACR Question 2) doesn't mean we can assert the existence of a relationship between our actions and the documented changes in student performance.

Earlier, we discussed the relationship between dependent and independent variables, the dependent variable being those things we wanted to see changed and the independent variables being the actions we undertook to effect those changes. In the natural sciences, one observes the interaction of independent and dependent variables as a straightforward cause-and-effect relationship. Any changes observed in the dependent variable (the achievement target) can be unambiguously attributed to adjustments in the independent variables. Under experimental conditions in the natural sciences, these are justified conclusions because in laboratory situations, it is possible for the researcher to fully control the environment.

However, when we are dealing with human behavior and with social interactions, things are never quite that simple and straightforward. For us to claim that *A* caused *B*, we would have to be able to prove that *nothing* else could possibly have influenced the final result but *A*. This is impossible to prove. Let's say Richard's target is to have one of his students, Sam, become more diligent in editing his written work. Richard may be trying to accomplish this by following a theory of action that had him providing students with detailed teacher feedback after the first draft of each of their essays. As it turns out, the data Richard assembled reflected a clear pattern: The quality of the editing in Sam's final papers improved considerably over the course of the term. The relationship seemed clear to Richard, as illustrated in the following figure.

Independent Variable   **Dependent Variable**

Detailed teacher feedback → Improved editing of Sam's final drafts

It seems apparent that when Richard changed his feedback process, Sam's editing improved. From this data, Richard started feeling pretty confident in his tentative assertion that his actions had caused Sam's improvement.

But what Richard didn't realize was that at the same time that he began providing intensive feedback, other factors independent of his actions had also changed. Coincidental with his provision of intensive feedback, Sam's father began offering him a twenty-five-dollar reward for every *A* he received on a major school project. Once Richard became aware of this data, a new question emerged: How might I determine if the improvement in Sam's work was due to my teaching or the result of his father's bribe?

Two categories of factors can interfere with a direct relationship between dependent and independent variables. Researchers call these *extraneous* and *intervening* variables. An extraneous variable is something that has nothing to do with the phenomenon being studied (our teaching) but gets in the way in a manner that influences the result. The bribe provided by Sam's dad was separate and apart from the phenomenon Richard was studying (the relationship between intense teacher feedback and the quality of Sam's editing), but nevertheless, it may well have influenced the dependent variable being measured (the quality of Sam's final papers).

An intervening variable is a phenomenon that is also influenced by the independent variable (our intervention) while having its own separate effect on the outcome (dependent variable). For example, let's say Richard is a PE teacher who notices that students whose homes are located north of the river are better golfers than students living on the south side. He concludes that housing location improves one's golf game. The causal relationship might be illustrated this way:

However, what Richard didn't take into account is that the north end of town is also where the more affluent families live, as well as where all of the town's golf courses are located. Consequently, the factor that may more powerfully influence students' skills with golf isn't their housing location per se; rather, it may be the increased practice that results from access to golf courses and the financial ability to play the game. The influence of these extraneous variables is illustrated as follows:

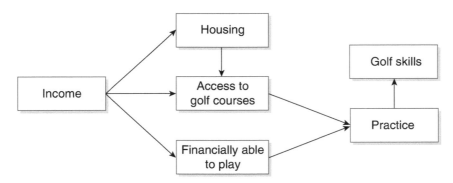

In the next chapter, where we will be working on developing valid and reliable data collection plans, we will spend considerable time on strategies designed to enhance our confidence in the relationship between our specific actions and documented outcomes. Having that confidence will be important as we plan changes in our actions based on our action research data.

DEVELOPING YOUR OWN RESEARCH QUESTIONS

In the last chapter, you worked through a set of processes designed to help you articulate your theory of action. You visually illustrated your theory with an implementation road map, a graphic reconstruction. Often, our theories of action are robust. By this, we mean they involve dozens, sometimes even hundreds, of different assumptions. In human endeavors, nothing is ever certain. So realistically, every item on your road map is an assumption: The role of each individual activity is an assumption, the way you sequenced the activities is based on assumptions, and the relationship of individual activities to each other and ultimately to the achievement of the priority achievement target are assumptions. As cynics like to point out, nothing in modern society is ever certain but death and taxes.

Some of the assumptions in your theory of action are easy to see because they are right on the surface. For example, a graphic reconstruction could contain a relationship as illustrated in the following figure.

The connection between these variables is clear and direct; the action researcher is asserting a belief that there is a dynamic relationship between self-esteem and grades. But that is only the surface assumption. That same dynamic presupposes numerous other underlying assumptions. For example, there are several implied assumptions in this relationship, including the following:

- Self-esteem is important.
- Good grades are valuable.
- Different students are awarded different grades.
- Self-esteem is malleable.

As an inquiring educator, you may have an interest in investigating and developing a deeper understanding of some of those assumed relationships. But rarely is one person equally interested in or capable of exploring every one of the assumptions contained within his or her comprehensive theory of action. When one considers that there may be literally hundreds of assumptions that could be investigated, the question for the part-time action researcher becomes this crucial one:

What are the specific assumptions that are worth me spending my finite time and energy investigating?

We will now explore a systematic process designed to help you go about responding to that question.

TWO-STEP WALK-THROUGH

The last thing you did when completing your graphic reconstruction (implementation road map) was to proof your theory by walking through the road map in the shoes of different types of students or participants to see if you could identify obstacles or omissions and make adjustments. We are going to repeat the walk-through process once again, but this time, you will be asking slightly different questions as you walk through your completed graphic reconstruction.

Hopefully, when you proofed your theory by walking through it and searching for problems, the process resulted in a final theory of action that represented your best thinking regarding a comprehensive strategy to get everyone to the desired destination. Now that you are ready to implement your theory and begin the action part of the process, there is another overriding issue you need to be concerned with: determining if your best thinking, as represented in your theory of action, was, in fact, adequate to produce success with your priority achievement target.

The role of the research questions is to help you accomplish that task. Earlier, we said that everything on your graphic reconstruction was an assumption, and you could, if you had both the time and interest, go about systematically validating or refuting each one of those assumptions. Assuming that you do have a life outside of being an action researcher, you probably want to narrow the scope of your inquiry. This is done by focusing exclusively on those issues that you truly *need* or *want* to know more about.

You can identify these issues by walking through your theory two more times. On each walk, you will be asking one of the following questions:

1. Is this factor, issue, variable, or relationship significant?

2. How confident am I regarding the influence of this factor, issue, variable, or relationship?

Based on your answers to these two questions, one or more meaningful action research questions should emerge.

Walk-Through 1: Determining Significance

Everything that makes up your theory of action is something you believe, and everything illustrated on your graphic reconstruction is something that, in your opinion, plays a role in realizing success on the achievement target. However, as we noticed when developing the priority pies, everything involved in the work on our targets is probably not of equal importance to the end result.

On this first walk-through, you should question the relative importance of every single element of your theory. This includes every box, circle, square, arrow, line, and so forth that appears on your graphic reconstruction. Specifically, you should ask,

Is this factor, issue, variable, and/or relationship significant?

To be deemed significant for action research purposes, a factor or relationship needs to meet two qualifications. First, you must believe that this factor or relationship exercises a powerful influence over your ability to influence the phenomenon under study. For example, if your focus is on developing student self-esteem, and you have an arrow that shows a relationship between parenting skills and the level of self-esteem, one might conclude that you feel this relationship is significant, meaning you believe the relationship between parenting practices and a child's self-esteem is a powerful one. But that is only one aspect of significance for an action researcher.

The second aspect refers to whether you feel this factor can be significantly influenced by *your* actions. This is a good time to remind ourselves that action research should focus on investigations into the effect of *our* actions and not other concerns or phenomena, regardless of their importance, that fall outside of our sphere of influence. While we may have deemed parenting to be a powerful factor in the development of a young person's self-esteem, we might also conclude that our ability to influence the parenting received by our students is quite limited. For our purpose as action researchers, we will only declare something to be significant if it qualifies under both aspects of this definition. Therefore, the relationship of parenting to self-esteem *would not* be classified as "significant" when using the two-step walk-through process.

Now, let's imagine an arrow that reflects a relationship between grades received and self-esteem. In all likelihood, we would conclude that this relationship meets both definitions of significance: It plays a powerful role in the development of self-esteem, and since grading is a practice we have control over, it is a factor that can be significantly influenced by our actions.

Figure 6.3 is the graphic reconstruction created by Ms. Montgomery. It illustrates her plan to use effective questioning and discussion techniques to help her students achieve proficiency with two priority achievement targets: learning to contribute meaningfully to class discussion and her ability to provide equitable distribution of high-quality and high-quantity response opportunities. Those components of her theory that she deemed significant are indicated on her graphic with the letter *S*. It isn't surprising that she identified eleven of the *elements* and five of the *relationships* illustrated on her theory as significant. (We generally find significance in most components of a theory we authored since, intuitively, when designing our theory, we tended to focus on those issues we deem important.)

Your task now is to take out a copy of your graphic reconstruction and ask Question 1 of every single item (box, cluster of boxes, arrows, and so on) that makes up your theory. Then, indicate your judgment on each item's significance by writing an *S* by or on every item that satisfies the two-part definition.

Aspects of your theory that you designate as significant could very well be worth spending time investigating. Other aspects of the theory, those that didn't meet the definition of significance, shouldn't be dropped from the theory, and they should stay where they are on your graphic reconstruction; but in all likelihood, they won't justify any further investment of the limited time and energy you have available for data collection.

Walk-Through 2: Your Confidence in the Assumptions

Now, walk through your theory a second time. However, this time, consider only those aspects of your theory that you deemed to be significant. The question you will be asking of these items is,

How confident am I about the workings of this factor, variable, or relationship?

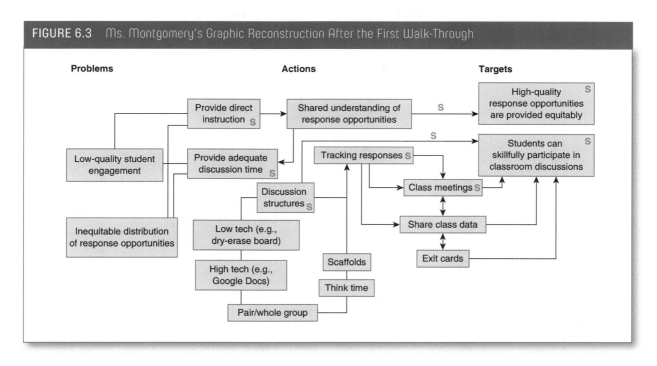

FIGURE 6.3 Ms. Montgomery's Graphic Reconstruction After the First Walk-Through

No doubt there will be some factors or relationships about which you are quite confident, such as the earlier example of the relationship between self-esteem and grades. While you might have already decided that this is a significant relationship, you may also feel that you already have a pretty complete understanding of the way this phenomenon works. It is possible that you already possess a great deal of confidence in this assumption, and there are a number of things that could justify this confidence. For example, when you did your literature review, you may have read considerable research on the role of grades and self-esteem, or the source of your confidence could emanate from years of personal experience.

Alternatively, as you reflect on this question, you might conclude that while you feel this is a matter of significance, and you *believe* this assumption is correct, you recognize that it is still only a matter of conjecture, and you might well be mistaken. When this is the case, indicate your uncertainty by placing the letter *U* (for uncertain) next to the *S*.

Once you've completed the second walk-through, your graphic reconstruction likely has several items marked with an *SU*. These are factors that you have deemed *significant* and about which you are *relatively uncertain*. Figure 6.4 is Ms. Montgomery's graphic reconstruction after her second walk-through.

Significant issues that you are uncertain about are precisely the things that justify further investments of your finite professional time and energy. The one remaining task is to take the items that were flagged (earning an SU) during the two-step walk-through and rephrase them as action research questions. Figure 6.5 shows a list of seven elements and two relationships that Ms. Montgomery identified as *significant*. The elements and relationships in bold print are those that she deemed both *significant* and *uncertain* and consequently worthy of incorporating into research questions.

FIGURE 6.4   Ms. Montgomery's Graphic Reconstruction After the Second Walk-Through

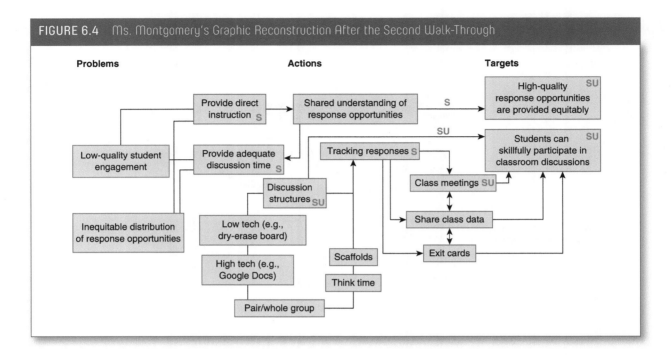

DRAFTING THE QUESTIONS

The way a research question is worded is not just a matter of semantics. Wording can make a big difference because the precise way a question is stated plays an important role in determining the nature of the data that will be required to provide an adequate answer. A set of guidelines follows, for your consideration while drafting your action research questions.

Avoid narrow questions that could be answered with a simple yes or no (such as, Does teacher feedback influence student motivation?). One way to determine if a question is too narrow is to ask yourself,

> Will a definitive answer to this question, in and of itself, provide helpful direction for my/our further action?

Let's assume the answer to the example given was,

> Yes, teacher feedback does influence student motivation.

Would you say that this answer provides enough direction for you to plan your next steps, and would it inform your future professional action? Probably not. This is because the simple "yes" answer neither illustrated how and why teacher feedback influenced student motivation, nor how different forms of feedback might differentially influence motivation.

Do ask open-ended questions, where a large number of potential answers may surface (such as, What are the relationships of different forms of feedback to changes in student performance?). When this question is evaluated through the criteria for its *potential for informing future action*, we will be much happier with the result. This is because the data collected in answer

> **FIGURE 6.5**   Significant Aspects of Theory and Significant Relationships
>
> **Significant Aspects of Theory**
>
> 1. Direct instruction of expectations on response opportunities in class
> 2. **Shared understanding of response opportunities and expectations**
> 3. Sufficient discussion time
> 4. A variety of discussion and response structures
> 5. Responses are tracked
> 6. Teacher elicits feedback from students in class meetings
> 7. Teacher elicits feedback from students individually through exit cards
> 8. Teacher shares results of feedback and progress toward goal
> 9. **Students possess skills to participate in discussions at high levels**
> 10. **Equitable distribution of high-quality and high-quantity student response opportunities**
>
> **Significant Relationships**
>
> 1. The relationship between feedback from students and the shared understanding of response opportunities and expectations
> 2. The relationship between discussion time and discussion techniques
> 3. The relationship between explicit direct instruction and creating a shared understanding of response opportunities
> 4. **The relationship between the discussion structures and the students possessing the skills to participate in discussions at high levels**

to that question will undoubtedly provide insights into the specific nature of the feedback a teacher should consider providing in an effort to enhance student motivation.

Avoid using causal language. Many beginning action researchers feel that conducting scientific research means uncovering definitive cause-and-effect relationships. This is understandable. Most of us learned what constitutes research in our science classes. In the basic and natural sciences, it is actually possible to control for all relevant variables and consequently determine what causes what. However, in social science, this is never possible. When it comes to human behavior, results are influenced by such a wide array of variables that no one could ever control for every possible factor.

Fortunately, there are ways to enhance validity and reliability in social science research, and these will be elaborated on in the next chapter (Chapter 7).

Frame questions in a manner that is likely to highlight observable patterns and correlations between the strength of the independent variables and changes in the dependent variables. (For instance, what are the characteristics of teacher feedback that correspond to increases in the quality of student work?) The answer to a question like this one can help the action researcher recognize those specific teacher behaviors (feedback) that consistently accompany the desired student outcome.

Having completed the two-step walk-through of her theory, Ms. Montgomery was now ready to draft a set of research questions to guide her study. These questions will become the heart of her inquiry. Ms. Montgomery's questions were the following:

- How has this effort influenced the provision of high quality equitable response opportunities? (This question focuses on a critically important outcome and an aspect of the theory rated SU: *the equitable provision of high quality response opportunities.*)
- How did the class meetings on response opportunities impact student participation? (This question focuses on two of the significant aspects of the theory rated SU: *class meetings and students skillfully participating in classroom discussions.*)
- In what manner did emphasizing discussion structures influence the ability of students to skillfully participate in class discussions? (This question focuses on the one significant relationship rated SU: *the relationship of discussion structures to skillful student participation.*)

It has often been noted that the most time-consuming aspect of the action research process is the work that leads up to the development of research questions (Hubbard & Powers, 1999). We have heard many first-time action researchers assert that it took them an entire year or more to come up with a really good question. Look at how well you did; it only took you six chapters!

Sometimes, we go through an extensive and lengthy process to find meaningful questions. However, if the questions that emerge end up guiding us to information that helps us move ahead with our priorities, then the time invested is time well spent.

Ms. Montgomery can now look forward to the rest of the action research process knowing that everything she engages in from here on will be focused on helping her to better illuminate answers to three very meaningful questions.

SURFACING RESEARCH QUESTIONS FOR LEADERSHIP PROJECTS

The two-step walk-through process for surfacing meaningful research questions works in precisely the same manner when the action research is focused on work being engaged in by a school leader. In Chapter 3, we heard about Dr. Hernandez and her interest in studying her efforts to create a more collegial school. In Resource C (Exhibit 5), you will find a copy of her theory of action, along with the results of her application of the two-step walk-through process and the research questions it produced.

7

Building a Data Collection Plan

On the surface, no aspect of the action research process appears more daunting than data collection. While the planning you've engaged in thus far has been time consuming, there is nothing new about that. Teachers are accustomed to spending considerable time planning their instruction, units, and programs. While the work you've completed in Stages 1 and 2 of the action research process may be somewhat more extensive than what is required for other, more routine types of planning, hopefully, the additional clarity and focus you received from this reflective practice justified the extra expenditure of energy. However, at first glance, the time required for data collection often doesn't seem that worthwhile to a busy educator.

When anticipating the collection of data for action research, first-time researchers are often legitimately concerned about two things:

1. The time required

2. The need for precision

Because of the importance of these concerns, we will begin our discussion on data collection by addressing each one separately.

DATA COLLECTION AND THE COMPETING DEMANDS FOR YOUR TIME

If devoting time to data collection means taking time that could have been invested in other learning activities, that cost is greater than most dedicated educators are willing to pay. Fortunately, this is not a choice you have to make. These two categories of professional action appear to be in conflict only if one holds a limited view of what qualifies as teaching and what qualifies as data.

WHAT QUALIFIES AS TEACHING?

As every teacher knows, there is more than one way to produce learning. One mechanism educators have historically used to stimulate student learning is direct instruction. This is the model where the teacher is positioned in front of the learner and is responsible for demonstrating or telling the student how to accomplish a specific task and providing the student with immediate feedback as he or she practices the new skill or recites the new information. There is much to commend this approach, especially when teaching certain types of straightforward basic-skill content. And many teachers have found that the direct-instruction model works well with learners who need consistent and immediate oversight. However, many teachers have also found that there are an even greater number of circumstances when direct instruction is not the only or even the best pedagogy. Many times, a reliance on direct instruction comes at a heavy cost: It is an all-consuming task, leaving teachers with little time and energy for monitoring, assessing, and adjusting.

Increasingly, teachers are finding out that we serve our students and ourselves best when we act as the *facilitators* of student learning, no longer being the sage on the stage but becoming the guide on the side. In this model, the students' role is transformed; they become what Ted Sizer (1984) defined as *knowledge workers*. Every day, knowledge workers wake up and go to their workplace (your classroom) understanding that they will be expected to fulfill their job description, which is to do what is necessary to acquire new knowledge and develop greater skill. In this model, the teacher's role becomes analogous to the supervisor's function in the adult workplace. Our job becomes supplying whatever is needed to help our knowledge workers complete their job successfully—in this case, the acquisition of knowledge and the development of skills. In this relationship, the ultimate responsibility for learning becomes shared and no longer rests solely on the teacher's shoulders.

In the adult workplace, supervisors occasionally will demonstrate new techniques, but they spend far more time observing the workers and providing feedback. Supervisors also engage in planning, gathering data on worker productivity and adjusting individual and group work plans accordingly. They attempt to monitor everything critical to the work being attempted so they can knowledgably and purposefully intervene when necessary. Lastly and most importantly, when the supervisors' goal is increasing worker productivity, they implement practices and procedures that result in the workers being motivated to put forth their very best efforts.

We need to approach data collection in the spirit of the action researcher as the supervisor of a cadre of knowledge workers. Most of the data collection strategies presented here can occur during the workday, while your students are purposefully and actively engaged in their own learning.

Properly implemented, most of the suggested strategies will also support student achievement by providing encouragement, direction, and motivation for your learners.

WHAT THINGS QUALIFY AS DATA?

If you think of a piece of data as something artificial, something that only comes into existence if and when we decide to solicit it, then generating and collecting data becomes a job unto itself. This isn't a productive way for an action researcher to view data collection.

As practitioner researchers, you are well served by applying a broad definition of data. Much action research methodology has been heavily influenced by anthropology. The primary work of anthropologists is observing, documenting, and attempting to understand human cultures that are different from their own. The strategy most often used by field anthropologists is direct immersion into the cultures they are studying. While doing their work, they try to take in everything encountered, from one-on-one discussions to social activities to local rituals. Even mundane activities, such as eating habits and home decor, are considered data. When all of these observations are taken together and analyzed through a sensitive and thoughtful lens, these disparate bits of data can illuminate a complex culture that was the focus of the study.

DATA IN DESCRIPTIVE RESEARCH

When we are conducting descriptive research, our work is nearly identical to that of field anthropologists. Just as they hope to understand what is going on in other cultures by unearthing the meaning of the behavior, habits, and beliefs demonstrated by the members of that culture, the descriptive action researcher is trying to understand the particular circumstances, norms of behavior, and meanings attached to certain behavior by the participants in a specific school, classroom, or academic setting. For this reason, when we are engaging in descriptive action research, nearly everything that occurs in the setting we're studying has the potential to be meaningful data for our understanding of the following questions:

- What is going on here?
- Why is it happening?
- What impact is it having?

DATA IN QUASI-EXPERIMENTAL RESEARCH

Action researchers conducting quasi-experimental studies will also be well served to view data collection through the anthropologist's lens. Undoubtedly, quasi-experimental researchers will want to monitor changes in performance on their priority achievement targets and, therefore, will almost always be using some quantitative methods. But that is only part of the process. The quasi-experimental action researcher needs to understand more than simply whether or not the priority targets were hit. It is equally important, if not more important, to understand the following as well:

- Why was the target hit or missed?
- How did various elements of the theory of action contribute to success or failure?
- What could be learned from this undertaking that might help illuminate other related aspects of the teaching and learning process?

To address these issues, the quasi-experimental researcher has the same need as the descriptive researcher to deeply understand the context and the nuances of the environment where the action took place.

We can hear some of you asking, "Are they crazy? Did they just say I ought to be acting as an anthropologist and collecting data on *everything* going on in my school or classroom?"

Not to worry. While it is true that the range of things that you may want to document is vast, the good news is that much of the necessary data are already being and will continue to be collected, whether or not you had ever decided to conduct action research.

One of our primary tasks as action researchers is identifying *efficient* ways to collect and compile the data that already exist in our environment. But before we examine ways to accomplish this, we should spend a few minutes considering the other big concern regarding data collection: achieving adequate precision.

DATA COLLECTION AND CONCERNS ABOUT PRECISION

It is unwise to collect flawed data and even worse to make use of it. None of us want our physicians making our treatment decisions based on faulty data, nor do we want to fly in aircraft designed by engineers who relied on imprecise data. Equally important, none of us wants our students to receive inadequate instruction simply because inaccurate data suggested an unwise strategy. Even those of us with the most minimal backgrounds in research and statistics probably recall from Ed Psych 101 the two key conditions that must be met if data are to be considered accurate: validity and reliability.

- *Validity* refers to whether the data actually reflect the phenomena they claim to. For example, we would all agree that a measuring tape is a valid way to measure height, and a scale is a valid mechanism for determining weight.
- *Reliability* refers to the accuracy of data. For example, even though a scale is a valid way to measure weight, any particular scale could malfunction and consequently provide unreliable reports on the weight of an object.

As professionals, we want the data that we use to influence our decisions on teaching and learning to be both valid and reliable. While there

FIGURE 7.1	Triangulation Matrix		
Research Question	**Data Source 1**	**Data Source 2**	**Data Source 3**

Source: Reprinted with permission from Richard Sagor, *How to Conduct Collaborative Active Research* (Alexandria, VA: Association for Supervision and Curriculum Development, 1992).

are a number of techniques researchers use to establish validity and reliability, the strategy used most frequently by action researchers is called *triangulation.* As pointed out earlier, triangulation is similar to the strategy used by trial lawyers to prove a case beyond a reasonable doubt. In planning their cases, lawyers strive to find corroboration for every critical bit of testimony or evidence presented. Corroboration is accomplished by offering additional independent pieces of evidence that lead to the same conclusion. While any single bit of evidence might be flawed or imprecise enough to raise suspicion, when enough separate and independent pieces of data all point in the same direction, the face validity of the conclusion can become inescapable. Figure 7.1 is a *triangulation matrix* for use with action research. The left column is where we list our research questions. Then, like a trial lawyer preparing a case, we consider all of the independent sources of data (witnesses) that might be collected, consulted, and presented so that when taken together, they will provide a credible answer to the research question. Then, after reviewing all of the potential sources of evidence, the separate sources of data we plan to use are listed in the row corresponding to the appropriate research question.

As we proceed through this chapter, it is suggested that you use the triangulation matrix to build a case worthy of your confidence. If you build and follow a triangulated data collection plan, it is likely that the findings and conclusions that emerge from your research will possess both validity and reliability.

FISHING IN A SEA OF DATA

Schools and classrooms are data-rich environments. In any situation where life exists, data are continuously being created. Data represent what people choose to do and what they elect not to do. It involves who is doing an action, what they are doing, and their explanations for why they chose to engage in that action. In places where work is undertaken, such as schools, even more data are produced. Where people work, they produce products; those products are data. Here are just a few of the work products typically created in schools that you could use as sources of action research data:

Work Product	Data Regarding
Lesson plans	What I intend to teach
Grade book	Grades earned, test results and assessments of my students
Attendance book	Who was and was not present
Faculty meeting agendas	The scope of faculty business
PTA attendance	Parental interest in the PTA's work
Walk-through notes	Instructional activities in the building

Such a list could go on endlessly. The point is simply this: Data are swirling around the schoolhouse, and these data relate to nearly everything that goes on inside. Collecting these data is much like catching fish with a net. If a fine enough net is cast, it will catch every living organism in the environment. Even if we could cast such a net in our classrooms and catch every minute thing that transpires inside, the time it would take to sift through all those data, separating those which are of value from those which are mostly irrelevant, would certainly take more time than we have available.

The fisherperson solves this problem by designing a net that allows undesirable items to flow through while hopefully only retaining those that were intended and desired. This is analogous to the task before us as we make our plans for data collection.

SECURING RESEARCH ASSISTANTS

This chapter began with a discussion regarding the time issue. Frequently, the way professors and other research scientists deal with limitations on their time is by employing research assistants, generally abbreviated as RAs. In grant-supported research teams, the individual responsible for the study is known as the PI, or principal investigator. In most cases, RAs are highly motivated graduate students who willingly do much of the grunt work of data collection for the privilege of working and learning alongside the PI. So you might be asking, where are you, the poorly paid and overworked educator involved in the conduct of unfunded action research, going to find the motivated RAs to help you with your data collection? Fear not; the solution is nearer than you might think.

Earlier, we touched on the difference between providing direct instruction and facilitating learning. We mentioned that when the teacher becomes the facilitator of learning, and the students perform as knowledge workers, they share the responsibility and accountability for the achievement of results.

Research in adult work settings has clearly established that when workers are involved in systematically monitoring their own progress and self-assessing their own work, performance improves (De Pree, 1997; Hersey & Blanchard, 1993). This happens because when workers are delegated responsibility for monitoring their own work, they tend to hold themselves accountable to higher standards. Equally as important, they tend to enjoy their work more and show more pride in their ultimate accomplishments. So when we ask our students to become the primary collectors of data (our research assistants) on their own learning and to document the activities they are engaged in, we are setting ourselves up for a classic win-win situation.

We would wager that you already know through personal experience that having students compile portfolios, self-assess their work, maintain logs and journals (on their learning activities), and prepare for student-led parent conferences is anything but a waste of time. By having the students monitor their own work, we are helping them learn and internalize what constitutes productive work, as well as gain insight into how they learn best (the skill of metacognition).

It would be nice if we could promise that by turning your students into RAs, you will free yourself from all data collection responsibilities. But that isn't the case. Having RAs on staff doesn't eliminate the participation of the principal investigator in the data collection process, but it does transform the work of the PI. As the lead researcher, the PI's job always begins with fleshing out the theory (what you did in Chapters 4 and 5), determining the research questions (what you did in Chapter 6), and creating the research design: determining what data are to be collected, who will collect them, when they will be collected, and how they will be analyzed. Those are the tasks we will concern ourselves with for the remainder of this chapter. As you proceed to build your research design, our primary focus will be on strategies that

- emphasize the use of *available data*,
- emphasize data that can be collected *while you are facilitating learning*, and
- maximize the value for students of *monitoring their own performance*.

BUILDING A TRIANGULATED DATA COLLECTION PLAN

There are no limits to the variety of things that qualify as data or the techniques that action researchers can use to collect those data. There is, however, a limit to how much can be covered in one book. For this reason, we will work through the process of building a triangulated data collection plan with a few sample strategies that are frequently used and can be efficiently implemented by school-based action researchers.

To begin, we will return to Ms. Montgomery's action research project. As you recall, Ms. Montgomery was investigating the use of effective questioning and discussion strategies as mechanisms to create equitable response opportunities and improve the quality of student work. While in the midst of this study, something occurred that motivated Ms. Montgomery to conduct a second descriptive action research study inside her quasi-experimental study.

During the first nine weeks of the school year, Ms. Montgomery became deeply concerned about a particular young man, Allen Freeman, who was a very bright African American. Allen was diagnosed as ADHD and had a history of low academic performance tracing back to his fourth-grade year. Despite medication, his off-task behavior and academic problems continued unabated during the first quarter, and whenever the class engaged in discussion activities, Ms. Montgomery noticed that Allen was off task and frequently disruptive. Ms. Montgomery was at a loss as to what to do. She decided that since she didn't fully understand what was going on with Allen, she would be well served by conducting a descriptive action research study on Allen's experience in class. She chose social studies as the setting for her study, as some of the discussion activities she planned on using in social studies this quarter would likely prove problematic for Allen. She felt that if she could understand what was happening with Allen during second-quarter social studies, she might gain valuable insights on how to better meet his educational needs. She decided to frame her inquiry around the three ACR questions discussed in Chapter 6. Figure 7.2 is a triangulation matrix set up for use with the three ACR questions.

The process of constructing a data collection plan begins by taking one research question at a time and then asking this question:

> What is one source of data that could be *efficiently* collected that would provide good information to illuminate the answer to this question?

After surfacing a first answer to that question, the process calls for continued brainstorming by repeatedly asking, *What is another source? And then another? And then another?* This process continues until the action researcher believes that when taken together, the multiple sources of data identified will provide a comprehensive, credible, valid, and reliable answer to that research question.

Ms. Montgomery began this process with this paraphrased version of *ACR Question 1: What exactly did the class and Allen do?*

She started by considering sources of data that were already available. She recognized that her plan book, weekly annotated to reflect what she

FIGURE 7.2   Triangulation Matrix: Three ACR Questions

Research Question	Data Source 1	Data Source 2	Data Source 3
What did we actually do?			
What changes occurred with our priority achievement targets?			
What was the relationship between the actions taken and changes in performance on the achievement targets?			

actually taught, was one source of data. She realized that by cross-referencing Allen's *attendance records* with her plan book, she could determine what specific activities Allen experienced, and this could serve as a second data source. As her brainstorming continued, it occurred to her that since all of her students are required to keep their daily work in a portfolio, Allen's *daily work* could serve as a third source of data.

At this point, she paused and asked herself, Will this be enough to create a credible report in answer to this question? She responded with a yes; a record of what was going on every day Allen was in attendance, as well as what he missed on the days he was absent, triangulated with the work he completed and failed to complete when he was there, would provide adequate information to answer the first ACR question.

She then moved to *Question 2: What changes occurred with Allen on my priority achievement targets?* Once again, Ms. Montgomery began her brainstorming with readily available information. The first thing that came to mind was her *grade book*. This is a treasure trove of data, as this is where she records grades on all assignments, quizzes, tests, projects, and student journals. She then added Allen's *daily work folder* to her list of data sources. (Note: A single data source may assist in answering multiple questions. For example, Allen's portfolio can help answer both Questions 1 and 2.) Her thinking then shifted to include data she could collect during class while facilitating student learning. She remembered that she regularly carries a pad of paper and writes notes to herself while walking around the classroom.

She realized her *observational notes on Allen's behavior*, as well as the *narrative comments she wrote on Allen's assignments*, would be data. Remembering that she required all of her students to *self-assess their major assignments*, she added that to her list of data sources. Lastly, since one of her priority achievement targets (for her quasi-experimental study) was increased productive engagement during class discussions, she had already developed a rating scale for use each Friday to produce a *teacher rating of engagement*. She then had her students use this same rating scale to create a *weekly student rating of engagement*.

Once again, it was time for Ms. Montgomery to stop and consider if, when taken together, the multiple sources of data she had just brainstormed would be adequate. She looked at her list asking, Will an examination of the information in my *grade book*, *Allen's daily work*, *my written notes on Allen's behavior*, *my comments on his papers*, *his self-assessments of his work*, and *weekly comparisons of Allen's and my engagement ratings* give me a good enough picture of any changes occurring in Allen's performance? While one can always collect more information, Ms. Montgomery was satisfied that the picture that would likely emerge from these data would capture most of the pertinent changes occurring in Allen's performance.

Now, she moved to the final action research question: What was the relationship between the actions taken and any changes noted in Allen's behavior?

It immediately struck her that the data she would be using to answer the first two questions would also assist her in answering this last question. Specifically, she realized that looking at the activities engaged in (her plan book and Allen's attendance) and comparing them to what was

FIGURE 7.3	Descriptive Study of Allen Freeman's Experience in Social Studies		
Research Question	Data Source 1	Data Source 2	Data Source 3
What did we actually do?	Lesson plan book	Attendance record	Allen's portfolio of daily work
What changes occurred with our priority achievement targets?	Grade book (quizzes, home work, journals, reflection papers, projects, tests, weekly assessments)	Teacher observations, observation notes, ratings of engagement, and comments on assignments	Allen's portfolio, daily work, Allen's ratings of his engagement, and self-assessments
What is the relationship between the actions taken and changes in performance on the achievement targets?	Contrast lesson plans with performance data from grade book.	Correlate lesson plans with observation notes and comments on papers.	Correlate lesson plans with materials in Allen's portfolio and Allen's self-assessments.

accomplished (Allen's work, her grade book, her written comments on Allen's work, Allen's self-assessments, her anecdotal notes, and both student and teacher engagement ratings) would enable her to identify any patterns that might exist between specific classroom activities and Allen's performance. In the next chapter, when our focus shifts to analysis, additional processes for tracking the relationship between actions and outcomes will be discussed.

Figure 7.3 shows Ms. Montgomery's completed triangulation matrix for the descriptive study on Allen Freeman's second-quarter experience in fifth-grade social studies.

DATA COLLECTION PLANNING FOR LEADERSHIP PROJECTS

While there are few places that are as rich in data as classrooms, when one is conducting a study pertaining to school leadership, the process of planning for data collection should be governed by the same principles as with classroom research:

1. It is important that the data collection plan utilize enough independent sources of data to produce both validity and reliability.

2. Data should be collected in an efficient manner.

As a rule, most members of a school staff will appreciate it when they see leaders collecting data on the impact of their leadership. Such behavior not only models a belief in the value of assessment, but when people see their leaders acting on data, it demonstrates the leader's commitment to the instructional ethic of monitoring and adjusting. That being said, leaders need to be mindful of limitations on their own time, as well as the time of those they are working with. Therefore, as much as possible, data collection for leadership projects should be based on available and easy-to-collect data. In Resource C, you will find two data collection plans prepared by Dr. Hernandez: Exhibit 6 is a plan developed to answer the three ACR questions, and Exhibit 7 is a plan prepared on the assumption that she was pursuing the three questions that surfaced through her application of the two-step walk-through process.

Now, it's your turn. Using the blank triangulation matrix (Figure 7.4), start developing a viable data collection plan that you believe holds promise for producing the insights you will need to answer *your* action research questions.

Although each of the data collection strategies Ms. Montgomery planned to use involve data that were either already being collected or could easily be collected while teaching, the amount of work involved in pulling all of this together could still prove significant. Earlier, it was mentioned that one way to manage the data collection workload is by enlisting your students as research assistants. That will certainly help. But there are other efficiencies (both electronic and manual) that can help one manage the work of data collection. We conclude this chapter and our work on *Stage 3: Implementing Action and Collecting Data* with a look at how classroom technology can help you manage your work while implementing your theory of action and collecting the data needed to answer your research questions.

INTEGRATING EFFICIENCIES INTO YOUR DATA COLLECTION WORK

Ms. Montgomery's data collection plan made use of several sources of written material that are routinely produced in classrooms:

- The comments she wrote on Allen's papers
- Notes she wrote to herself when walking around the classroom
- Notes she might occasionally send to Allen's parents, the school's special ed teacher, and the school administration regarding Allen
- Conversations with those listed above
- Allen's self-assessment

Compiling and organizing these data can become a project unto itself. However, over the years, Richard had a great deal of success using a particular low-tech strategy to tackle this problem. His strategy involved the use of sets of carbonless paper.

Keeping File Copies of Narrative Data

Figure 7.5 is an example of a form Richard printed on two-part carbonless paper. (Any school district or commercial print shop should be able to create documents for you on carbonless paper.)

Whenever he was writing something to a student, including comments he normally would have written on the student's tests or on an assignment prior to returning it, he did it on the carbonless paper. Then, he would give the top sheet to the student or staple it to the paper being returned and

FIGURE 7.4 Triangulation Worksheet

Research Question	Data Source 1	Data Source 2	Data Source 3

FIGURE 7.5   Carbonless Paper

A note from the teacher . . .

keep the yellow copy for his own records. When he was writing a note regarding a student to a parent, to another teacher, or to himself, he would use the same paper. Richard maintained a folder for each student, and at the end of each day, he simply dropped any yellow copies of the notes he'd written into the appropriate folder, always making sure that each note was dated. If, as it turns out, he never had a reason to review these notes, nothing was lost. After all, it took just a few minutes each day to file them. But should he ever need to review these notes as data for his action research, to prepare for a parent or administrative conference, or simply to refresh his memory regarding what transpired with a student, he could simply open the file and arrange the notes in chronological order, and it was easy to quickly identify patterns in his comments or observations regarding a student's behavior or performance.

An alternative to the carbonless-paper strategy is to write everything pertaining to your project (comments on student work, notes to parents, office referrals, etc.) on the computer and then keep electronic files of this material for later review.

Keeping Running Records of Behavioral Ratings

In Chapter 3, we developed rating scales for measuring changes in performance on our achievement targets (the dependent variables). Earlier in this chapter, we discussed having students become RAs for our action research. Having students keep running records on their performance, as measured on your teacher-created rating scales, is one excellent way to do this. This is an especially powerful strategy because of the motivational impact of students monitoring the direct relationship between their effort and the results obtained. Self-monitoring builds an internal locus of control, an essential component of student success (Curtis-Fields, 2010; Shepherd, Owen, Fitch, & Marshall, 2006). It is no surprise that fitness buffs, weight watchers, and bridge players all keep running records of their results. Observing patterns of improved behavior motivates people to keep trying, or conversely, data that reflect stagnation or decline can provide motivation for changing old habits.

Action researchers can effectively and efficiently turn their students into RAs by first teaching them the use of the appropriate rating scales. When working with younger children, this might mean translating the scales you developed in Chapter 3 into "kid language" and then providing each student with a copy of the scale or placing it on a poster on the wall of your room. With prereaders, teachers often do this by creating a scale with a range of smiley to frowny faces.

You recall that Mr. Johnson, the principal, and the faculty at the AR Academy were committed to co-constructing a shared definition of engagement. Part of this process was developing a rating scale they could use to document the levels of student engagement. The rating scale they developed through this process is reproduced here as Figure 7.6. Since Mr. Johnson, the AR Academy principal, was conducting his own action research on the effect of his leadership, he was in need of teacher feedback regarding which of his leadership practices were most impactful on the

FIGURE 7.6	Rating Scale: Engagement				
Low	**Basic**	**Developing**	**Meeting Expectations**	**Productive**	**High**
The student didn't disrupt and interfere with others' learning.	The student did some of the assigned work. Worked productively for much of the period.	The student completed most of the assigned work. Worked productively for most of the period.	The student completed all of the assigned work. Was on task for the entire class period.	The student was on task for the entire period, completed all the assigned work, and went beyond expectations.	The student was on task the entire period and put forth a maximum effort.
1	2	3	4	5	6

teachers' ability to enhance student engagement. To help answer this question, he created another scale for the AR Academy teachers to use in providing feedback on his leadership practices. Figure 7.7 is a copy of Mr. Johnson's leadership rating scale.

To answer his research questions, on a monthly basis, Mr. Johnson asked the AR Academy teachers to rate student engagement and principal leadership using those two rubrics.

Circumstances such as these, when we need to collect opinion data over an extended period, are another example of where we have found carbonless paper to be extremely helpful. Figure 7.8 is an example of a form we have students use for recording their daily or weekly self-assessments. Then, we have the students turn in the original and keep the carbonless copy in their portfolios. Ms. Montgomery might well have had her students use forms such as Figure 7.8 for their weekly assessments.

By using these carbonless assessment forms, we will have a running record of how each one of our students viewed her or his performance on our priority targets, and because these forms are dated, we will be able to correlate those ratings to what was transpiring in class. (There will be more specificity on establishing the relationship between actions and performance in the next chapter, when we work on data analysis.)

After a period of time, usually a set number of weeks, we provide our students with another set of carbonless forms (Figure 7.9), which they use to produce line graphs reflecting the direction of their self-assessments over this time period. These line graphs provide us with trend data for each one of our students over an extended period. As a further bonus, we are able to use these forms to effortlessly gather one additional piece of data. Once the students have graphed their performances, we ask them, on the same form, to review the slope of their graph and provide their explanations for any patterns or trends.

By having the students keep the original rating forms in their portfolios, they are able to compile these longitudinal summaries with little extra effort on our part. This way, our RAs (our students) are responsible for

FIGURE 7.7	Rating Scale: Principal Johnson's Support to Increase Student Engagement			
	Not Helpful (1)	**Somewhat Helpful (2)**	**Helpful (3)**	**Very Helpful (4)**
Observation and feedback	Observations were minimal, and the feedback added some value.	Observations were inconsistent, but the feedback related to student engagement was somewhat useful.	Observations were consistent, and the feedback was clear, relevant, and provided specific strategies for enhancing student engagement.	Observations were consistent, and the feedback was clear, thorough, and relevant; it provided specific strategies that would work in my classroom, enabling me to increase the quantity, quality, and equity of student engagement.
Training and support	Some training and support was provided. It provided some new information to improve my practice.	The training and support provided was acceptable, and I was able to find at least one strategy that will help with student engagement.	The training and support was timely, relevant, and well facilitated. The training and support provided new insights I will use to improve student engagement.	Training and support were exceptional. This assistance was timely, directly on point, and will enable me to make significant progress in the quality, quantity, and equity of student engagement in my classroom.
Materials and other resources	Some limited materials were made available to support student engagement.	When materials and other resources were provided, they added some value to my work on improving student engagement.	When materials and other resources were requested, high-quality materials and resources were promptly made available.	The leader effectively anticipated teacher needs and was able to provide high-quality materials and resources in a timely fashion so they could be used for planning purposes.
Response to teacher feedback	Feedback on leadership was solicited inconsistently, and it appears to have been received and accepted.	Feedback on leadership was solicited inconsistently, and it appears that occasionally it resulted in changes in how leadership is handling the student engagement issue.	Feedback on leadership was consistently sought and incorporated into how leadership is handling the student engagement issue.	Feedback on leadership was consistently sought and incorporated into improved leadership behavior. The leadership of the student engagement initiative is being carried out with full transparency and disclosure.

creating the statistics and charting the trends on their own ratings. Obviously, this saves us a great deal of time. But more importantly, by doing it this way, we have provided our students with a chance to take stock of, assume responsibility for, and justify to themselves their own choices of behavior. These are powerful lessons on the road to building an internal locus of control.

FIGURE 7.8   Rating Scale: Principal Johnson's Support to Increase Student Engagement

Name: _____

Date: _____

Rating of Engagement

Today _____

1	2	3	4	5	6

Why?

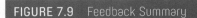

FIGURE 7.9   Feedback Summary

Name: _____   **Date:** _____

Feedback Summary

Scale #2

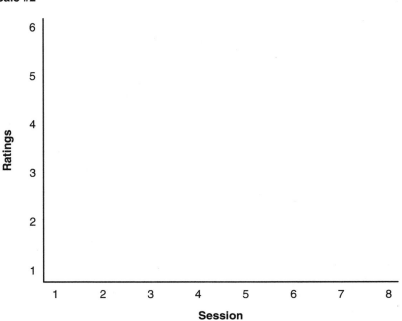

Explain?

To see the power and time saving of this one simple strategy, consider the following scenario. We'll assume we are doing action research with a class of thirty students, compiling daily ratings on two different scales over a three-week period. This amounts to thirty assessments per student, nine hundred assessments per class. Yet if we provide our students with just one minute per day to jot down their daily ratings and then give them fifteen minutes to complete their summaries at the close of the three-week period, we will have all of these data compiled and summarized with an expenditure of a mere thirty minutes of class time. Most importantly, this meager time investment will provide the students with an opportunity to internalize ownership of their own improvement. (Resource A contains detailed instructions on the use of carbonless reporting forms for collecting and analyzing data.)

USING TECHNOLOGY TO COMPILE AND ASSEMBLE ACTION RESEARCH DATA

The beauty of the time-honored teacher grade book is that in this one easy-to-maintain document, a host of different types of information regarding the performance of each of our students can be compiled. In one set of columns, we have attendance data; in other columns, we have a record of their homework, as well as quiz grades and major assignments. And the list goes on. Data input is easy. When taking roll, we simply check if the student is present or absent, and before we return papers, we jot down the grade we assigned. Of course, pulling all of this together (adding up each column and figuring the averages) can take considerable time at the end of the grading period. Fortunately, many school systems have moved to computerized grade books, where the compilation of statistics and the graphing of trends in student performance is made much simpler.

Those readers who don't have access to computer grade books can accomplish many of the same things by using a spreadsheet on their computer. It is now commonplace for computers to be delivered with spreadsheet software preinstalled. If you don't own spreadsheet software, it is easy and inexpensive to acquire. Basically, a spreadsheet is no more than a grade book with an unlimited number of expandable columns. However, it is superior to a hard-copy grade book in three big ways:

1. It will automatically compile statistics (such as averaging the scores in each column), making end-of-term grading easier.

2. The cells of the spreadsheet can expand infinitely. In traditional grade books, each cell is just a fraction of an inch wide, not providing too much room for data. But in a spreadsheet, you can enter an entire note or comment, even copy a photograph or a scanned image of student work into a cell.

3. Lastly, with a spreadsheet, you can easily ask the computer, on virtually any assignment, to compute averages for subgroups, allowing for disaggregation by gender, ethnicity, past performance, and so forth. This is extremely helpful when you are conducting data analysis, which will be discussed in the next chapter.

One really good thing about using a spreadsheet as your electronic grade book is its portability. By using a netbook or a tablet computer, teachers can input data as they move around the room. Technologies, most notably tablet computers, now enable teachers to write longhand notes or score student work and later have these data automatically converted into print for placement in their computerized grade book. Tablets can take photographs of student projects, and with voice recognition software, teachers are even able to dictate notes into their computer, tablet, or cell phone and later convert those comments into text.

What enables doctors to provide personalized treatment for each one of their diverse patients is the availability of an accessible running record of all the pertinent data on each patient's condition. Of course, the doctor has a support staff to transcribe the doctor's notes, input the lab data, and place the various items into the correct patient file. It is unlikely that we will see that type of support provided to teachers in the near future. But fortunately, spreadsheets and portable computing technology increasingly can do nearly the same thing for the overworked educator.

This brings us nearly to the close of our discussion on Stage 3 of the action research process, *Implementing Action and Collecting Data*. It is now time for you, the action researcher, to begin the fun stuff: implementing your theory of action and collecting the data as indicated in your triangulated data collection plan. There is only one little task that needs to be discussed before you commence action on your theory.

KEEPING A RESEARCHER'S JOURNAL

We strongly suggest that during this upcoming period of implementation, you keep a researcher's journal. Needless to say, the more observations you collect in your journal, the more information you will have available when you arrive at the final stage of the process, *Stage 4: Reflecting on Data and Planning Informed Action*. Even if your data collection plan doesn't call for using information from a teacher's journal or if journaling isn't something you are comfortable doing, keeping a researcher's journal isn't a big commitment, and it takes very little time. In fact, you needn't even write in your researcher's journal on a regular basis. What is important, however, is that you make notes in your journal whenever you depart from the theory of action you articulated in *Stage 2: Articulating Theories of Action*. When this happens, in your notes, you should indicate the date, the specific actions that differed from your original theory, and your rationale for making these adjustments.

As an educational action researcher, your first and most sacred duty is to the first part of your title, your work as *an educator*. Because that is your most important job, you should always feel comfortable deviating from your previously enunciated theory of action wherever and whenever you think it is in your students' or school's interest. However, later, when you put on your researcher hat, you will find it essential to document what actually transpired and the reasons why you felt it necessary to make adjustments to your theory of action. Unless you have an accurate record of what took place and why, you will be unable to learn from your experience.

Keep in mind that often, the best learning comes from serendipity. You should stay open to letting this happen. Your researcher's journal will allow you to understand the significance of unanticipated events, as well as enable you to share this learning with others.

Last Word on Data Collection
The data collection sources mentioned in this chapter are simply examples. You are encouraged to use them to stir your imagination while keeping in mind that there exists a virtually unlimited universe of data selection strategies for your use as a creative action researcher.

8

Analyzing the Data

We are now ready to begin our work on the final stage of the action research process, *Stage 4: Reflecting on Data and Planning Informed Action*. There are three distinct activities that occur during this stage:

1. Analysis of data

2. Planning for future action

3. Reporting and sharing what's been learned

The process begins by *analyzing* all the data that have been collected. Then, the insights gained from that analysis are used to prepare a *plan of action*. This is followed by *reporting and sharing* what was learned with colleagues. In this chapter, we focus on the first of those activities, analyzing the action research data. In the two chapters that follow, the focus will shift to strategies for action planning and reporting.

Every action research project is a story of what transpired during the course of the research. As in the world of literature, each story has its own theme, plot, and set of characters. Our stories can range from a report on a single student's experience in class to the story of what was learned while teaching familiar content in a new way, or it could be the saga of a faculty and its attempt to become more collegial. Now that you have arrived at *Stage 4: Reflecting on Data and Planning Informed Action*, the events of your story have already occurred. Every element (the characters, conflicts, setting, and themes) can hopefully be understood through the data you collected. The task before you, when engaged in data analysis, is to figure out a strategy to liberate the story that is lying dormant inside your data and give it an opportunity to take form and reveal itself. In this chapter, we review several ways to accomplish this.

Just as the nature of your research questions influenced the types of data you collected, the nature of those data will influence the strategy you will use for analysis. When you prepared your data collection plan (Chapter 7), we discussed the use of a set of three generic ACR research questions and saw how effective they could be with a wide range of research foci. We will now examine a few generic approaches to data analysis, all of which have the power to effectively bring to the surface the stories residing in most sets of school data. The first approach is called a *trend analysis*. This is a versatile strategy that can easily be modified and adjusted for use with an array of data sources and should help you answer a broad range of action research questions.

TREND ANALYSIS

Above all, education is about growth and development. Students, classes, and schools change over time. When things are proceeding as we'd like, the direction of those changes is positive. As educators, our hope and professional assumption is that the longer someone is engaged in the educational process, the greater will be his or her development. In this book, we framed the rationale for engaging in action research as a means to help us find the best routes for fostering that development and to assist us as professionals learning from our own experience as we travel ever closer to the achievement of universal success.

The specific areas of development you will want to document are changes in performance on your priority achievement targets. When analyzing action research data, your goal will be to accomplish two things:

1. Trace any and all changes in performance that occurred in the effort to reach your priority achievement targets.

2. Understand the pertinent factors, circumstances, and/or actions that contributed to those changes.

Conceptually, the way action researchers usually approach the analysis of data is very similar to the way historians and other reporters of naturally occurring events approach theirs. What first attracts the attention of a historian or a reporter is the awareness of a compelling event. Whether that event is a conflict, a discovery, a scandal, an accident, or an election, the analysis process begins with the reporter (that is, the historian or researcher) becoming aware that something has happened that he or she wants to know more about. Invariably, the aspect of the event that made it noteworthy was that it appeared unique or, at the very least, appeared significantly different than what had gone before. After an event has been initially reported or brought to the surface, the focus of the reporter, historian, or researcher switches to understanding the event. After describing what occurred, historians train their eyes and ears backward, trying to understand what factors contributed to or otherwise influenced the event. The consuming questions at this point become the following:

- Why did this occur?
- Why did it occur here and not elsewhere?
- Why did it happen now and not at some other time?

The events we action researchers want to report on are changes in performance on our priority achievement targets. The factors or circumstances that led up to the events are the things that transpired as the learner, the class, or the program developed to its current level of performance. Our job when conducting data analysis is to use available data to deepen our understanding regarding which of all of the infinite number of things that transpired (all the potential independent variables) actually influenced the changes in performance that were recorded on the dependent variable.

Since change occurs over time, we can pictorially illustrate the analysis process as a line graph, such as that shown in Figure 8.1. In Figure 8.1, the vertical axis represents performance on the achievement target, and the horizontal axis represents the events that occurred over the term of the study.

Figure 8.2 is a graph representing the rates of highway fatalities in the United States from 1988 to 1998. An examination of this graph reveals something quite positive. Fatalities per 100 million vehicle miles dropped dramatically during this decade.

If you were working in the field of transportation safety and had selected as one of your priority achievement targets reducing highway fatalities, you would be delighted by this trend in performance. In all likelihood, you and your colleagues had been taking many different actions designed to reduce the fatality rate. At this point, you would have significant interest in determining which of those actions, if any, contributed to this positive change on your priority achievement target.

No doubt, you and your colleagues have been collecting data on several aspects of driver behavior, and you would now be interested in seeing if those data might help you understand what, if any, of those specific changes in behavior corresponded to the drop in fatalities. One of the sets of data you have available is the annual reports on the use of seat belts. Wondering if there might be a relationship between seat belt use and highway fatalities, you decide to contrast seat belt use from 1988 to 1998 with the fatality data. Figure 8.3 shows these two data sets side by side.

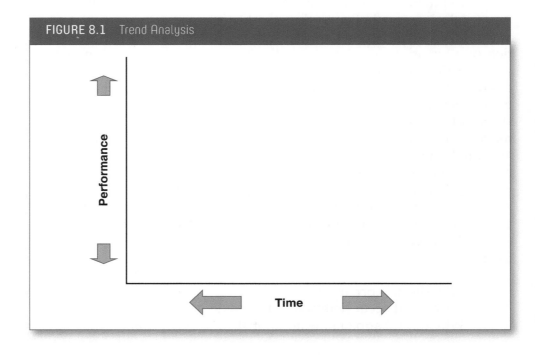

FIGURE 8.1   Trend Analysis

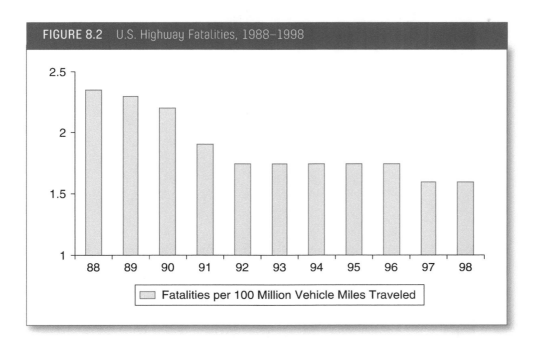

FIGURE 8.2   U.S. Highway Fatalities, 1988–1998

A cursory look at these graphs reveals a clear pattern: The decline in fatalities (the dependent variable) appears to correspond almost precisely to the increase in the use of seat belts (one of the independent variables). Needless to say, you would want to do further analysis employing other sets of data before you claim to have demonstrated this relationship as irrefutable, yet at this point, it is beginning to appear that the actions you and your colleagues took to encourage seat belt use appear to be paying dividends.

ORGANIZING DATA TO HELP ANSWER THE THREE GENERIC QUESTIONS

When conducting a trend analysis with the data collected in response to the three ACR research questions, it is helpful to compile and review the data in the same order as we posed the questions. To illustrate how this is done, we will look at studies conducted by four action researchers, three of whom you met earlier in this text: Charlene and her action research on the efficacy of the leadership coaching she is providing her principals, Mr. Johnson and his efforts to understand his leadership of the student engagement initiative, Ms. Montgomery and her efforts to better understand the educational experience of Allen (the student with ADHD in her class), and Mr. Seeker, a high school teacher who was studying his efforts to improve his students' writing of the persuasive essay.

ACR QUESTION 1: WHAT DID WE DO?

Action researchers who took the time to detail their personal theory of action will already have in their possession important historical documents with good data regarding what they *intended to do*. The priority pies

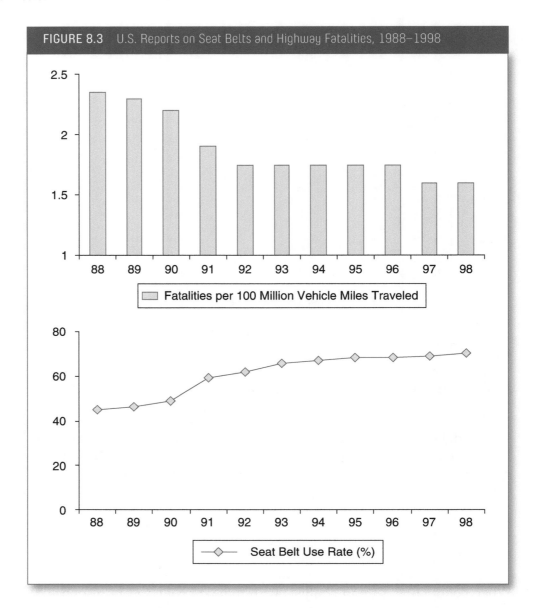

FIGURE 8.3   U.S. Reports on Seat Belts and Highway Fatalities, 1988–1998

and graphic reconstructions produced during *Stage 2: Articulating Theories of Action* provide accurate data on what you had planned and what you intended to do (as of the date you created those documents). Therefore, the first step of this part of the analysis process is to revisit your original theory of action and then critically review your data on implementation for evidence of four things:

1. Was the theory of action (as illustrated on the graphic reconstruction) implemented as designed?

2. In what fashion was the theory of action implemented?

3. What, if any, elements of the theory were omitted or changed?

4. What, if any, significant actions were taken that were not part of the original theory?

There are several ways we can go about answering these questions. One is to examine the sum of our actions and determine the degree to which our investments of time and energy corresponded to the percentages we had anticipated spending and illustrated on our priority pies (see Chapter 4). A second strategy is to see if we faithfully followed through on the theory of action as displayed on our graphic reconstructions (see Chapter 5). If you elected to use the Time Priority Tracking Form (Figure 6.2) and kept a researcher's journal or an annotated set of lesson plans (or both), you will have all the data you need to answer ACR Question 1. The following three-step process will help you synthesize these data and complete this part of your analysis.

Step 1: Allocating Time

Using the worksheet provided (Figure 8.4), enter the data you collected on your weekly Time Priority Tracking Forms (Figure 6.2).

The next step is to illustrate the time actually spent over the course of your study. This is done by creating a line graph. Figure 8.5 illustrates the ebb and flow of the time spent by Mr. Seeker while engaging in his action research on improving his students' writing of five-paragraph essays.

Now, it is time to examine the *time allocation graph* by category to see if any notable patterns or outliers can be identified. For example, was there an extended period of time (perhaps an entire month) when nothing was done in a particular category of action, or was the time spent on each category consistent throughout the project? When we look at Figure 8.5, we can see that Mr. Seeker spent significant time early in the term on mechanics and grammar, and the time he devoted to instruction on editing increased as the term progressed.

You may want to use Figure 8.6 to plot the actual allocation of time across the categories of action identified on your original priority pie.

Another valuable use of the data on the summary sheet (Figure 8.4) is to determine if the actual expenditure of time was consistent with what you had anticipated when planning your project. This is done by producing a grand total of the hours spent working on the project and then creating subtotals for each category of action. To calculate the percentage of time invested per category, divide each subtotal by the grand total. Then, using the percentages produced, draw another pie graph; this one will illustrate your actual expenditure of time.

By placing the priority pie, constructed prior to commencing action, next to the pie graph you just produced, you will have created a visual that clearly and succinctly contrasts your original assumptions regarding time allocation with the actual expenditure of your time. Figure 8.7 shows the two graphs produced by Mr. Seeker.

Contrasting Anticipated and Actual Energy Expended in Leadership Projects

The use of priority pies to contrast the anticipated versus actual expenditure of energy across independent variables is a valuable part of data analysis, regardless of the specific focus of one's action research. On

FIGURE 8.4 Summary Time Priority Form

Category of Action	Week 1	Week 2	Week 3	Week 4	Week 5	Week 6	Week 7	Week 8	Week 9	Totals
Total										

FIGURE 8.5 TIME-USE GRAPH: EIGHTH-GRADE WRITING IN HOURS

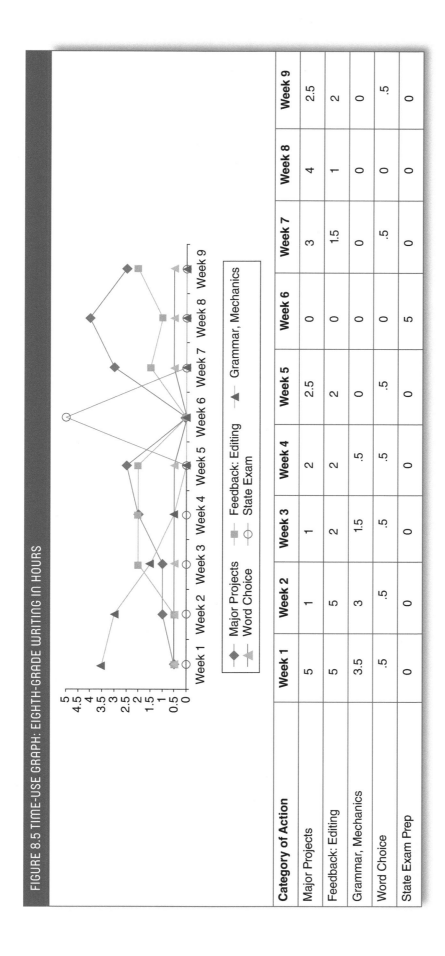

Category of Action	Week 1	Week 2	Week 3	Week 4	Week 5	Week 6	Week 7	Week 8	Week 9
Major Projects	5	1	1	2	2.5	0	3	4	2.5
Feedback: Editing	5	5	2	2	2	0	1.5	1	2
Grammar, Mechanics	3.5	3	1.5	.5	0	0	0	0	0
Word Choice	.5	.5	.5	.5	.5	0	.5	0	.5
State Exam Prep	0	0	0	0	0	5	0	0	0

FIGURE 8.6 Trends in Time Use

Project: _____

Approximate Time Spent	Week 1	Week 2	Week 3	Week 4	Week 5	Week 6	Week 7	Week 8	Week 9
5 hours									
4.5 hours									
4 hours									
3.5 hours									
3 hours									
2.5 hours									
2 hours									
1.5 hours									
1 hour									
0.5 hour									

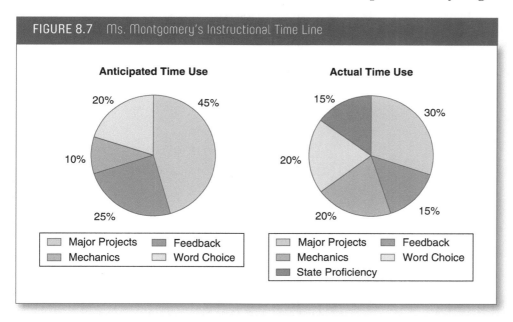

FIGURE 8.7   Ms. Montgomery's Instructional Time Line

those occasions when key actions took place during scheduled classes or at scheduled events, such as regular faculty or PLC team meetings, the use of strategies like the Summary Time Priority Form will enable the action researcher to create an accurate picture of how her or his energy was expended. This is because the Summary Time Priority Form process treats time and energy as if they were the same thing. But on other occasions, for example, when leaders are conducting action research on their facilitation of change, direct measures of time invested (for example, entries on one's calendar) may not produce an accurate portrait of energy expended.

For this reason, it is suggested that when conducting action research on leadership activities, the action researcher prepares contrasting pictures of *anticipated* and *actual* energy expended (as opposed to *time expended*). To create these contrasting pictures, we use a slightly modified process for generating the *actual energy expended data*. Resource C (Exhibit 8) contains instructions on how you can create contrasting priority pies of energy expended. Charlene used this process to analyze her data on the energy expended on instructional improvement activities with her principals. She recorded these data using the process outlined in Resource C (Exhibit 8) and used that information to prepare the contrasting graphs displayed in Figure 8.8. (See next page.)

After reviewing her data, it was clear to Charlene that she did not take into consideration the impact of using a structured agenda for her school visits. Additionally, due to the high stress levels of schools under pressure to improve student outcomes, she now recognized that if the goal is changing teacher practice, attending to the prevailing professional culture is an essential element. The data showed that she needed to spend significantly more time with principals, strategizing ways to enhance the professional culture in their schools.

Now, taking all the data you just compiled to answer ACR Question 1, it is time to summarize the data in clear, unambiguous, bulleted narrative statements. We call these narrative statements *findings*. For example,

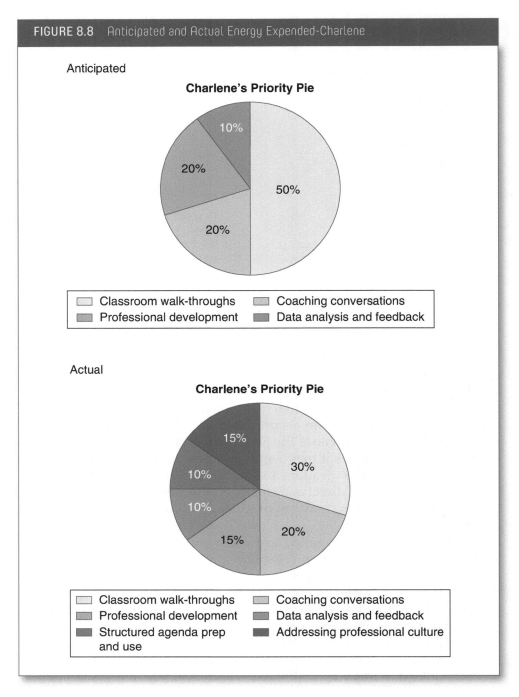

FIGURE 8.8 Anticipated and Actual Energy Expended—Charlene

Mr. Seeker's data would have enabled him to write statements such as the following:

- The project lasted for eighteen weeks.
- Approximately 16 percent of class time was spent each week on journal writing (thirty minutes per week).
- Overall, 30 percent of class time (an average of three hours per week) was spent engaged in work on major papers.

- Overall, 5 percent of class time was used for teacher feedback.
- Overall, 10 percent of class time was spent on group and peer feedback.
- Overall, 20 percent of class time was spent working on mechanics and grammar.
- During six weeks (three in October, two in November, and one in December), zero class time was spent on either drafting or revising major papers.

Step 2: Look for Patterns

Read through your researcher's journal, your annotated lesson plans, and/or your calendar, with paper and pen in hand. Whenever you notice something that appears to be a pattern (an observation or an activity that occurred three or more times), jot down a phrase that describes that pattern. For example, your list might contain items such as the following:

- Class discussions about grades
- Review of previously taught material
- Use of editing groups
- Parent conferences
- PLC team meetings
- Student-led classroom discussions

Now, reread the journal, annotated lesson plans, or your calendar, and using an analysis form like the one in Figure 8.9, note the date of the occurrence, and tabulate the frequency of the occurrences by category. (See page 140.)

Once again, it is time to summarize this information as bulleted findings. Examples of findings that Ms. Montgomery identified include the following:

- Class meetings were held at the end of each week.
- Discussion time was maximized six out of nine sessions.
- Eight distinct question and discussion strategies were used.
- Student responses were tracked on a daily basis.
- Feedback was elicited from my peers regarding the data on response opportunities at the end of each unit.

These are examples of the type of bulleted findings that emerged from Mr. Johnson's analysis of the data collected for ACR Question 1:

- I attended twenty-four grade-level PLC meetings.
- I organized seven professional development sessions on engagement strategies.
- Student engagement data were collected weekly; disaggregated by race, gender, and SPED and ELL status; and shared at our regular monthly faculty meetings.
- Each teacher conducted at least three peer observations.

FIGURE 8.9 Activity Analysis Form

Step 1. Read through your log, journal, or annotated lesson plans for activities or events that appear to recur. Jot down a phrase that describes the recurring event in the left-hand column.

Step 2. Reread the documents, jotting down the date for each occurrence of particular events or activities and a descriptive comment if necessary.

Event or Activity	Dates of Occurrence	Frequency	Comments
Example: Current events journal writing 10/6, 10/13, 10/20, 10/27, 11/4	9/8, 9/15, 9/22, 9/29, Nine times; once per week	Occurs first fifteen minutes of class every Monday	

Finally, Charlene reflected on the practices she engaged in with her principals to answer ACR Question 1, *What did I do?*

- I shared my theory of action with all eight principals.
- I visited every classroom with the principal in each building at least three times over the course of the year.
- Approximately 50 percent of our conversations were about classroom practices, student data, and training or resources related to improving literacy.
- I coached three principals through discussion protocols to support struggling teachers.
- I assigned technical support to three schools regarding curriculum support to improve reading achievement.
- I worked with teachers willing to use additional training and resources to design model classrooms.

Step 3: Creating a Time Line

The purpose of this step is to help you construct the equivalent of the horizontal axis for the trend graph (see Figure 8.1) by using your journal, annotated lesson plans, or calendar. First, read through your lesson plans or journal entries for each specified period of time (generally weekly), and then, write a brief summary of the key actions that occurred during that time period. Then, write this out on a long sheet of chart paper. Figure 8.10 (on the following page) shows Ms. Montgomery's instructional time line for her second-quarter class.

Now, review your time line, as well as your sets of bulleted statements of findings, and write a short narrative describing what was done by you and the participants in your project. Typically, narratives might read something like these examples that could have been written by Mr. Johnson, the middle school principal, and Mr. Seeker, the high school writing teacher.

Mr. Johnson might have said the following about what he did to foster enhanced engagement schoolwide:

I had intended to devote fewer professional development sessions to the focus on engagement strategies. I had committed myself to delivering two sessions during the first quarter, accompanied by walk-throughs, with feedback provided to individual teachers in one-on-one conversations, along with brief engagement status updates on the project during faculty meetings. I expected this to take 20 percent of my time but recognized, based on teacher feedback and classroom observations, that more training was requested and needed. I added two additional training sessions, resulting in 40 percent of the time dedicated to the project. I also spent less time doing walk-throughs and providing feedback than expected. I originally planned on doing weekly scans of engagement per grade level; however, I wasn't able to follow through on this as I had intended due to a host of calendar interruptions. I hadn't anticipated needing to help teachers get prepared for the engagement training, and as a result, that wasn't included in my original theory. In the end, preparation for training ended up consuming 20 percent of the time and energy I devoted to this project.

FIGURE 8.10 Ms. Montgomery's Instructional Time Line

Week 2	Week 3	Week 4	Week 5	Week 6	Week 7	Week 8	Week 9
Students were assigned collaborative pairs. Three discussion structures were introduced using the pairs, followed by writing prompts. The week ended with a whole-group discussion.	Research topics were selected, and student pairs, jigsaw activities, and pair jeopardy were methods used to promote discussion and understanding of key learning targets.	Students explicitly taught levels of questions and ways to probe or deepen levels of questions posed to each other in class. Several practice sessions. Students critiqued peer and teacher questions based on Costa's levels of questions.	Structured discussion activities regarding Baltimore protests. Teacher led and created.	Research on violence in various cultures and communities and use of deadly force. Student-facilitated discussions using technology.	Student presentations with peer edits and feedback. Proposal submitted to local police and elected officials around community safety.	Persuasive-essay topics selected. Students discuss various methods to persist in writing lengthy papers. Provide feedback on thesis.	Students prepared for fish-bowl-style Socratic seminars. Time was given for triads to prepare questions for the discussion.

Week 1

Students were given a choice of one of four articles they found interesting. Students worked in jigsaw groups, using close reading and Cornell note strategies. Students used graphic organizers to collect and report out key concepts. Most lessons were whole groups with dry-erase boards and sticks of justice.

Mr. Seeker might have said the following in his summary answer to ACR Question 1:

> *My theory of action called for spending nearly half (45 percent) of class time on major projects and 25 percent on feedback. In practice, less than a third (30 percent) of class time was spent on major projects, and much less time than I had anticipated (15 percent) was spent on feedback. Significantly, more time was spent with direct instruction on mechanics and grammar (20 percent) than the 10 percent that I had intended. Lastly, 15 percent of class time was used to prepare for and take the state proficiency exam, a category of action that I hadn't even considered when planning this class.*

ACR QUESTION 2: WHAT CHANGES OCCURRED REGARDING THE ACHIEVEMENT TARGETS?

Using your grade book or whatever other records you've kept on performance on your priority achievement target over the term of the project, you should now place those data into a chronological sequence for any individual student, category of students, or other group whose performance you wish to understand. Figure 8.11 shows the grades earned during the second quarter by Allen, the hyperactive fifth-grade student in Ms. Montgomery's class. Ms. Montgomery recorded grades for homework, quizzes, journals, and group projects. She then used a line graph to ferret out any trends in these data regarding Allen's performance. Figure 8.12 reflects Allen's grades over the nine weeks of second-quarter social studies.

FIGURE 8.11   Allen's Grades for 2nd Quarter

Week	Journals	Homework Completion	Reflection Papers	Quizzes	Group Project Grades
1	55	80		70	
2	60	60		60	
3	50	60	65	70	85
4		60		80	
5	75	80		90	
6	80	100		90	
7		80		100	
8	90	80	85	90	95
9	100	80		100	

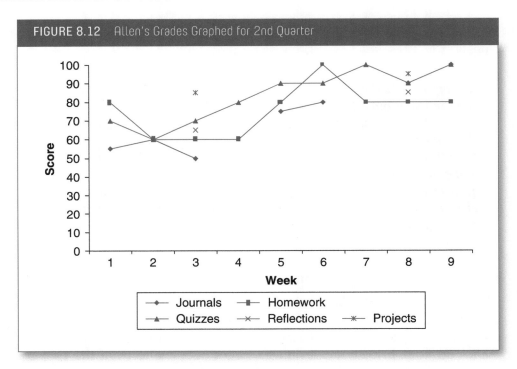

FIGURE 8.12   Allen's Grades Graphed for 2nd Quarter

The next step in a trend analysis is comparing and contrasting trends in performance to see if they might have been influenced by variables other than simply your actions. With classroom research, this is easily accomplished by graphing average class (or subgroup) performance over the same time frame and comparing the achievement of individual students with overall class or subgroup performance. Figure 8.13 is an

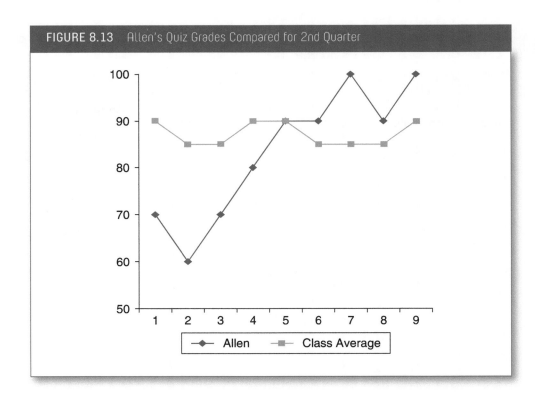

FIGURE 8.13   Allen's Quiz Grades Compared for 2nd Quarter

example of such a graph. It contrasts Allen's quiz grades with the average quiz grades earned by his classmates. Another illustration of this process can be found in Figure 8.14. This contrasts Allen's grades with his classmates' grades on each of the five categories of performance tracked in Ms. Montgomery's grade book.

Once you have graphed or otherwise summarized all of the performance data you have collected, it is time to review these data and summarize them as bulleted findings. For example, Ms. Montgomery might have generated the following list of findings:

- During the first semester, the average homework completion rate for the class was 95 percent while Allen's homework completion rate was 77 percent.
- Allen's homework completion rate went from 65 percent the first four weeks to 85 percent in the last four weeks.
- The class's average quiz grade was 87 percent; Allen's average quiz grade was 83 percent.
- Allen's quiz grades went from 70 percent in the first four weeks to 95 percent in the last four weeks.

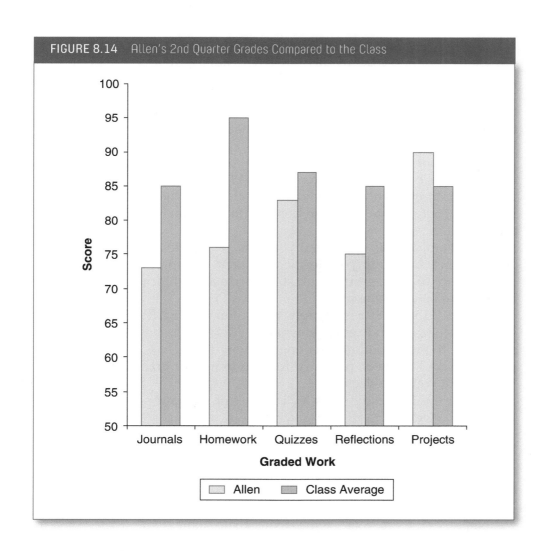

FIGURE 8.14   Allen's 2nd Quarter Grades Compared to the Class

Disaggregation

As educators concerned about making progress on the twin goals of equity and excellence, we will always want to see if, when, and how our actions might have had a differential impact based on the culture, ethnicity, gender, or other background or behavioral characteristics of the participants. This is called disaggregation and is accomplished by subdividing performance data by each category we deem to be potentially relevant. As a teacher, you start this process by reflecting on the different demographic subgroups represented by the students in your data set and any achievement differences between these groups that have appeared in the past. Then, ask yourself the question, Would it be worth comparing and contrasting performance across these groups? Considering past achievement gaps, many teachers have found it valuable to disaggregate their student data by categories such as the following:

- Gender
- Past level of academic performance
- Race or ethnic group
- Primary home language
- Years of attendance at your school or in your district
- Economic disadvantage (free and reduced lunch)

The fifth-grade PLC team from AR Academy that was working on increasing student engagement found it valuable to disaggregate their data by race, gender, special education, talented and gifted, and English language learner. They also found it helpful to compare each subgroup's engagement level with the averages for that grade level and content area. Often, schoolwide action research teams find it helpful to compare the performance of students by both their past performance (previous grades) and attendance history. For example, the PLC team might choose to contrast the data from those who attended schools in the district for five or more consecutive years with students who had more recently moved to the district.

Once you have disaggregated your data, compute and graph the averages for each subgroup you deemed relevant. Compare and contrast the performance of these groups, and summarize all significant observed patterns as bulleted statements.

Figures 8.15 and 8.16 are graphs that compare the AR Academy team's first-quarter schoolwide engagement data, disaggregated and reported by subgroup, to the second-quarter engagement data.

Figure 8.17 has been provided for you to use for graphing the performance data you've collected.

Repeat the foregoing steps for each set of relevant performance data you have collected.

FIGURE 8.15   PLC Teams First Quarter Data

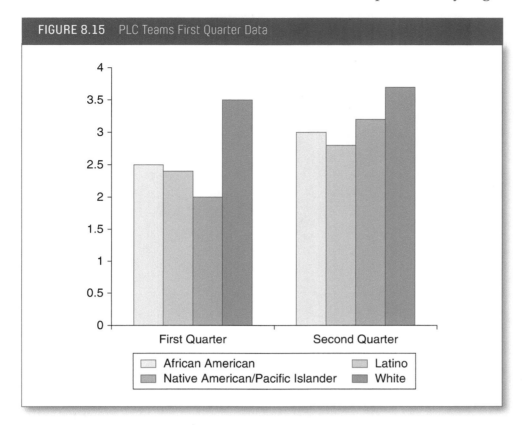

FIGURE 8.16   PLC Teams First Quarter Data

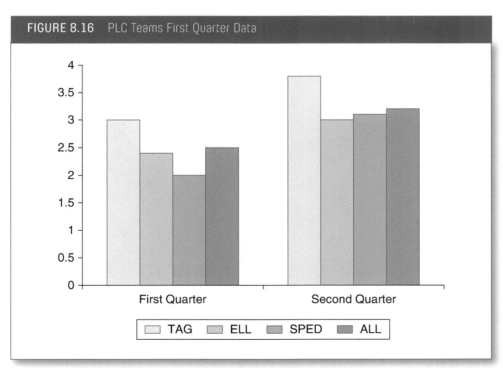

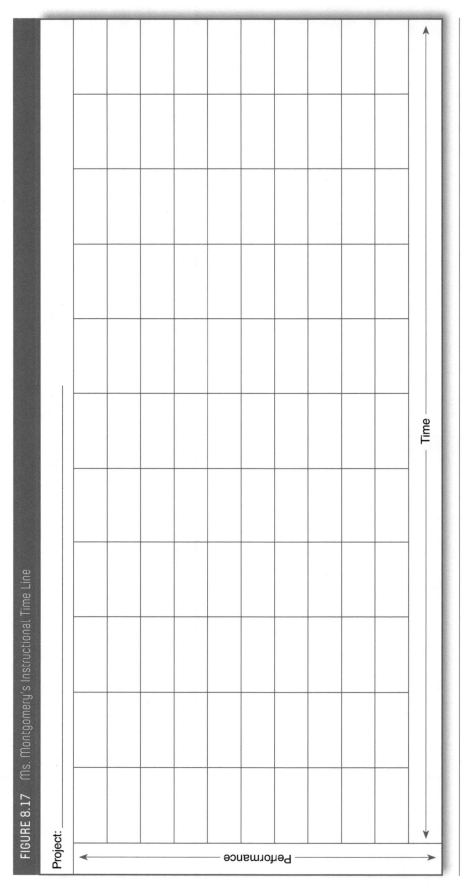

FIGURE 8.17 Ms. Montgomery's Instructional Time Line

Project: _____

Time

Performance

ACR QUESTION 3: WHAT WAS THE RELATIONSHIP BETWEEN ACTIONS TAKEN AND ANY CHANGES IN PERFORMANCE ON THE TARGETS?

You will need to do two things to answer this question. The first makes use of the findings you generated in answering the first two questions. Place the time line you developed (see Figure 8.10) when analyzing the data you collected in answer to Question 1 under the horizontal axis of a graph. Then, on the vertical axis, plot the performance data collected in response to Question 2. This step is illustrated in Figure 8.18, which tracks Ms. Montgomery's weekly assessments of Allen's response opportunities and Allen's weekly assessments during the nine-week quarter.

Ms. Montgomery actually has two sets of data to work with, both of which rightfully belong on the horizontal axis. One is the summary of her lessons (Figure 8.10); the other is the collection of weekly narrative comments she wrote regarding Allen's behavior. Figure 8.19 incorporates both of those sets of data on the same time line. (See pages 150–151.)

It is at this point that Ms. Montgomery can go back and look for changes in Allen's performance, either positive or negative, and check to see if there were any particular actions or activities that corresponded to those changes. The purpose here is to see if she can identify a trend, such as the one between seat belt use and fatalities (see Figures 8.2 and 8.3), to help her explain the story of Allen's experience in class. She was pleased to notice the tight correlation between her assessments and Allen's

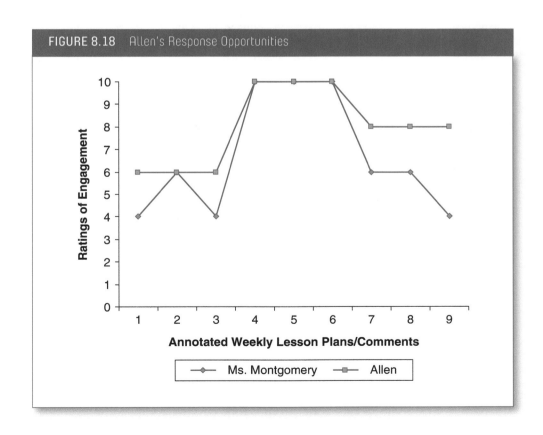

FIGURE 8.18   Allen's Response Opportunities

FIGURE 8.19 *Ms. Montgomery's Instructional Time Line, With Comments on Allen*

Week 1	Week 2	Week 3	Week 4	Week 5	
Students were given a choice of one of four articles they found interesting. Students worked in jigsaw groups, using close reading and Cornell note strategies. Students used graphic organizers to collect and report out key concepts. Most lessons were whole groups with dry-erase boards and sticks of justice.	Students were assigned collaborative pairs. Three discussion structures were introduced using the pairs, followed by writing prompts. The week ended with a whole-group discussion.	Research topics were selected, and student pairs, jigsaw activities, and pair jeopardy were methods used to promote discussion and understanding of key learning targets.	Students explicitly taught levels of questions and ways to probe or deepen levels of questions posed to each other in class. Several practice sessions. Students critiqued peer and teacher questions based on Costa's levels of questions.	Structured discussion activities regarding Baltimore protests. Teacher led and created.	
Allen seemed disinterested and appeared to be off task most of the week. He appeared busy when we were in the library, but I'm not sure he was doing the assigned work. I had to stay on him all period on Friday.	Allen was far more engaged this week than last. He seemed to take ownership of his group's work. He even showed some leadership. Later in the week, he needed prodding to stay on task.	I had trouble with Allen this entire week! He refused to attend when other students were presenting. Ultimately, I had him sit with me, just to keep him from disrupting others.	I think the computer is Allen's thing. He was excited the moment we entered the lab. A few times I had to ask him to curb his enthusiasm, as he occasionally took over for Ms. Johnson. I had to remind him it wasn't his class.	Allen assumed the role of group leader this week. At first, I thought the other kids would object to his bossy style, but they seemed to genuinely value his expertise with technology. What pleased me was that he stayed on task and focused on the assigned work! Further, I had an aha moment: Allen's occasional (mis)behaviors are likely signs of boredom.	

self-assessments of his engagement. She also noticed some dramatic improvement in Allen's engagement during Weeks 4–6. To get a handle on what might account for this, she looked at her instructional time line and noticed that Weeks 4–6 were when the regular curriculum was set aside, and the class focused on the Baltimore protests. It appears that the relevance of that topic may well have had a positive influence on Allen's level of engagement.

Let's return again to Mr. Seeker and his attempt to help his students write better five-paragraph persuasive essays. The graphs (Figures 8.20 and 8.21) reflect disaggregated data on the weekly self-report assessments

Week 6	Week 7	Week 8	Week 9
Research on violence in various cultures and communities and use of deadly force. Student-facilitated discussions using technology.	Student presentations with peer edits and feedback. Proposal submitted to local police and elected officials around community safety.	Persuasive-essay topics selected. Students discuss various methods to persist in writing lengthy papers. Provide feedback on thesis.	Students prepared for fish-bowl-style Socratic seminars. Time was given for triads to prepare questions for the discussion.
I'm glad I have monitored Allen closely. The counselor and I are moving forward with a recommendation for the talented and gifted program. It was another good week in class. Allen acted as though he was my aide, helping his classmates and solving problems.	This week had its ups and downs for Allen. For the first time, his teammates started showing frustration with him trying to control everything. I intervened; we had a short team meeting, and everything was amicably resolved.	Overall, this was an okay week for Allen. I did need to redirect him a bit, as we had moved on from the exciting topics from the previous weeks. On Wednesday, the party and unstructured format was a little too much stimulation for him. I don't think he liked the prep work for the writing assessment, but he stayed on task and was respectful.	Allen was cooperative during the preparation activities, although I don't know how well he did yet. He was absent for the movie and was cooperative on the field trip, but that may have been because his dad was one of the chaperones.

by his students on the effort they had expended in class. Figure 8.20 compares those students who had been average performers (previous year's GPAs of 2.00 to 2.99) with the low performers (GPA of less than 2.00) and high performers (GPA of 3.00 or more). Figure 8.21 contrasts this same class of Mr. Seeker's students, this time disaggregated by gender.

When Mr. Seeker examined these graphs, he could see that the effort expended by the middle and low performers began dropping during the second week of February and continued in this depressed state throughout the month of March. When he looked on the horizontal axis to see what, if

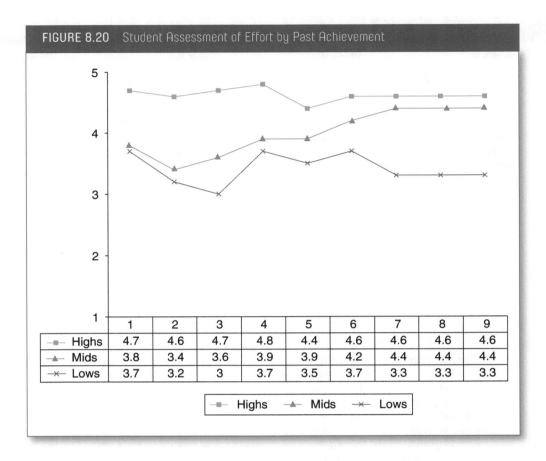

FIGURE 8.20   Student Assessment of Effort by Past Achievement

	1	2	3	4	5	6	7	8	9
■ Highs	4.7	4.6	4.7	4.8	4.4	4.6	4.6	4.6	4.6
▲ Mids	3.8	3.4	3.6	3.9	3.9	4.2	4.4	4.4	4.4
✕ Lows	3.7	3.2	3	3.7	3.5	3.7	3.3	3.3	3.3

■ Highs   ▲ Mids   ✕ Lows

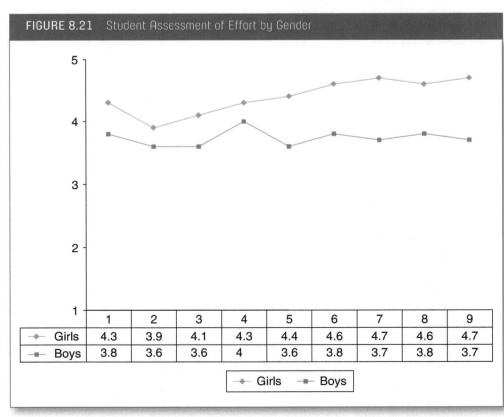

FIGURE 8.21   Student Assessment of Effort by Gender

	1	2	3	4	5	6	7	8	9
◆ Girls	4.3	3.9	4.1	4.3	4.4	4.6	4.7	4.6	4.7
■ Boys	3.8	3.6	3.6	4	3.6	3.8	3.7	3.8	3.7

◆ Girls   ■ Boys

any, events or actions corresponded with this drop in effort, it became apparent that his students reported putting forth less effort during the time when his regular writing program was temporarily suspended, and the focus of the class shifted to preparation for the state test. Based on this analysis, Mr. Seeker might have noted the following findings regarding the achievement target of *effort*:

- Average class performance declined during the period of preparation for the state exam.
- Average performance of the boys declined sharply during the period of preparation for the state exam.
- The performance of the average- and low-performing students declined during the period of preparation for the state exam.
- There was no significant change in the performance of the high-achieving students during the period of preparation for the state exam.
- There was a slight improvement in the performance of the girls during the period of preparation for the state exam.
- Average class writing scores were higher during the class periods where at least three types of response strategies were employed.

It is now time for you to look for changes in performance in the data you collected and see if you can identify a pattern or patterns of corresponding actions or events that might help explain these changes. Jot down, in narrative bulleted form, any changes in performance and any significant corresponding events.

DRAWING TENTATIVE ASSERTIONS

At this point, review the findings (bulleted statements) you've written, and reflect on how these findings might be explained. Your reflections at this stage are what action researchers call *tentative assertions*, and they combine two things:

1. Empirical data (what informed your findings)
2. Your intuition regarding the influence of actions on performance

You shouldn't be uncomfortable with the use of intuition in this context, even if you are a novice action researcher. After all, while you may be new to action research, you aren't new to the world of the classroom or the school. You've been an active participant in the actions that you've been studying, and in all probability, this is not your first year on the job; consequently, you are probably an experienced and sensitive observer of the educational process. If you have a sense of why one thing impacted another and why it did so in the particular way it did, it definitely warrants being noted as an educated hypothesis.

Mr. Seeker might tentatively assert the following concerning his study of improving effort and engagement in writing:

The drop in average performance appeared to be a reflection of a decline in student motivation, likely influenced by a shift of classroom focus from the writing process to review for the state exam. This observed drop in performance was most pronounced with the boys and with students with a history of moderate and low performance. I suspect the reason why there wasn't a comparable decline in the performance of the high achievers was that these kids have become so accustomed to doing what is required to receive good grades that it didn't matter to them if the work was particularly motivating or interesting. The girls in this class are a very cooperative and responsible group, and this may explain why they continued to put forth considerable effort, even though their feedback made it clear they found the work to be less then stimulating. My guess is that the slight improvement in the girls' performance (even though they didn't enjoy the work) was due to this fact.

After conducting a similar analysis of her data on her coaching of principals, Charlene tentatively asserted the following:

I noticed a significant increase in the quality of conversation around instruction when I began to provide structured agendas to principals ahead of time for our weekly meetings. Some principals who seemed defensive when asked to share evidence to support their evaluation of teacher practices seemed less so during my campus visits and learning walks, as well as following professional development activities and structured one-on-one sessions. Principals are now producing and discussing more concrete evidence on what practices are working in their classrooms and why.

As has been mentioned several times in this text, we can't prove, nor should we contend to have proven, causal relationships. This simply cannot be done in action research or in any other form of social science. Instead, our goal as practitioner-researchers is to identify relationships and correlations that appear so strong and occur so consistently that it only makes sense to adjust our future actions in ways that are supported by those findings.

The way we build confidence in the importance of a relationship is by establishing, as best we can, that the relationship or correlation was more than mere coincidence. As we live out our lives, we do this all the time, and we do it intuitively. In fact, we do it the same way that scientists do: through repeated trials and attempts to accomplish the same thing in the same manner as the original researchers—that is, to see if we can replicate the results. This is nothing new to the classroom teacher; we do this routinely with our teaching. When something appears to have worked, we try it again. If it works the second time and with another group, it builds our confidence, and we probably stick with it. The more this pattern repeats itself, the more confident we become regarding the efficacy of any particular approach.

That having been said, often, our action research is a first-time trial. Therefore, before we can comfortably and confidently move ahead with our answers to Question 3, we ought to consider how we might add more credibility and validity to our tentative assertions.

USING MEMBER CHECKING TO ADD CREDIBILITY TO THE TENTATIVE ASSERTIONS

Member checking is a strategy that qualitative researchers often use to add support for and provide insight into their tentative assertions. As the name implies, this is accomplished by checking one's tentative assertions with the members of the group whose behavior or performance was documented. As action researchers, we can accomplish this by following two sequential steps.

Step 1: Report the Findings

The researcher shares the *findings* with the members of the group whose work was chronicled. By findings, we mean the pertinent facts—the bulleted narrative statements—not your interpretations of those facts. For example, referring to the changes in performance Mr. Seeker observed as coinciding with time spent reviewing for the state test, the findings that he might member check with his students could be the following:

1. Average class performance declined during the period of preparation for the state exam.

2. Average performance of the boys declined sharply during the period of preparation for the state exam.

3. The performance of the average- and low-performing students declined during the period of preparation for the state exam.

4. There was no significant change in performance of the high-achieving students during the period of preparation for the state exam.

5. There was a slight improvement in performance of the girls during the period of preparation for the state exam.

6. All students reported that our class work was less fun and less stimulating during the time we were preparing for the state exam.

Step 2: Solicit Interpretations

This step can be done in either of two ways. The first is to follow your report of findings by posing an open-ended question to the members (in this case, the students in the class): *How would you interpret these findings?*

Another approach is to go further and share your interpretation of the facts—your draft statement of tentative assertions—and then ask the members, *Do you think my interpretation of these data is correct? And if not, how would you explain these findings?*

When the perceptions of an action researcher and the members of the group whose performance was documented are in agreement, significant credibility is added to the tentative assertions.

Occasionally, when we invite member checking, we find that members disagree with us. This could mean that our tentative assertions were, in fact, incorrect. Alternatively, it might mean there are other ways reasonable people could explain the same findings. Sometimes, after considering additional data that surfaced through member checking, action researchers will change their tentative assertions. Other times, they will feel justified sticking with their original positions. On still other occasions, the interpretations that surface though member checking are used to modify and add texture to the tentative assertions previously drafted by the researcher. Regardless of the outcome, member checking always provides valuable insights into our understanding of the impact of action on performance.

The preceding section focused on analyzing data, much of it quantitative, collected to answer the three generic ACR action research questions. Those strategies are also applicable for many other action research questions. However, the trend analysis processes that have been reviewed so far may not help you analyze all of the qualitative data you have collected. The tools in the following section will assist you in your search for the story embedded inside your qualitative and narrative data. Even if the trend analysis strategies presented thus far seem to have answered your action research questions, it is still suggested that you review the following section and consider the applicability of these qualitative-analysis techniques prior to concluding your work with data analysis, as these tools may help you develop a richer and deeper understanding of the stories to be found in your data.

ADDITIONAL TOOLS FOR QUALITATIVE DATA ANALYSIS

As we continue our discussion of data analysis, it would be helpful to consider a metaphor from the world of athletics. A key element of the preparation for competition in most sports is *scouting*, a systematic process of observing the competition, reviewing statistical data on their performance, and developing a list of their tendencies. Tendencies are for athletes what correlations are for statisticians—a set of findings drawn from data on past action that can be used to predict future action. A tendency reports a pattern as follows:

When x is the *context*, and y is the *action*, then z tends to be the *response*.

Having a good set of tendencies is important for an athlete or coach preparing for competition because it enables him or her to predict the consequences of an action with a certain degree of confidence. For example, let's assume I am a baseball pitcher. It is the ninth inning, there are two outs, and the batter has two strikes. I must decide where to throw my next pitch. Now, let's say I know that in this type of situation, this batter has a tendency to swing at an inside fastball 90 percent of the time. If I want him to swing at my next pitch, based on my knowledge of this past tendency, I would be wise to throw an inside fastball. In this example, *the context* is the behavior of this particular batter in ninth-inning pressure situations. *The action* is the throwing of an inside fastball, and *the response* is a swing (90 percent of the time).

Tendencies allow us to plan future action to be implemented in a given context based on a pattern of past responses to those same actions in that same context. That is precisely what most of us hope to gain from the analysis of our action research data. For this reason, as you go through the process of analyzing your data, think of what you are trying to accomplish as attempting to generate a reliable list of tendencies. This will necessitate sorting your data into three essential categories that will help with your final analysis:

1. Things that help you understand the *context* (especially as the context may have evolved over the period of the study)

2. Things that help you identify patterns of *actions*

3. The patterns of *responses* to those actions

To illustrate the necessity of including these three things in our analyses—*context*, *action*, and *response*—we'll use an academic example. Figure 8.22 illustrates the average length of first drafts produced by a group of students after their teacher introduced the use of the word processor for drafting weekly written compositions. The reason this teacher started having her students create their compositions on the computer was because she theorized it would result in increased fluency.

The story told by this graph shows that the average length of compositions actually decreased after the students began using word processing for their writing. *The action* in this case was the use of the word processor, and *the response* was fewer words per composition. These data could result in a finding that use of the word processor negatively influences the development of fluency. The problem with that finding is not that it is based on erroneous data; the data are irrefutable. The problem is that it ignores some important nuances of *context*. To illustrate, we will now add two additional bits of data:

1. This was the first time these students had been exposed to this word-processing program.

2. These data reflect only those papers written in the three weeks immediately following the introduction of the new software.

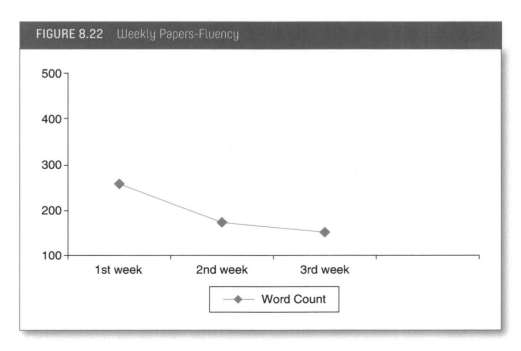

FIGURE 8.22   Weekly Papers-Fluency

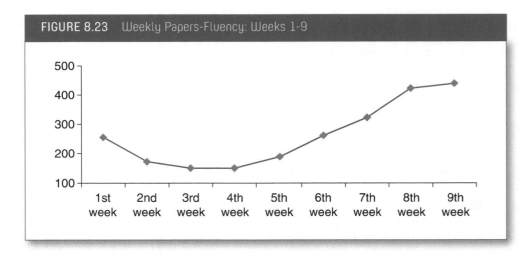

Figure 8.23 is a graph showing the average length of the weekly compositions, but with additional data, the data now have been extended to reflect performance over the full nine-week term.

With the addition of these two bits of context, these data end up telling a very different story. The decrease in fluency that occurred in the first three weeks is likely an illustration of what Michael Fullan (2001) has called the *implementation dip*, a temporary phenomenon that often occurs when a new skill is first learned. Because of the awkwardness of integrating something new into old routines, performance frequently drops initially, but this is often followed by improvement once the learner has become comfortable with the newly acquired skill.

QUALITATIVE DATA ANALYSIS USING BINS AND A MATRIX

We often find ourselves analyzing *qualitative* data that appear difficult or impossible to convert into *quantitative* terms. For example, we may have collected data from open-ended interviews, from student or teacher journals, from the minutes of meetings, and so on. In those cases, it might seem difficult to effectively use a graph to illustrate how our story is unfolding. Even so, our goal for data analysis is the same: We are attempting to report on the changes and the degree of change occurring over the period of time the actions took place. Our purpose when analyzing qualitative data is the same; we still want to identify patterns and tendencies, but we will need to use a different approach to accomplish this purpose.

The bins-and-matrix strategy, adapted from Miles and Huberman (1994), is a process of sorting and resorting qualitative action research data to identify and contrast tendencies and patterns as they evolve in a particular context.

Creating Bins for Your Data

Richard likes to describe this process as analogous to the process he uses to prepare his family's recyclables for curbside pickup. The waste management company supplied his family with four color-coded bins. The yellow one is where the family is expected to place paper, the blue is for clear glass, the green is for colored glass, and the red one is where they are expected to put all of the recyclable metals. The task Richard faced every time he carried a load of recyclables to the garage was to examine each of the items in his hands and determine which bin to put it in.

When using the bins-and-matrix process for sorting your action research data, you will basically be doing the same thing. Your first task is one that was done for Richard's family by the waste management company. Using their experience and data, they made a determination regarding what were the major categories of recyclables likely to be produced by families in his community. This resulted in their choice of four bins: paper, clear glass, colored glass, and metal. Of course, each of their customers probably also had other materials that could have been recycled (for example, wood products, engine oil, scrap metal, and plastic). Apparently, it was determined (after looking at many years' worth of data) that although many households possessed other recyclable materials, they weren't present in large enough quantities to make it environmentally justifiable to spend the fossil fuel to collect them at the curbside.

Whenever Richard would go to his garage with his family's recyclables, it was his job to sort the data he was carrying into the bins that the company deemed relevant. One could look at Richard's family's recycled items as data. In this particular case, the items accumulating in the bins in his garage constituted the raw data on his family's consumption habits.

At this stage of your analysis process, the task before you is to determine what bins or categories you deem as most relevant and will want to use for sorting your data. There are a number of things for you to consider when making this decision:

- The achievement targets your project was designed to address
- The specific phenomena that your descriptive study examined
- The significant activities you engaged in or had participants engage in

In addition to those items, you should skim through the data you've collected, looking for issues, ideas, and actions that tended to reappear frequently. On a sheet of notepaper, jot down a word or phrase that captures the item you see recurring. For example, if we were skimming through a set of student reading journals, we might notice repeated examples of students commenting on the following things:

- *Genres:* Fantasy, biography, and other nonfiction
- *Relevance to their lives:* Their reasons for being attracted to the work
- *Time issues:* Finding time to engage in recreational reading
- *Family attitudes:* Family attitudes toward reading

Now is a good time to go back and review your theory of action, looking for potential bins. Take another walk through your graphic reconstruction, this time looking for the events or phenomena that you had, once upon a time (back when you developed your theory of action), thought would be particularly relevant to your ultimate success. As you review these events, tasks, actions, or phenomena, add them to the list you have been building.

You are now ready to create a list of potential bins.

For example, the principal, Mr. Johnson, who was studying his leadership in enhancing student engagement in his school, might have generated a list of items like the following. Each of these will eventually become a bin for sorting his data:

- Training sessions
- High-interest content
- Low-interest content
- Principal actions
- Comments on the role of leadership
- High-engagement teaching strategies
- Teacher talk
- Student talk
- Student performance
- Teacher reflections
- Walk-through data
- Subgroup trends
- Planning

The next step of this process involves deliberately going through each individual piece of data you've collected and placing that piece of data into the appropriate bin. When using the bins-and-matrix method, it is appropriate to use all of the valid and reliable data you have available, even if they came from an unanticipated source. The actual sorting procedure can be accomplished with a variety of low-tech and electronic methods. We will begin by discussing the low-tech procedure, since it is the most concrete, and then will discuss how you can easily accomplish the same thing using either word-processing or spreadsheet software.

Tip on Bin Creation

As was the case with Richard's recyclables, there may not be a bin for each item or piece of data you collected. However, if you did a good job of choosing your bins, there should be a bin for all of the most important items. If you find you have a great deal of seemingly significant data that can't be categorized, you should consider establishing more bins.

LOW-TECH STRATEGIES FOR BINS AND MATRIXES

Low-Tech Strategy 1: Making a Receptacle for the Data

We have implemented this procedure in two ways. The first method is to purchase a set of small plastic bins, such as the ones shown in Figure 8.24, and label them with the categories of items to be collected in each.

A second approach is to take large sheets of chart paper, tape them to the wall, and create a column for each category (bin).

When using the plastic bins, we make sure that we have a large quantity of index cards on hand. When using the chart paper method, we make sure to have several big colorful pads of sticky notes available.

Placing the Data Into the Bins

We begin by rereading our data, looking for items that we believe belong in one or more of the bins. When we find a relevant bit of data, we write verbatim that piece of data on a sticky note or index card, always indicating

FIGURE 8.24 Sorting Data into Plastic Bins

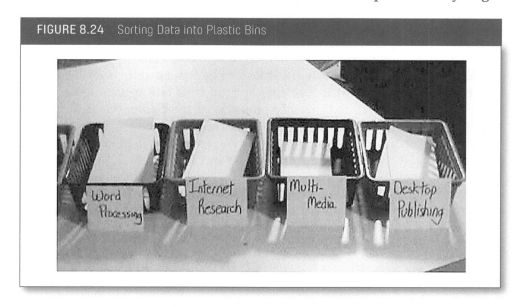

FIGURE 8.25 Sorting Data into Bins-Chart-paper

where it came from (such as, from Allen Freeman's journal, a parent's comment, or a note from the principal) and noting the date that piece of data was obtained or the date the event took place. The card is then placed into the appropriate plastic bin or attached (by sticky note) in the proper column on the chart paper. Keep in mind that when appropriate, the same piece of data can be copied and placed into multiple bins. Figure 8.25 shows an action research team placing their data into bins on chart paper.

This action research team in the picture was made up of a cohort of master's students undertaking a descriptive study designed to identify and describe the instructional practices most often used by a set of local teachers known for obtaining high levels of student performance. They obtained so much data from merely six classroom observations that they ended up needing an entire classroom wall to effectively sort their data.

Other Low-Tech Strategies: Cutting and Pasting and Using Highlighters

One very efficient strategy when using data collected from surveys or written work (provided the work doesn't need to be returned) is cutting and pasting. If you want to use this approach, it is important that your surveys or data be printed on only one side of the paper. (Unfortunately, this is not an environmentally friendly strategy; however, it does make analysis more efficient.) Then, whenever you encounter a piece of data that you feel belongs in a bin, you simply cut it out (always being sure to indicate, on the back, where it came from and when it was obtained) and then physically place it into or paste it onto the appropriate bin.

A similar approach makes use of highlighting pens. When we use this strategy, we assign a color to each bin. Should we have a very large number of bins, we will assign a symbol, as well as a color.

USING A COMPUTER FOR BINS AND MATRIXES

Using the Sort Command

It can be a time-consuming task to retype data already collected into a computer's word-processing program or onto a spreadsheet. For this reason, using this approach will not make that much sense unless your data were collected electronically, you are a proficient typist, or you have clerical support available. However, should you already have your data in an electronic format where they can be easily pasted into a word-processing program or onto a spreadsheet, then using the sort function found in virtually all word-processing and spreadsheet programs will enable you to organize your data into bins very quickly. To accomplish this, just follow these four simple steps:

- **Step 1: Assign a code number to each category.** For example, with Mr. Johnson's study on enhancing student engagement, these might be the code numbers he assigned:

  1. Training sessions
  2. Teacher talk
  3. Student talk
  4. Student performance
  5. Teacher reflections
  6. Walk-through
  7. Subgroup trends
  8. Planning and training

- **Step 2: Attach the correct code number.** Then, when typing or copying pertinent text, type the appropriate number at the beginning of the passage, and be certain to press the return key both before and after each "coded" item, thus transforming each coded item into a separate paragraph. For example, let's assume we found a quote from a teacher survey that we felt belonged in the bin for teacher reflections. We would make sure that item read as follows:

  5. Honestly, I hated going to meetings at this school; I even dreaded reading the staff bulletin. Nothing that we ever did seemed relevant to me. But now, I look forward to working together; the meetings have truly helped me learn how to increase engagement in my classroom.

- **Step 3: Sorting the data by bin**. Now, by simply selecting the "sort" command (all word-processing and spreadsheet programs contain a sort function), all of the items belonging in the bin with a particular number will become instantly grouped together. Another nice aspect of using the computer to sort your data is that you can always resort and subsort the data inside the individual bins—a very powerful tool for purposes of disaggregation.

- **Step 4: Disaggregating your data**. When we want to determine if there are differential trends in performance or when we want to see if defined categories of students outperform or underperform other categories of students, it is essential that we disaggregate data. This simple action can make a big difference in helping us determine where inequities still exist. Disaggregation is easily accomplished electronically. All we need to do is think through in advance each demographic subcategory we might want to sort by and consider the order in which we would want to have them sorted. For example, the order we might want to sort the data we collected in the bin titled "attitudes towards elementary school reading" might be

  - first, by bin;
  - second, by whether the item is positive or negative ;
  - third, by the grade level where it originated;
  - fourth, by gender;
  - fifth, by ethnicity; and
  - sixth, by date obtained.

Then, we assign a number to each of the subcategories (such as, 1 = positive, 2 = negative; 1 = first grade, 2 = second grade). Finally, using our prearranged order of sorting, we input these code numbers. Using the foregoing codes as an illustration, if the passage we quoted above had come from a second-grade teacher, the item would be prefaced by the numbers 5.1.2, meaning it is a teacher reflection (5), it is a positive comment (1), and it came from a second-grade teacher (2).

There is virtually no limit to how many subcategories can be created. And whatever process you ultimately decide to use for sorting your data, be sure to create a coding key for easy referencing later on. What follows is an illustration of a sample key that Mr. Johnson might have established to assist with the sorting of his data.

Create Factoids From the Information in the Bins

After you have sorted all of the data you deemed relevant, it is time to go through the items in each bin, generating brief bulleted statements of fact that can be supported by the data contained inside that bin. Write each of these bulleted statements, which we call factoids, on a separate index card. Ultimately, what qualifies something as a factoid is based upon your professional judgment regarding its significance. We find that we generally report two kinds of factoids:

1. *Statistical*. These are statements that reflect both the quantity and percentage of items reporting on the same thing. For example, we might create a factoid saying, "Thirteen comments, from 20 percent of the teachers, were complimentary of the principal's leadership."

Level 1	Level 2	Level 3	Level 4	Level 5	Level 6
Bin	Tone	Grade Level	Gender	Race or Ethnicity	Date Obtained
1 = Training sessions	1 = Positive	1 = First	1 = Male	1 = White (non-Hispanic)	1 = September
2 = Teacher talk	2 = Negative	2 = Second		2 = Hispanic	2 = October
3 = Student talk		3 = Third		3 = African American	3 = November
4 = Student performance		4 = Fourth		4 = Asian	4 = December
5 = Teacher reflections					5 = January
6 = Walk-throughs					
7 = Subgroup trends					
8 = Planning and training					

2. *Illustrative.* We are always alert for a particular comment or vignette that will help bring a statistic to life. When we find one, we write the comment or retell the vignette verbatim on a separate card and explain its relevance. An example of such an illustrative factoid would be, "Typical of the positive comments regarding principal leadership was the following comment from a sixth-grade teacher: 'It was clear that Elena [the principal] protected us from district demands on the faculty that could otherwise have drawn us away from our school goals. I really appreciate that. It showed me that she truly was supportive of our priorities.'"

Assuming Richard's waste management company wanted to prepare a report on Richard's family consumption habits, some of the factoids they would have been able to create after reviewing the weekly data from his family's recycling bins (their findings) might read like the following:

- In an average week, this family disposes of
  - forty-seven mail order catalogs,
  - sixty-four pop cans, 40 percent of which are sugar free,
  - fifteen newspapers (none of which appear to have been read), and
  - no more than one tin can.
- Most weeks, the man of the household can be seen running out of the house in his bathrobe with additional items to be added at the last minute.

The data in the bin on walk-throughs in Mr. Johnson's study might produce factoids like the following:

- Eighty percent of girls were engaged in note-taking.
- Sixty percent of the boys were on task in group discussions in September and 75 percent during October.
- Fifty percent of English language learners volunteered answers to teacher questions in September and 65 percent in October.
- Eighty five percent of special-needs students responded correctly when sentence frames were used regularly in the classroom.
- One hundred percent of the teachers reported appreciation of the peer observations and feedback.

Sift the Data Using a Matrix

Keep in mind that the main purpose of data analysis is to identify and communicate an evolving story. Every story has a context and occurs over time. To find the story, we need to see the patterns of meaningful action and identify the tendencies of the responses that followed those actions. Occasionally, this happens by the simple sorting of data into bins. However, more often, further sorting of the data is needed to enable the complete story to emerge. One good way to accomplish this is to make use of two-dimensional matrixes to further sift your data. Figure 8.26 shows the general structure of a matrix set up for analyzing the data collected in Mr. Johnson's study of building faculty proficiency with increasing student engagement.

Each bin becomes a column in the matrix while the rows can be assigned to a variety of different values. Since we are often interested in understanding how a story unfolded over time, we often like to begin by assigning time frames to the rows (fall, winter, spring, monthly, weekly, and so on). Then, all the factoids that were generated are placed into the appropriate cells of the matrix.

FIGURE 8.26 Mr. Johnson's Two-Dimensional Matrix

	Training Sessions	Teacher Talk	Student Talk	Student Performance	Teacher Reflections	Walk-Throughs	Subgroup Trends
September							
October							
November							
December							
January							
February							
March							
April							
May							
June							

Summarize and Draw Tentative Conclusions

Once our time frame matrix has been completed, we review the rows and columns and ask ourselves whether these data adequately answer our research questions. If they do, then we summarize the data in the form of tentative assertions.

Often, the answers to all of your questions will not be apparent from one matrix, and you will need to repeat the process using different categories for the rows. Keep in mind, your purpose is always the same: identifying meaningful patterns and tendencies. The time frame matrix will highlight the relationship between changes in performance and time. Likewise, a gender matrix would highlight the relationship between gender and changes in performance. To properly answer your questions, you might want to examine other relationships; you will be able to do so relatively easily by simply changing the categories for the rows. Some of the categories that others have found helpful are as follows:

- Categories of Participant
  - High achievers, middle achievers, and low achievers
  - Gender
  - Ethnicity
  - English language learners and English-proficient students
  - Special education or learning challenged
  - Primary teachers, intermediate teachers, middle school teachers, and high school teachers
- Type of Data
  - Interviews
  - Surveys
  - Portfolios
  - Teachers' journals
- Source of Data
  - Students
  - Parents
  - School staff

Use Member Checking to Add Credibility to Your Findings

Once you have generated a set of tentative conclusions that you feel adequately respond to your research questions, it is time to test your perceptions against those of other participant-observers of the same process. This is done by using the one of the member-checking procedures that was discussed earlier in this chapter.

This concludes our discussion regarding the analysis of action research data. Analysis ends with our acknowledging what we've learned through our actions. In the next chapter, our focus shifts to the second element of our Stage 4 work, where we will deal with the bottom-line question for all action researchers,

So now that we know what we know, what do we plan to do about it?

9

Turning Findings Into Action Plans

In Chapter 8, we began working through the final stage of the action research process—*Stage 4: Reflecting on the Data and Planning Informed Action*. This stage has three parts: analysis, action planning, and reporting. In the last chapter, we covered data analysis, where our purpose was discovering the story embedded in our action research data. The analysis portion of this stage concluded with you generating a list of findings and tentative conclusions backed up by your data.

Whether your action research was descriptive or quasi-experimental, the analysis process should have helped you gain greater clarity on what occurred as you endeavored to realize your achievement targets. Hopefully, the insights generated through analysis proved meaningful for you on a number of levels.

The greatest value of what we learn from our action research lies in the power of the new knowledge and insights we gained to inform our future actions and thereby provide benefits for our students. Those benefits won't be fully realized until we make use of our findings and conclusions to adjust our professional practice and create new operative theories of action.

MODIFYING YOUR THEORY OF ACTION

If we are to become truly reflective practitioners, the thing we must always do prior to commencing action is pause and deeply consider what we already know about the challenges before us so we can use that thinking to design thoughtful theories of action to guide our future work. The process you employed to accomplish this when you began your action research project involved two visual aids, the priority pie, and the graphic reconstruction. Now that you have concluded this initial round of action and analyzed your data, it is time to return to those two documents and adjust them based on what you have learned.

A classic way to illustrate change over time is by contrasting *before* and *after* pictures. Your graphic reconstruction will serve as a type of before picture. It is, after all, a sketch of your best thinking *before* you initiated action and conducted your investigation. The *after* picture will be a portrait of your best thinking now that you have completed your study. In Chapter 5, we discussed how the first voyage of Christopher Columbus could be viewed as a form of action research. At that time, we suggested that a map by Henricus Martellus, circa 1489 (Figure 9.1), was the type of graphic reconstruction or theory of action that guided Columbus when planning his first voyage—for this discussion, that map might be considered his before picture. For a comparison *after* picture, we might use Figure 9.2. This is a map made by Martin Waldseemüller in 1507, not very long after Columbus's first voyage and considered by most historians to be the first map incorporating the findings from Columbus's voyage.

When we initially articulated our theories of action, we constructed a priority pie and produced a graphic reconstruction. At this point, we suggest that you reconstruct both of these documents based on what you've learned through your analysis of the data on your actions (Chapter 8). However, this time, we suggest that you prepare these two visuals in reverse order: draw your graphic first, and then, bake your pie.

FIGURE 9.1   Henricus Martellus's 1489 Map

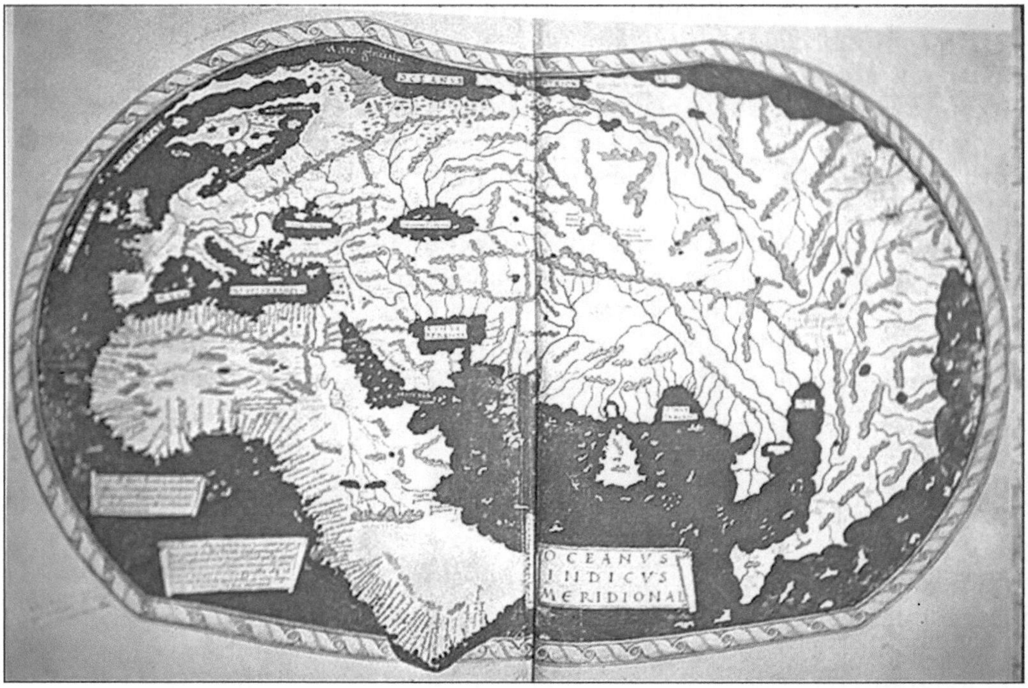

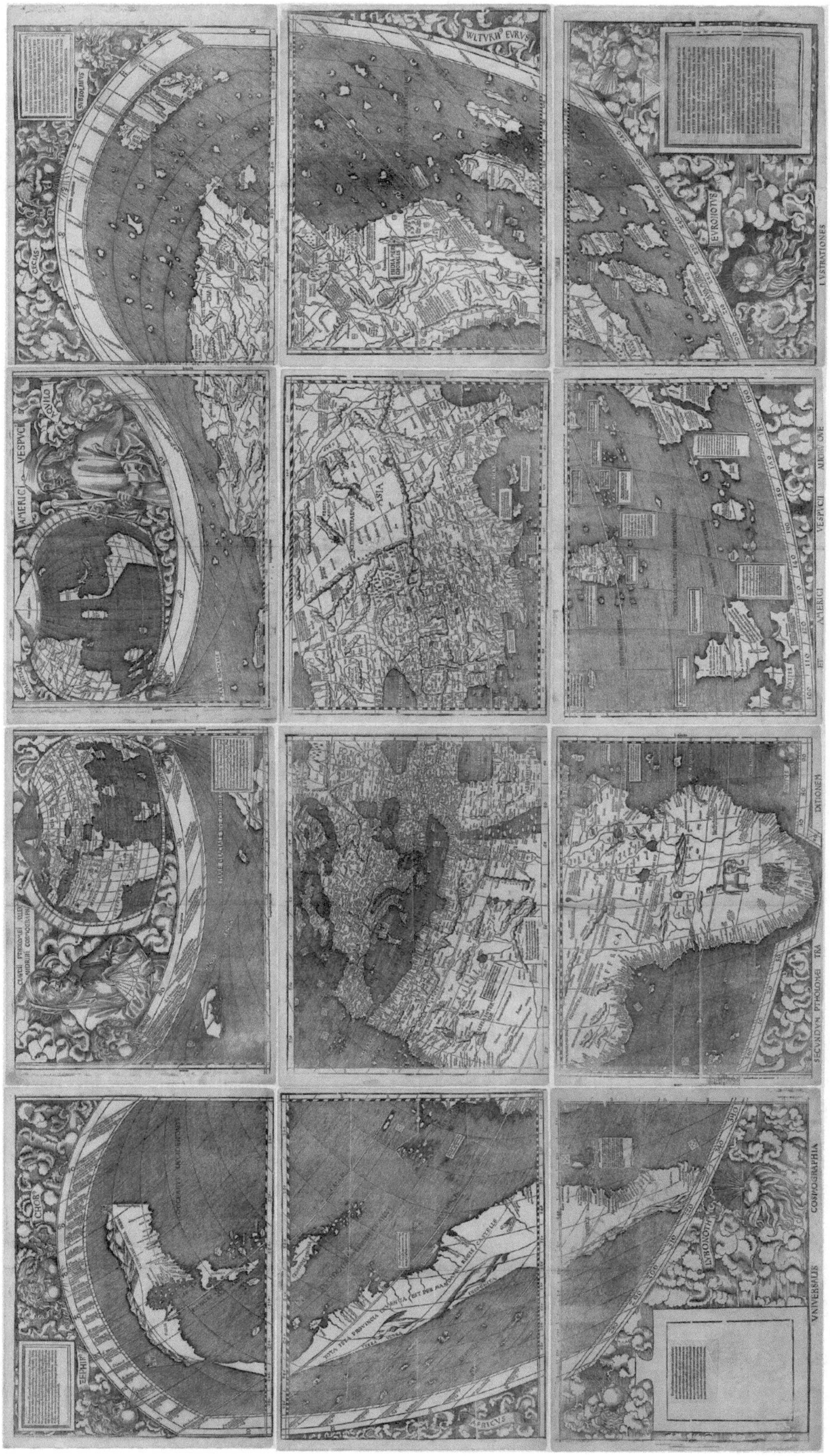

FIGURE 9.2 Martin Waldseemüller's 1507

Step 1: Taking Stock of What You Have Learned

Review the list of findings and the tentative assertions you drafted (see Chapter 8). Then, take out the graphic reconstruction—the implementation road map you designed prior to the implementation of your project (Chapters 5). Now, one last time, take a slow and deliberate walk through your graphic reconstruction, asking a set of questions of every event, activity, relationship, or cluster of relationships you encounter along the way.

For every activity or event, ask yourself, *Based on what I've learned, do I now think that*

1. There are other critical events or activities that should occur prior to this activity?

2. This activity is still essential for success on this target?

3. There are additional activities that I now think should be included to improve performance on this target?

For each relationship or cluster (arrows, linking lines, and groups of events), ask yourself, *Based on what I've learned, do I now think that*

1. This relationship is still important?

2. These activities or events influence each other in the manner illustrated?

3. There are other relationships that should be added to this theory?

Based on your answers to those questions, make any needed additions, deletions, and alterations to your graphic reconstruction.

Once you have made the changes you feel are warranted, proof your new theory of action, just as you did in Chapter 5. (Walk through it in the shoes of different categories of students or participants.) Once you are satisfied that your new graphic reconstruction illustrates a theory of action with real promise for producing universal student success on your priority achievement target, you will have created your *after* picture.

Now, place your before and after pictures side by side. Figure 9.3 contains Ms. Montgomery's two graphic reconstructions, before and after her action research on improving equitable response opportunities through effective questioning and discussion techniques.

Upon close examination of Figure 9.3, one can see that Ms. Montgomery made two significant changes in her theory of action based on her analysis of the data:

1. Student leadership. Prior to conducting her research, she felt it was a good idea for the teacher to mediate most of the early class discussions to ensure each student truly had equitable response opportunities. But the data from student exit cards and regarding the class meetings revealed that students preferred leading and facilitating their discussions earlier in the process, at both the group and class level. In fact, she noticed the best responses occurred when she allowed student choice of the questions she would use.

FIGURE 9.3   Before and After Graphic Reconstructions

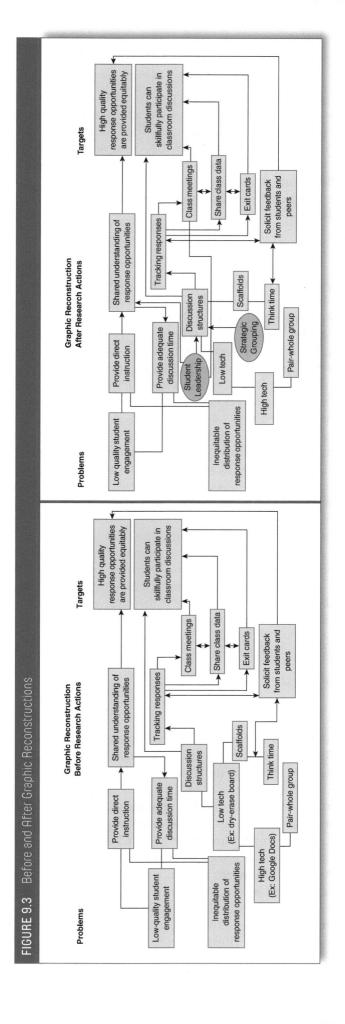

2. **Strategic grouping**. Prior to conducting her research, she felt it was a good idea to randomly group and regroup her students periodically as a way to enhance discussions. But her data revealed a significant disparity between the functioning of the groups. It seemed that random assignments didn't always result in groups with a productive chemistry. Based on these data, she now believes that student groups will function better if she strategically assigns students based on her analysis of their strengths and needs.

Step 2: Reconsider the Time Issue

To begin this step, locate your original priority pie, which represents how you had once believed your time and energy should be allocated to achieve universal success on your priority achievement target. If you completed the Time Priority Tracking Form (Figure 8.4) and constructed a second pie that reflected actual time usage, this is a good time to review those two graphs. Now, taking a good look at the graphic reconstruction you just developed (your after picture) and considering the theory of action depicted on this visual, conduct another intuitive regression analysis by using Figure 9.4 (this is the same form that was used earlier in the text as Figure 4.1) to create a third pie chart. This chart will illustrate how you now believe time (after conducting your research) *should* be allocated.

Figure 9.5 shows the before and after pies created by Ms. Montgomery. You can see that based on the data from her action research, she determined it would be necessary to create an entirely new category of action (a brand new slice of pie): *coaching students on facilitating discussions*. You might note that she found the time for this new activity by reducing the time she had previously devoted to class meetings and direct instruction.

Now, place your original priority pie next to the one you just produced. A comparison of these two pie charts should visually illustrate a number of the insights gained through your research and help you better allocate your finite time and energy when you next attack this target.

DATA-BASED DECISION MAKING

The Use of Ed Specs

Frequently, when organizations such as schools begin planning for a major purchase or enter into a long-term contract, they start the decision-making process by developing a set of bid specifications. In the case of school architecture and school facility development, those specifications are frequently called educational specifications (ed specs). The ed specs later become the criteria used to assess competing proposals. Using a quality set of ed specs can go a long way toward ensuring that sound and transparent purchasing decisions are ultimately made.

As you plan future action in your focus area, you will likely have many programs and alternative strategies to consider and consequently would be well served to craft a sound set of criteria (ed specs) to guide you toward wise decisions. One very good place to find sound material for developing such criteria is in the insights gained from the action research

FIGURE 9.4 Intuitive Regression Analysis

Using the following form, make a judgment regarding the relative importance of each of the factors you identified as critical to success on this achievement target. Use a separate form for each target you are pursuing.

Achievement Target: _____

List Each Factor Deemed Critical to Fostering Success with This Achievement Target	Importance of This Factor (%)
Total: 100%	

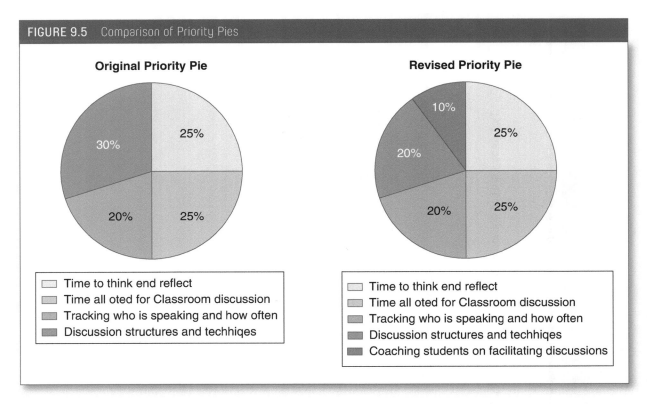

FIGURE 9.5   Comparison of Priority Pies

Original Priority Pie

30%
25%
20%
25%

☐ Time to think end reflect
☐ Time all oted for Classroom discussion
☐ Tracking who is speaking and how often
☐ Discussion structures and techhiqes

Revised Priority Pie

10%
20%
25%
20%
25%

☐ Time to think end reflect
☐ Time all oted for Classroom discussion
☐ Tracking who is speaking and how often
☐ Discussion structures and techhiqes
☐ Coaching students on facilitating discussions

you just conducted, as well as any related research that may have been conducted in the recent past by you and your colleagues.

To understand precisely how selection criteria can be used to inform instructional decision making, it would be instructive to review how it is often applied in other educational arenas (such as school facility development and purchasing) and then adapt it for our work with performance, program, and process targets.

Ed Specs and School Facilities

Generally, the process begins by convening a meeting of individuals with the most up-to-date knowledge of the school's situation and needs. At this meeting, these key individuals are asked to take stock of the context and any highly valued operative theories of action. Then, they use that information to develop a list of specific things they will want to see accomplished by the new facility or equipment.

A few years ago, Richard was working for a school district that was about to commence construction on a number of new elementary schools. A staff committee had reviewed everything they knew about best practices for elementary education and theorized that in future decades, in effective schools, children would be spending nearly equal portions of their school time engaged in individual, small-group, and large-group learning. Therefore, they wanted their new elementary schools to be designed to effectively accommodate all three types of learning.

There were also several givens (what we might call contextual issues) that needed to be taken into account. One was the state funding formula, which established the maximum square footage of the buildings and the amount of money available for construction. This meant that the designs produced by the district's architect would have to fit within the state's cost and size restrictions. The school board wanted the architect to create several alternative designs for district consideration; however, each of the alternatives had to accommodate the perceived future needs of staff and students. Consequently, every design proposal was required to address the future program, as envisioned by the ed specs committee (specifically, equal opportunities for individual, small-group, and large-group instruction), as well as to conform to state regulations.

By considering only designs that addressed both categories, the district was able to ensure that whatever design was finally chosen would meet state requirements and the district's educational needs. Before we translate this process to your action planning, it will be helpful to look at one other educational application of criteria-based decision making, one that may be somewhat closer to the issues you will be dealing with.

Ed Specs for Purchasing Computers

This second example of ed specs involves what, at first, may seem like a routine purchasing decision. In all likelihood, you work in a school system that regularly purchases significant numbers of computers, laptops, and tablets for student and teacher use. Since there are a number of manufacturers that produce and market educational technology and since there are a number of competing operating systems to choose from, there are always alternative proposals to consider. Since a great deal of money is at stake, and since, for budgetary reasons, schools know they must live with the computers they purchase for several years, it is important that these decisions be made wisely. Therefore, prior to soliciting bids, most school systems create a set of purchasing criteria to be used in evaluating the alternative proposals submitted by prospective vendors. Usually, those criteria cover a multitude of factors, including the following examples:

Cost and Reliability

- The purchase price per computer or tablet
- The past defect record of this company's products

Service

- Availability of on-site personnel for routine repairs
- Turnaround time for repairs

Versatility

- The ability of the computers to run the desired software
- Ease of use
- Availability of professional development and technical support for staff
- Quality of documentation and user manuals

Those charged with making the final decision on which computers should be purchased will insist that every vendor's bid address each one of these criteria, and ultimately, they will choose the vender whose proposal scores best on the criteria. Inevitably, some proposals will score better on certain elements than others. This is why it is crucial that each assessment criterion be weighted based on importance.

Weighing Assessment Criteria

When you look at the above list of criteria that might be used by a school district purchasing classroom computers, you can easily see that they are not of equal importance. For instance, although having high-quality user manuals would be nice, however, even the most well-written documentation won't make up for computers that turn out to be unreliable, break down frequently, and take forever to get fixed.

This is why, when developing ed specs, one needs to take special care to determine, in advance, which factors are deemed the *most critical*—matters so important that going ahead with a plan that does not satisfy these criteria is simply foolhardy. Other criteria, while not absolutely essential, might be deemed *highly desirable*. Lastly, there are criteria that are *valuable*, involving things we would like to have but which, like superlative user manuals, are not absolutely crucial to program success. When we are making data-based decisions, those distinctions need to be considered and made *prior* to evaluating competing proposals.

Now, we will return to concerns more central to the life of the classroom teacher and school leader, the type of program-planning decisions that you are asked to make on a regular basis and that ultimately have significant influence over the success of the actions we take in our schools and classrooms. In doing so, we will explore how the principles of data-based decision making can be applied to instructional and program planning.

TURNING YOUR FINDINGS INTO ED SPECS

The list of findings you generated in Chapter 8 will now become your first draft of ed specs to use when assessing proposals and ideas for new programs or the design of novel innovations for use in your school or classroom. The form shown in Figure 9.6 was designed to help you convert your action research findings into ed specs.

In the left-hand column, write all of the bulleted findings that emerged from your action research data (see Chapter 8). Then, convert those bulleted findings into ed specs; this is done in the middle column of the worksheet. Once you have listed all of the findings as ed specs, it is time to ask of each one,

> How important is this particular ed spec to the decisions I must make on my future actions?

Based on your answer to that question, rate each item using the following scale:

> 5 = *Essential Factor* (Programs or actions that do not address this ed spec aren't appropriate for use here.)

FIGURE 9.6   Turning Research Findings Into Ed Specs

Step 1. List all the pertinent findings from your and other relevant research in this focus area.

Step 2. Write the essence of each finding in the form of an educational specification.

Step 3. Determine the weight to be assigned to each ed spec, with 5 indicating the highest effectiveness:

Pertinent Action Research Finding	Finding Rewritten as an Ed Spec	Weighting: 5, 3, or 1
Example: Time for writing was limited due to preparation for the state assessment.	The need for additional time for use with the writing process.	5 = Essential factor

3 = *Important Factor* (Programs or actions that address this ed spec should be of significant value in our efforts to improve performance with this priority achievement target.)

1 = *Worthy Factor* (Programs or actions that address this ed spec are better than those that don't.)

Tip on Formulating Ed Specs

When using action research findings for ed specs, you needn't limit yourself to the findings from your most recent study. Findings from other studies conducted by colleagues or any other relevant data on the needs of your program or students can justifiably be added to your list of specifications.

SOLICIT AND BRAINSTORM
ACTION ALTERNATIVES

At this point, it is time to return to the graphic reconstruction you completed at the end of the data analysis process (Chapter 8). This is the graphic that illustrated your *revised* theory of action. Take a look at the changes you made to your original theory, and ask yourself (or your teammates), Are there strategies we are aware of that have been implemented elsewhere in an effort to achieve success with our achievement targets? To illustrate how this might be done, let's return once again to the case of Ms. Montgomery.

In her revised theory of action (Figure 9.3), she noted two significant changes in the way she believed this unit should be implemented next year:

1. The necessity for strategic grouping of students

2. The need for student leadership and involvement on topic selection, focus questions, and discussion strategies

For dealing with the issue of strategic grouping, she was able to quickly come up with a list of possible alternative approaches:

1. My students could submit a "most wanted to work with" list, and I could use these data to make group assignments.

2. I could rank the students by past performance and select groups to maximize heterogeneity (to increase diversity).

3. I could rank the students by past performance and assign groups to maximize homogeneity (to reduce diversity).

4. I could assign the students to single-gender groups.

5. I could use random assignments modified by my personal perceptions of student compatibility.

The different strategies on her list are what we call action alternatives. Each one is an approach that, on the surface, appears to have promise for fulfilling Ms. Montgomery's needs. What she now needs to do is to choose which one of these action alternatives will likely work best for her students and her program.

Tip on Surfacing Action Alternatives
If the list you have generated seems adequate, it is okay to proceed with that list. However, if you sense that you are unable to find strategies that hold real promise to solve your problem, it is a good idea to conduct another literature review (see Chapter 3 if needed).

USING ED SPECS TO EVALUATE ACTION ALTERNATIVES

Having collected a comprehensive set of action alternatives, it is time to evaluate each one using the weighted ed specs you developed from all of the relevant findings. One way of doing this is by constructing a chart for each action alternative like the one shown in Figure 9.7 on the following page. We usually do this by creating posters on large sheets of chart paper for each action alternative.

Now you need to review the elements of each action alternative through the lens of your ed specs (Figure 9.6). This is done by standing in front of each action alternative poster with your ed specs in hand and asking yourself the following question regarding each of your ed specs:

Is the implementation of this action alternative likely to have a positive influence, negative influence, or no influence on this criterion?

Whenever your answer is *positive*, that ed spec and its weighted score should be placed on the top portion of the chart. If the answer is *negative*, then that ed spec and its number should be placed on the lower portion of the chart. If the answer to your question is *no influence*, then nothing is written on the chart.

Repeat this process with each of the action alternatives. Once all of the action alternatives have been assessed using your set of ed specs, add the positive points (top portion of the chart) and subtract any negative points that have been assigned (the lower portion) to produce a score for that action alternative. Then, list the action alternatives in rank order based on the point totals awarded.

At this juncture, your decision-making process will differ from the bid procedure used by school business offices. Frequently, state or provincial laws require that public entities award contracts to the lowest bidder. This is a reasonable requirement that ensures fiscal accountability. However, as

FIGURE 9.7   Sample Action Alternative Poster

Action Alternative: _____

Ed Specs in Support of AA	Points
Total Points Supporting:	

Ed Specs Not Supporting AA	Points
Total Points Opposing:	

professionals who are using action research findings to improve our teaching and our students' learning, it makes no sense to bind ourselves to a decision simply because one particular strategy achieved a marginally higher score than a competing one.

When applying this approach to data-based decision making, you will generally find that the scoring of your action alternatives will fall into three groups:

Group 1: Weak Proposals. Some action alternatives will have very low scores; some could even have obtained a negative score. A low or negative score means that this particular approach would likely make things worse than the current situation.

Group 2: Adequate Proposals. A second group of alternatives will have received positive scores but a significant number of negative ones as well. Consequently, the total score is still rather low. It likely is not worth the effort to alter your current approach and go through all of the work and possible expense of implementing a new program that, at best, will turn out to be only marginally superior to the approach you've been using.

Group 3: Strong Proposals. There will, however, likely be certain action alternatives that received many positive scores and attracted very few, if any, negative ones. These are proposals that appear to hold real potential for making a difference with your efforts to produce universal success on your priority achievement targets.

Making a Final Decision on Action

It is now time to consider the applicability of each of the action alternatives in Group 3, the strong proposals. This is another point in the process where it is appropriate to use intuition. For each alternative, ask yourself these three questions:

1. How well do these strategies fit with my or our teaching style?

2. How might the students in our school respond to this program or approach?

3. What, if any, additional problems or expenses would this program entail?

USING ED SPECS TO EVALUATE ACTION ALTERNATIVES FOR SCHOOLWIDE PROJECTS

Facilitating collaborative decision making is one of the most challenging issues for school leaders. Many times, leaders feel torn between two equally unpleasant alternatives. They could invite faculty to propose ideas they are passionate about, but by doing so, they might risk a vote that could split the faculty into opposing camps. Alternatively, they could try to broker a compromise that everyone can live with yet no one is particularly passionate about. Neither of these approaches is very helpful for a school that wishes to have a collegial culture while energetically pursuing universal student success. Another option is to use the Action Alternative process.

If the project you are working on is a collaborative effort, it is well worth taking some faculty meeting time to discuss how you will decide which high-scoring "strong" action alternative best fits your situation and should be adopted. In our experience, this is rarely a contentious decision. While, on occasion, some of us might hold a preference for one of the high-scoring alternatives, and some of our teammates might find themselves attracted to another, it is unlikely that we will have strong objections to going along with their choice since every proposal being given final consideration was one that scored "strong" on criteria drawn from "our" collaborative research findings.

The open, collaborative assessment of action alternatives with the use of ed specs built from locally generated data is an ideal way to minimize conflict. When decisions are made in this manner, it is rarely contentious. This is because these decisions are being made by data, not by personalities. Furthermore, the data that are being used to inform decision making will be deemed credible because they were generated by and for the people making the decisions. We often hear school leaders express a desire to see their workplaces transformed into professional learning communities (Dufour, Dufour, & Eaker, 2008).

There is no better way for a faculty that is committed to becoming a learning community to assume ownership of decisions than to have those decisions informed by ed specs derived from their own reflective practice (Sagor, 2010).

COMPLETING THE CYCLE: REVISED THEORY OF ACTION 2

Unless you discovered the magic elixir that succeeded in getting every single student or every participant in your project to excellent performance on your target, your work as a reflective practitioner and as an action researcher can't be considered complete.

What you have accomplished, however, is the completion of one full lap around the action research cycle. (Reporting, which will be discussed in the next chapter, does not necessarily need to occur prior to beginning another cycle of action research.)

Figure 9.8 illustrates the relationship between the steps of repeated cycles of action research when done on the same targets by the same researchers. You are now nearly ready to restart the process. However, this time, you will be able to jump ahead and begin your work at *Stage 3: Implementing Action and Collecting Data* by developing a new set of research questions to guide your next study (see Chapter 6).

As you may recall, the process of developing meaningful action research questions required having a clear and unambiguous theory of action that you were committed to implementing. Therefore, the only thing left for you to do before commencing your second round of research is to do one final review of your revised theory.

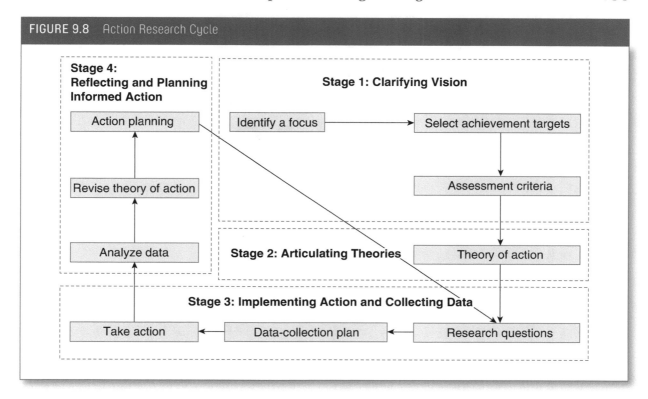

FIGURE 9.8   Action Research Cycle

It is now time to examine the revised theory of action you developed earlier in this chapter and ask if it requires any further modification in light of the action alternatives you may have just adopted, considered, or rejected for your program. If it does, you should insert those changes into your graphic and alter your priority pie, indicating any necessary revisions to the proposed allocation of time and energy.

Once you are satisfied that you have a revised theory of action that captures your best current thinking, is consistent with the findings of your research, and incorporates any action alternatives you will be adding, you are ready to select a new set of research questions and rejoin the action phase of the process.

Hopefully, you aren't in too great a rush because in the next chapter, we will discuss the very important topic of *reporting and sharing action research findings*. Many action researchers—we are among them—have found that whenever our findings are presented to colleagues, much is learned from their reactions and comments. For this reason, we generally like to share our findings with our peers and solicit their ideas before jumping into our next round of action.

10

Reporting and Sharing Action Research

There is nothing in the world of scholarship and science less controversial than the need for faithful and accurate reporting of results. From our earliest experiences studying science in school to our professional endeavors and even in our lives as consumers, we have all learned how important it is to be able to access accurate summaries of the experience of others to inform our own future actions and decisions.

In science class, we learned that it isn't enough to conduct an experiment correctly; the results of that experiment must also be presented competently in a lab report. These are reasonable expectations for the science student because they parallel the real world of scientific practice. Reporting is so crucial to advancements in science that the scientific community has institutionalized processes for the sharing of findings, and these processes are rigorously followed throughout the world.

Presentations of findings are made at professional meetings, and studies are reported in widely circulated journals. Papers are only accepted for publication or presentation after careful peer reviews for comprehensiveness, clarity, and accuracy. After initial review, research reports are publicly presented to knowledgeable and skeptical audiences who are expected to examine the findings, as much to identify fatal flaws as to validate the accuracy of the findings. Scholarly debates are publicly reported in conference proceedings, as well as in the pages of refereed journals and throughout the halls of academe.

As much as these processes are an esteemed part of the culture of the world of science and as much as citizens have come to depend on the results of scientific sharing for the development of the products and services we consume, being an active participant in the scholarly presentation of research while simultaneously working as a full-time K–12 educator probably appears daunting or unrealistic.

However, if we overlook the crucial importance of the reporting process and choose not to engage in it, we do so at our own and at our sacred profession's peril. When we don't share what we've learned through our experience, we are forcing every other educator and every other faculty to reinvent the same wheel all by themselves. Furthermore, as sound as our analysis may have been, when we have additional eyes and ears considering and debating our findings, it inevitably leads us to deeper and sharper understanding.

All students suffer when those who are guiding their education aren't in possession of the very best information when making instructional decisions. This is especially true when it comes to the challenge of universal student success. Clearly, many of the instructional strategies currently used in schools have failed to meet the educational needs of large numbers of minority and disadvantaged children. For those of us committed to the pursuit of excellence and equity, there is nothing more important than the sharing of information on practices that get us closer to universal student success. Finally, when educators don't share with colleagues what they're learning, it perpetuates professional isolation and reinforces the myth that this amazingly complex work is actually rather simple and can be mastered by people working alone in their own cubicles.

The good news is that while our self-interest, as well as our professional interests, and the best interests of our students require the reporting of our action research, the process for sharing need not be onerous. There are as many ways and as many formats for reporting and sharing action research as there are educators conducting these studies. In this chapter, we take a look at a few reporting processes and formats, ranging from the simple to the complex, and discuss the circumstances that call for using different approaches. But first, we examine a set of common issues that should be considered whenever you are planning a report on your action research.

COMMON ISSUES

Common Issue 1: Consider the Audience

As stated at the outset of this book, the primary reason for any of us to engage in action research is to help *us* learn from *our* practice to inform *our* future actions. Defined this way, every action research study already had an audience before it ever began, even if it was a small one: the actor/researcher himself or herself. But even when working in a remote and isolated location, this is likely not the only potential audience for our work. Even if we are working in a one-room schoolhouse, our students, their parents, and the community will have a keen interest in the results of our inquiries. And if there is at least one other professional working in our school, there likely is someone else who is trying to teach a similar curriculum to similar students. It is a fair guess that our immediate colleagues will have at least a passing interest in hearing the story that was told through our data. Lastly, since we are all part of the larger community of educators who are collectively engaged in a search for the most promising practices to move us toward universal student success, we can be certain that there are other educators in other places who are grappling

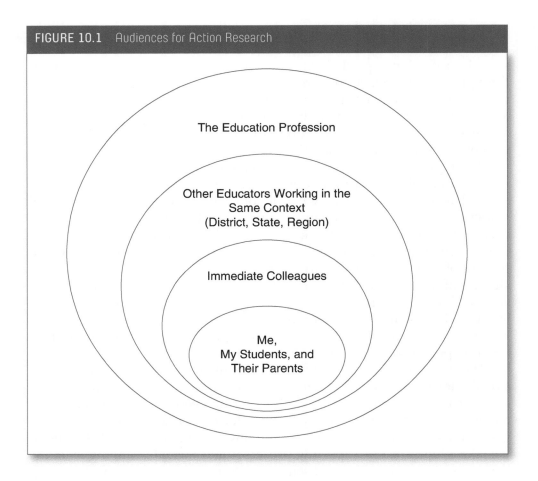

FIGURE 10.1   Audiences for Action Research

The Education Profession

Other Educators Working in the
Same Context
(District, State, Region)

Immediate Colleagues

Me,
My Students, and
Their Parents

with the same issues and consequently will find our insights of particular interest.

One way to conceptualize the different potential audiences for our action research is to look at them as nested circles, as illustrated in Figure 10.1.

The first consideration when preparing for sharing and reporting one's action research is determining who the principal audience (or audiences) will be for your report. Your answer will help you determine both the form and format that will work best for reporting on your project. Frequently, we are able to use our action research to kill multiple birds with a single stone. For example, let's assume Tanis was studying the use of problem-based learning (PBL) in her science classes. She is doing this primarily to improve her own teaching skills. In addition, her school's annual school improvement plan is focused on making the science curriculum more relevant and accessible to their diverse student body. The school's implementation of PBL is an integral part of that plan. Coincidently, Tanis is also enrolled in a master's program where students are expected to complete an action research project to fulfill the research requirement for their degree. In a circumstance like this, the same piece of research—looking at the implementation of PBL and its impact across the diversity of her students—could become the subject of three different research reports. However, each of these reports will need to satisfy different criteria.

Consider the levels displayed in Figure 10.1, and ask yourself, To which audience or audiences will I be aiming my report?

- *Immediate Audience:* Only those people with a direct interest in me, my teaching, my students, and this class
- *Immediate Colleagues:* The other teachers and educators with the responsibility for teaching this subject or these students (my grade level or department)
- *Other Educators in the Same Context:* Others in my district, region, state, or province
- *The Larger Educational Community:* All K–12 educators and policy makers with an interest in educational settings similar to mine

Common Issue 2: Purpose— What Decisions need to Be made?

All action research reports share one purpose: to help inform decisions on future action. In some cases, there is only one decision to be made. However, there are occasions when a number of different decisions are influenced by the reports of our action research results. For example, if you were planning to submit your action research project as part of a graduate program, in addition to providing you with information to inform your instructional decision making, your report would also help your professor make a decision on your grade.

Many times, action research is used as part of the evaluation of an externally funded project. In such cases, the report is likely to influence decisions on whether this work should be continued and encouraged elsewhere. On occasion, educators are also interested in developing their own scholarly publication record. These levels of decision making that might be influenced by action research reports can be illustrated by another series of nested circles, as illustrated in Figure 10.2.

Common Issue 3: Degree of Detail

Every consumer of an action research report won't need or want the same degree of detail. The superintendent might have a keen interest in the efficacy of the school's new "standards-focused homework hotline" program and whether the three goals established by the school board for that program were being achieved:

1. Enhanced parent–school communication
2. Continuous improvement on the state standards
3. More effective use of homework for learning

However, reports on other aspects of the school-based study may be more than the superintendent needed or wanted—for example, the specific nature of the homework assigned, how homework grades were determined, the patterns in homework completion rates, and assessments across individual teachers and categories of students.

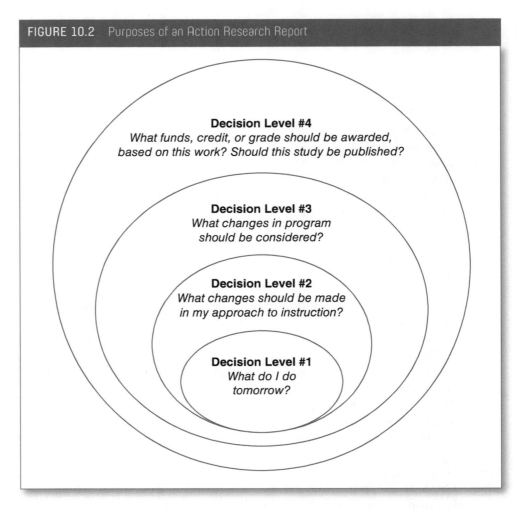

FIGURE 10.2   Purposes of an Action Research Report

Decision Level #4
What funds, credit, or grade should be awarded, based on this work? Should this study be published?

Decision Level #3
What changes in program should be considered?

Decision Level #2
What changes should be made in my approach to instruction?

Decision Level #1
What do I do tomorrow?

Here's another example: When presenting our research to our immediate department colleagues, it might be enough to describe the context by simply saying, "This research was conducted with four sections of sophomore basic writing we taught last semester." But if we were presenting the same research study at a national conference for English teachers, we would need to begin by providing significantly more detail on the nature of our school, its curriculum, and the type of students who tend to be enrolled in basic writing as sophomores.

As you prepare for sharing, it is important to realize that you probably have already generated a great many documents and artifacts as you conducted your research:

- Your reflective writing
- Your priority pies
- Your graphic reconstructions
- Your data collection matrix
- Any graphs or charts you made while analyzing data

All of these documents are items that you might choose to include in a report on your research.

Occasionally, an action researcher will use the series of activities engaged in and the documents prepared as they went through the four stages of action research as the *outline* for their report. By doing it this way, all that will remain to be done is for you to add a few transitions, as well as an explanation for the thinking behind your professional actions. Don't forget that last part because you will definitely want your audience to clearly understand the rationale and analysis that informed your professional decisions.

The Report Planning Form (Figure 10.3) is a good place to begin the planning for your report. It should help you focus on the three common issues discussed earlier: audience, purpose, and detail.

FORMATS FOR REPORTING

We have seen compelling reports of action research projects presented in a wide range of formats. We've read articles written by teacher-researchers in refereed journals, and we've seen action research shared informally in a teachers' lounge with a few colleagues sitting in a circle. We've watched teacher-produced videos that visually told the story of a research project, and we've seen research teams present their work on stage at national conferences. We've attended poster sessions held in school libraries, with audience members moving from display table to display table, informally discussing the projects with the researchers.

At action research presentations, we've been given one-page handouts summarizing the findings, and at others, we've received colorful, bound, fifty-page written reports. Determining the appropriate format is a decision for you to make, based on your needs and those of your audience. While formats may differ, we have found that there is a general flow and sequence that ensures that attendees will benefit from what was presented. This is a good time to once again remind ourselves that a completed action research report is basically a story. And just as there are infinite ways to write or tell a story, every story still contains a plot, starts with a beginning, and moves through a middle on its way to the end.

The report on your action research is the story of your trip through the four stages that framed this book:

Stage 1: Clarifying Vision and Targets

Stage 2: Articulating Theories of Action

Stage 3: Implementing Action and Collecting Data

Stage 4: Reflecting on Data and Planning Informed Action

As an audience member, we have found it particularly helpful when the person, video, or paper led us through the story of the researcher's inquiry in the same sequence as the four stages. Even when we're unfamiliar with the focus area, we find it easier to follow a story that begins with this foundation:

- This is the context where I work (where my action takes place).
- This is what I was trying to accomplish (the vision I was pursuing and my targets).
- This is how I thought I could best achieve my targets (my theory of action).

FIGURE 10.3 Report Planning Form

Step 1. Determine who your audience will be.

Step 2. Reflect on the reason for their interest in your inquiry.

Step 3. Using the following table, review each of the steps you took in conducting your research, the activities you engaged in, and the documents you produced.

Step 4. Based on your determination of the audience's need (Step 1), decide which documents to share and which activities to describe.

Stage or Process	Documents, Events	What Will You Share?
Identify focus	Reflective writing, journaling, reflective interview	
Select achievement targets	List of priority achievement targets	
Literature review	Information gathered	
Develop assessment criteria	Rating scales for targets	
Develop theory of action	Priority pies and graphic reconstructions	
Research questions	List of questions	
Create data-collection plan	Triangulation matrix	
Action, collection of data	Raw data, vignettes	
Analysis of data	Revised graphic reconstruction and revised priority pie	
Action planning	Review of action alternatives	

Step 5. Using the following table, make a determination on both the detail called for and the presentation technique you will use for presenting the information you have decided to share.

Thing to Be Shared (from the right-hand column in the foregoing table)	Detail Needed (summarized or with specifics)	Method for Sharing (handouts, displays, graphs, discussion, and so on)

Once we have heard that background information, we are prepared to learn what happened next:

- This is what I did (the implementation of my theory of action).
- These are the data I collected along the way.

Finally, once we know what the action researchers were trying to accomplish and how they went about it, our appetite has been whet to find out the ending:

- This is what I learned (my reflection on the data).
- This is what I intend to do about it (my action plan).

The Action Research Report Checklist (Figure 10.4) contains items that are often (although not always) present in an action research report. It is a good idea to go through this checklist prior to preparing your report. It should help alert you to items that you may want to consider including in your final product.

CREATING A BANK OF ABSTRACTS

Much has been written about the current knowledge explosion. In virtually every field, more and more information is being produced every single day. Finding efficient ways to access this information is becoming a necessity for people who want to stay current on their field's knowledge base. The increased sophistication and ease of use of information technology, including publicly available Internet search engines, are making locating information much easier and will continue to do so. But there are other, more low-tech techniques that you and your colleagues might wish to consider.

One low-tech strategy for sharing, which many school systems have had success with, is the production of a readily accessible book of abstracts of locally conducted action research. For example, in the Madison (Wisconsin) Metropolitan School District, the books of action research abstracts now contain virtually hundreds of projects, spanning all grades and every academic discipline. In many districts, each teacher is given a personal copy of the district's action research catalog (in hard copy or on a disk), or catalogs are made available in faculty rooms, through the district's media centers, or on the district's website. These action research compilations are made user friendly through cross-referencing by focus area, school subject, grade level, and program. Short abstracts provide enough information to enable a prospective user to get an idea of what has been investigated without having to wade through a great many details. Then, if and when more information is desired, contact addresses, phone numbers, and e-mail addresses are provided. A particularly nice aspect of this approach is that writing a brief abstract doesn't take very long.

It is helpful to limit the length of an abstract. We have found the guideline of five paragraphs and three hundred words works quite well. It can

FIGURE 10.4 Action Research Report Checklist		
Characteristic 1: Explanation of Context, Problem, Issue		**Include? Yes or No**
Elements	Significance of issue for other educators and students	
	Unique or general factors impacting issue	
	Potential for change/improvement	
Characteristic 2: Theoretical Perspective		**Include? Yes or No**
Elements	Summarize applicable literature	
	Logic behind this particular approach	
	Why not another approach?	
Characteristic 3: Research Design		**Include? Yes or No**
Elements	Why is it valid?	
	Why is it reliable?	
	How does it deal with extraneous or intervening variables?	
Characteristic 4: Analysis of Data		**Include? Yes or No**
Elements	The support and logic of the conclusions	
	Alternative explanations of data	
	Limitations explained	
Characteristic 5: Action Planning		**Include? Yes or No**
Elements	How is the plan supported by findings?	
	Is the potential for improvement theoretically sound?	
	Plans for further action research	
	Outline of potential value for self and others	

be accomplished by writing a straightforward paragraph in response to each of the following five prompts:

1. State the problem or the challenge that was being addressed by this research.

2. Provide a brief description of the setting of the research and the researchers (the context).

3. Briefly describe the methodology used to collect data for this study.

4. Summarize the principal findings.

5. State the conclusions, action plans, or additional research that resulted from this research.

Figure 10.5 provides an example of an action research abstract written in response to the five prompts.

Now it's your turn. Try writing a three-hundred-word abstract describing the study you just completed, using Figure 10.6.

FIGURE 10.5 Sample Three-Hundred-Word Action Research Abstract	
Begin with a statement of the problem or the challenge being addressed by the research.	As a faculty, we decided that we wanted to increase the quality, quantity, and equitable distribution of student engagement opportunities at AR Academy. We felt it was a good idea to create a shared conception of student engagement and its impact on achieving the simultaneous goals of equity and excellence. Personally, I wanted to get a clear picture of how effective my leadership was in supporting the faculty's work in this area. (72 words)
Then, provide a brief description of the context of the research and the researchers.	Our school has rich racial and linguistic diversity, nestled in a low-income, urban community in the Pacific Northwest. The school has experienced a reduction in resources, high staff turnover, and low morale. I surveyed staff to see what they wanted as a focus for their professional development. Overwhelmingly, teachers identified attacking student apathy and disengagement as priorities for professional development. (60 words)
Briefly describe the methodology of the study.	After working with teachers to co-construct a definition of engagement, I provided training and resources, conducted classroom walk-throughs, and provided feedback to teachers on what was observed. The faculty was surveyed on a regular basis to ascertain how my leadership practices were impacting their instruction. (45 words)
Summarize the principal findings.	Teachers valued collegial and administrator observation and feedback. They rated this as the most effective support. Teachers appreciated having input and sharing responsibility for planning professional-development experiences. Teachers appreciated my interest in learning what strategies they believed most enhanced their practice. As the year progressed, the teachers increased their skills at critiquing their engagement practices through an equity lens and became more adept at addressing the unique needs of diverse students. (71 words)
State the conclusions, action plans, or additional research that resulted from this research.	After I presented the project findings, the faculty identified several specific hurdles that were still hindering student engagement. As a result, a team volunteered to identify additional culturally relevant resources to supplement the standard curriculum. The staff enthusiastically agreed to continue the project during the next school year. (48 words)

FIGURE 10.6 300-Word Action Research Abstract Worksheet

Topic	Response
Begin with a statement of the problem or the challenge being addressed by the research.	
Then provide a brief description of the context of the research and the researchers.	
Briefly describe the methodology of the study.	
Summarize the principal findings.	
State the conclusions, action plans, or additional research that resulted from this research.	

CREATING A DISTRICT ARCHIVE

Several years ago, the Killeen (Texas) Independent School District began building the professional-development capacity of their district by providing two-year grants to volunteer teachers who were willing to document their work on priority innovative projects while engaging with a network of colleagues working in the same focus area. At the end of the two years, participants prepared a written report for presentation to their colleagues, and that report then became part of a district-maintained knowledge base. The reports prepared by the Killeen teachers all focused on the five characteristics found in Figure 10.4. Resource B contains a copy of the rubric that the Killeen teachers used as their guide when preparing their written reports.

Tip on Evaluation Criteria
It is strongly recommended that whenever one of the purposes of your action research report is to satisfy a requirement, mandate, or external expectation, you *request in advance the criteria by which the project will be evaluated.* In most cases, the college, funder, or agency requiring the report will have pre-established criteria that will help guide you through report preparation. If no criteria are available, you may want to consider using the rubric provided in Resource B as you develop your report.

11

Conclusion
The School as a Learning Organization

Dickens began *A Tale of Two Cities* with the line, "It was the best of times, it was the worst of times." The same thing could be said for the situation in which most of us K–12 educators currently find ourselves. We began this book discussing the context confronting the modern educator. The expectations have never been higher, and it has never been more important that we help all students to graduate and that all of our graduates be well educated. And while it is true that some of our graduates are now leaving school better educated than ever before, we still have a long way to go if we are to realize the twin goals of equity and excellence. If we wish to see a world where the fruits of a good education are enjoyed equally by all, where all students prosper regardless of their family background, race, culture, ethnicity, gender, or learning challenges, we still have a lot to learn about how each of us can do better to meet student needs.

Becoming adults in our society without adequate language, reasoning, and learning skills places young people at risk of not being able to support themselves or their families. Students who leave school without a moral compass, an ability to appreciate beauty, and an adequate supply of self-confidence and self-esteem will find living a fulfilling life difficult at best. And modern democratic societies need citizens who are well grounded in the natural, social, and behavioral sciences.

Beyond the moral imperative of eliminating achievement disparity, increasingly punitive public policies are subjecting students, teachers, and the public schools to high-stakes sanctions if arbitrary benchmarks aren't met on a preordained schedule. None of this would be problematic if only we knew everything we needed to know to make universal success a reality. If it were possible that a fix for every teaching and learning problem could one day surface like a cure for a terrible disease, we could simply support the scientists working on these breakthroughs and eagerly await their great discoveries. But alas, the solution to education's challenges isn't likely to be found that easily.

As was discussed at the opening of this book, the acts of teaching and learning present problems that are among the most complex endeavors any professional ever has to deal with. And the frontline workers in the education enterprise—the teachers and administrators working in schools—are the only people in a position to design adequate solutions to these challenges. Recruiting the best and brightest people to educate our children is arguably the most important issue facing modern society, and the future of public education rests largely on our ability to do so. Meanwhile, securing adequate funding for our schools and providing support for the people working in them is more tenuous than ever.

But there is also ample reason for optimism. Bright and capable people choose their careers based on an assessment of how rewarding they think the work will be. There are few things in the world of work more rewarding than working with colleagues trying to solve complex and important problems. It wasn't hard to persuade the rocket scientists at NASA and the medical researchers at the Salk Institute to work on their monumental breakthroughs. Likewise, nothing provides more joy for educators than seeing evidence of our students' growth and development. The best and most reinforcing thing about action research is that it creates a system for providing regular, credible data on student development while simultaneously enabling us to appreciate the role we have played in nurturing and facilitating that growth.

As a result, educators who integrate the four sequential stages of action research into their professional routines tend to be happy and satisfied professionals. Educators who are working toward the realization of the twin goals of equity and excellence will find the four sequential stages of action research to be a valuable tool, enabling them to understand the impact they are having on students in real time. Beyond the benefits for their students, this should add to their job satisfaction. After all, who wouldn't feel a sense of satisfaction when she has in her possession credible data and evidence demonstrating that she is being successful in overcoming problems that have perplexed others for generations?

Anyone who has been involved in public education in recent years has been inundated with the surface trappings of modern organizational theory. It is a rare school or district that hasn't developed a vision and mission statement, backed up by a strategic plan. Those things are important, but inspiring words and elaborate plans are not what make organizations successful; rather, what makes a real difference in school performance are the routine habits of productive professional behavior consistent with an organization's core values.

THE TWO KEYS: COHERENCE AND CONGRUENCE

Nobody needs a mission statement to know what the core value of schools should be in a democratic society. Surely, the business of public schools is maximizing the human potential of the next generation through growth, development, and mastery of a wide array of knowledge and skills. Accomplishing this requires organizational behavior that is consistent with the belief that everyone can learn, grow, and accomplish more than he or she has ever been able to do in the past. The two critical factors that determine whether an organization is staying true to its core values (behaving in accordance with its theory of action) are captured by the words *coherence* and *congruence*. Deliberate attention to the essence of the four stages of the action research process is one way for educators to ensure that the schools they work in manifest both of these elements.

Coherence

Schools are busy places. The typical teacher makes more decisions in one hour than most other people make in a day. Yet the question so often heard in the schoolhouse is, "Why are we doing this?" Principals ask this of the central office, teachers ask it of the curriculum department, and students ask it of their teachers. When people are busy and are asked to do something but they are not sure why they are asked to do it and why they are required to do it a particular way, it is more than frustrating. It should be no surprise that a lack of clarity on goals and methods generally leads to increased alienation and a decrease in organizational effectiveness.

Fortunately, coherence is never lacking where teachers, schools, and students have integrated into their routines the first two stages of the action research process—*clarifying the vision and targets* and *articulating a rationale for pursuing a specific plan of action*. Publicly sharing the rationale behind what they are doing further builds coherence for all those who are affected by their work.

Congruence

The educational process is about learning, and most every school's mission statement includes a recitation of the school's commitment to lifelong learning. But unfortunately, the behavior at many schools is far from consistent with that belief. The reality is that behavior is a far more powerful teacher than words. When schools behave as though the authorities (teachers, administrators, professors, and so on) already know all that one needs to know and have all of the answers to the issues of practice, they are modeling a very different set of beliefs. The best way to convince our students of our commitment to the value of lifelong learning is to invite them to see us cast in the role of learners. When students see the significant adults in their lives being curious, goal-driven people, trying to gain insight and knowledge from each experience they are engaged in, they will come to believe that we mean it when we say that learning is forever.

PUTTING THE PIECES TOGETHER

Jane Stickney, the former principal at Willamette Primary School in West Linn, Oregon, uses the phrase *the ethic of action research* to refer to the norms of collaboration and experimentation that prevailed at Willamette Primary School as she and her colleagues helped that school effect a remarkable turnaround in academic performance (Sagor, 1995). In schools such as Willamette, where the ethic of action research has taken hold, the system itself transmits many powerful lessons. First, it teaches that it is okay to dream, to create, and to believe in the achievement of visions and targets. Second, it teaches that through action research and thoughtful reflection, it is possible to design strategies that can help us realize those dreams. Most importantly, it teaches that the die is never completely cast. We can always learn from experience and get better at whatever it is we truly care about and value.

Institutionalizing the Ethic of Action Research

The Washoe County School District is a large school system serving the city of Reno, Nevada, and its surrounding communities. For several years, the district embraced action research as part of its strategy to foster continuous improvement, collaboration, and professional development.

A few years ago, the staff in the district began carrying cards in their wallets that captured the essence of what they were working to accomplish (see Figure 11.1). On one side of the card it says, "*Washoe County School District—Our Goal: Continuous improvement in student performance based upon disciplined use of data.*" On the reverse side it says, "*What Constitutes Sound Decision Making: 'The Big Five.'*"

1. What do you want to accomplish? (Vision, Target)

2. What criteria will determine success? (Assessment Criteria)

3. What do you think it will take to achieve success? (Theory of Action)

4. What data will you collect? (Data to Inform Decisions)

5. How will you share your learning? (Community of Learners)

In Washoe County, they dream of a day when the Big Five becomes a mantra chanted by everyone to everyone, over and over, throughout the schoolhouse.

Those questions can frame discussions with students, helping them to visualize and strategize achieving their goals. They can structure discussions between classroom teachers and, in doing so, reinforce the experience that colleagues are interested in and excited to be working alongside one another and want to learn from each other. And finally, the Big Five forms the outline of a process for school improvement and provides a structure for ongoing discussions with parents and the community.

Recently, the Portland (OR) Public Schools, another large urban district, made a decision to put collaborative inquiry at the heart of its efforts to simultaneously pursue excellence and equity. Now, the expectation in Portland is that all of its district and school-based school improvement efforts will be conceptualized, implemented, monitored, and revised using the inquiry process. The district supervisors follow a process the district calls the cycle of inquiry to guide them and help them improve the support they are giving building administrators with the improvement of their schools. Principals and other building administrators use similar inquiry processes to look at their own work and use data to become more effective instructional leaders. In the Portland schools, no one person is seen as

FIGURE 11.1 Washoe County School Goals and Endeavors Card

WASHOE COUNTY SCHOOL DISTRICT

OUR GOAL:

Continuous improvement in
student performance based
upon disciplined use of data

WHAT CONSTITUTES SOUND
DECISION MAKING: "The Big Five"

1. What do you want to accomplish? (Vision, Target)
2. What criteria will determine success? (Assessment Criteria)
3. What do you think it will take to achieve success? (Theory of Action)
4. What data will you collect? (Data to Inform Decisions)
5. How will you share your learning? (Community of Learners)

Source: Used with permission of Washoe County School District.

knowing all the answers. Rather, the continuous use of the inquiry cycle is a statement to all stakeholders (students, parents, teachers, administrators, and community members) that at every level of the organization, the professionals are involved in learning what they need to know to help every child reach his or her potential.

We truly hope that while reading this book, your participation and involvement with the four stages of action research have made you a believer in the power of this process. Whether it is publicly chanting the Big Five mantra, adopting your own district cycle of inquiry, or finding some other way to share your belief in the empowerment that flows from practicing the action research process, it is important that you find a way to celebrate the centrality of learning. Whenever you are discussing *your* visions, *your* theories, *your* data, and *your* action plans, you are providing testimony to the empowerment and professional satisfaction that one receives through engagement in the role of learner.

Building learners is more than noble work. When one believes in the innate human capacity to learn, then anything seems possible. Paraphrasing Christa McAuliffe, when you chose teaching for your career, in no small way, you were choosing immortality. When your students and the educators you work with learn from you how good it is to be a learner, they will have gained something that will stay with them for a lifetime. Through the model you are providing, they will get to see their own future: one filled with excitement, curiosity, and unlimited possibilities and one where they, like you, can use their own learning to help others grow and develop, thereby making this a better world for us all.

Good luck and a heartfelt thank you for all that you do.

Resource A
How to Use the Feedback Forms and Summary Reports

FEEDBACK FORMS

- These forms were designed for use with a class in order to efficiently collect regular feedback on students' perceptions on things of interest to their teacher. Carbonless paper is used so the students can maintain a record of their responses over time.

- When using this process, it is important to think through the nature of the student perceptions you wish to collect—there are infinite possibilities. In the past, teachers have used these forms to collect data on such things as *enjoyment of the class, engagement in activities, how much students felt they learned, how difficult they found the material, how they felt during class,* and so on.

- After selecting the nature of the perceptions you want to collect, develop a rating scale for the students to use. Provide them with a copy of the scale, or post it on the wall of your classroom, or do both. When doing this with students who aren't able to comprehend the meaning of a number scale, you might choose to build a scale with a sequence of smiling or frowning faces.

- It is often a good idea to have the students look at their previous feedback reports prior to filling out new ones. This makes it more likely that they will apply the scale consistently, and it will reduce the chance that changes in ratings are influenced by temporary changes in mood.

- Encourage students to provide comments to explain their ratings because often, there can be several different explanations for the same score. This enables you to know the specific justification for a student's choice of score. Also, these comments will later assist the students in recalling what they were thinking when they provided the feedback.

- Be sure the students date their feedback forms. This will prove important when you and they attempt to interpret any trends found in the ratings (for example, a relationship between their reactions and the teaching technique being used).

SUMMARY REPORTS

- These carbonless forms serve two purposes. They save you, the teacher-researcher, the time required to ascertain patterns of changes as you look for trends with individual students or within particular classes. Second, they cause your students to reflect on the changes that occurred in their perspectives over the course of the class or the term of your study, which enables them to develop a deeper understanding of themselves as learners.

- Another value of the summary form is that it provides you with additional and important pieces of triangulated data: the students' personal explanations of the reasons behind changes that occurred in their perspectives. Later, you will be able to compare and contrast their explanations with your own observations.

- When having students fill out the summary reports, use the following steps:

1. Have the students plot their numerical ratings on the two graphs. If you are doing this with students who don't yet understand how to plot scores on a graph, have a parent volunteer or older student plot the scores for the student.
2. Ask the students to look for changes in the direction and slope of the lines on their graphs and make tentative conclusions about the trends. For example, a student might conclude something like, "I enjoyed this project more and more as time went on," or, "I got frustrated in the middle of last week."
3. Ask the students to sequentially review the written comments they provided on the feedback forms and reflect on the reasons for changes in perceptions. The student should then record those explanations or thoughts in the space provided below the graphs on the summary form. Should you be doing this with students who are unable to write their own responses, ask an adult or older student to pose the questions to the students and then write down their responses.

Resource B

Five Characteristics of a Quality Action Research Project

CHARACTERISTIC 1: EXPLANATION OF CONTEXT, PROBLEM, AND ISSUE

Elements

- Significance of issue for teachers and learners
- Unique or general factors impacting issue
- Potential for change or improvement

Basic	Developing	Proficient	Strong
Declares the hope for change and improvement	Demonstrates awareness of possible benefits for teaching and learning	Adequately explains the benefits for the researcher's teaching or the student's learning	Makes strong case for the need and desirability for improvement
Doesn't address applicability beyond the case at hand	Seems unsure or unclear about relevance beyond the case at hand	Recognizes and explains the applicability of this inquiry to other educators	Perceives and explores a broad range of implications beyond the case at hand
Reports on context but leaves out several critical details	Provides accurate but incomplete report on research context	Recognizes and addresses the relevant and unique characteristics of the researcher's context	Provides readers with enough contextual data to take into account the uniqueness of the context

CHARACTERISTIC 2: THEORETICAL PERSPECTIVE

Elements

- Understanding or awareness of applicable literature
- Logic behind and reasonableness of approach
- Clarity of expression

Basic	Developing	Proficient	Strong
Demonstrates awareness of the procedures recommended by developers of an intervention	Shows a basic understanding of major premises behind intervention	Demonstrates an understanding of key research findings or commentaries on the issue or problem	Provides a thorough literature review presented in a logical, clear, and concise manner
Explains how the researcher intends to implement the intervention	Explains the rationale behind proposed intervention	Provides a logical and clear explanation of the researcher's theory	Detailed, logical, and clear explanation for the theory informing the proposed intervention
		The proposed intervention is justified based on the researcher's theoretical stance	The proposed intervention logically follows from the findings of others and the researcher's own theory

CHARACTERISTIC 3: RESEARCH DESIGN

Elements

- Potential for yielding valid findings
- Potential for yielding reliable findings
- Consideration of extraneous or intervening variables

Basic	Developing	Proficient	Strong
A technique or techniques are proposed to demonstrate impact	The research design uses authentic or recognized techniques to determine impact	The research design makes appropriate use of triangulation to corroborate and support findings	The research design takes into account and adequately controls for most apparent and possible extraneous or intervening variables
The techniques have the potential for accurately reflecting performance	The research design reflects an awareness of the risk of inaccuracy	The research design makes use of multiple data points to increase accuracy	The research design uses sampling techniques that make accurate findings highly likely

CHARACTERISTIC 4: ANALYSIS OF DATA

Elements

- Supportable and logical conclusions
- Alternative explanations addressed
- Limitations explained

Basic	Developing	Proficient	Strong
Conclusions are not contradicted by the available data	The conclusions are logical and generally supported by the available data	All findings are supported by credible pieces of data	All reported findings and conclusions are supported by multiple and credible pieces of data
	The potential for alternative interpretation is recognized	Reasonable alternative interpretations of the data are reported	Reasonable alternative interpretations of the data are recognized and discussed
	The researcher shows an awareness that possible limitations exist	Reasonable limitations are addressed	Reasonable limitations are recognized and addressed, along with suggestions for overcoming them

CHARACTERISTIC 5: ACTION PLANNING

Elements

- Supported by findings
- Potential for improvement theoretically sound
- Contains an action research assessment design
- Outlines potential value for self and others

Basic	Developing	Proficient	Strong
The plan is consistent with a theory	The plan has reasonable face validity	The plan is consistent with the data and conclusions	The plan is a direct and logical extension of the findings and conclusions
The plan is not contradicted by available data	The available data appear supportive of the plan	The findings suggest that the plan will make a difference in student performance	Based on the available data, it appears likely that student performance will improve if and when the plan is followed
	The plan seems logical	The theory behind the plan is addressed	The theory behind the plan is clearly outlined and addressed
		The action plan contains a viable assessment strategy	The assessment plan should provide valuable evidence of the effectiveness of the plan
		The researcher should benefit from data on the implementation of the action plan	The researcher and other educators are likely to benefit from data on the eventual implementation of the plan

Resource C
Applications for Leadership Projects

Exhibit 1: Target Identification Form for Leaders

Exhibit 2: Post Hoc Analysis of Leadership Form

Exhibit 3: Rating Scale for a Collegial School

Exhibit 4: Rate-of-Growth Charting With Leadership Projects

Exhibit 5: Using the Two-Step Walk-Through With a Leadership Project

Exhibit 6: Data Collection Planning Matrix

Exhibit 7: Data Collection Planning Matrix (ACR Questions)

Exhibit 8: Creating a Comparison Graph of Actual Energy Expended

EXHIBIT 1: TARGET IDENTIFICATION FORM FOR LEADERS

Reread your report, your journal, or your interview, asking the following questions (write your responses under each one):

What were the specific accomplishments (such as improved climate, improved morale, greater collaboration, or improved behavior)? These are *performance targets*.

_____

_____

_____

_____

_____

_____

_____

What specific changes did you observe in your leadership skills (for example, better facilitation of discussions, improved questioning skills, or greater delegation)? These are *process targets*.

_____

_____

_____

_____

_____

_____

_____

What specific changes did you observe in your school or program (for example, greater sense of community, improved behavior, or greater proficiency with state standards)? These are *program targets*.

_____

_____

_____

_____

_____

_____

_____

EXHIBIT 2: POST HOC ANALYSIS OF LEADERSHIP FORM

Briefly describe the goal of this initiative.

_____

_____

_____

_____

_____

State the way you had hoped things would change or evolve as a result of this initiative.

_____

_____

_____

_____

_____

If this initiative had been completely successful, what would a colleague (or a staff member responsible for carrying out this initiative) be saying about this project?

_____

_____

_____

_____

_____

What is this colleague (or staff member) now saying about this initiative?

_____

_____

_____

_____

_____

Using the table provided, list, in sequence, all of the significant activities and facilitation you provided during the implementation of this initiative and this colleague's (staff member's) reaction to that activity.

Use additional space if necessary.

EXHIBIT 3: RATING SCALE FOR A COLLEGIAL SCHOOL

Trait	Emerging (1)	Basic (2)	Developing (3)	Proficient (4)	Fluent (5)
1. Universal excellence in student performance	There is at least one arena (academic or behavioral) where more than 90 percent of the students demonstrate proficiency.	There are arenas (both academic and behavioral) where more than 90 percent of the students demonstrate proficiency.	The mean performance of students in every demographic category is at or above proficiency in reading, math, and writing.	Sixty-seven percent of students in every demographic category are at or above proficiency in reading, math, and writing.	More than 90 percent of students are proficient in every subject and arena of importance. Performance is equally excellent across demographic groups.
2. Excellent staff morale	There are staff members who report being personally and/or professionally satisfied with their work at this school.	Many staff report enjoying their work at this school and being personally and professionally satisfied with their work.	Most staff report enjoying their work at this school and being personally and professionally satisfied with their work.	More than 90 percent of the staff report being personally and professionally satisfied with their work at this school.	Everyone reports loving their work at this school.
3. Team culture	Some people work regularly with colleagues.	Some people work regularly with their colleagues. Collegial work is thought of in a positive way.	Every staff member is engaged in at least one significant collaborative endeavor. The staff reports enjoying collegial work.	Every staff member is engaged in multiple collaborative endeavors. Collegial work is cited by most staff as characteristic of the school.	Every staff member is repeatedly engaged in numerous collaborative endeavors. Collegial work is cited by all staff as characteristic of the school.
4. Staff as skilled problem solvers	Teachers identify and articulate educational problems.	Teachers bring educational problems to the attention of other professionals.	Teachers routinely seek the input of colleagues when dealing with educational problems.	Teachers routinely seek the input of colleagues and collaboratively develop alternative approaches when dealing with educational problems.	Solutions to complex problems always involve solicitation of input, action research, and the collaborative development of alternatives.

(Continued)

(Continued)

Trait	Emerging (1)	Basic (2)	Developing (3)	Proficient (4)	Fluent (5)
5. Alignment of curriculum, instruction, and assessment	Teachers choose instructional strategies in consideration of the content being taught and monitor student performance.	In several disciplines, the faculty follows a common curriculum, chooses instructional strategies based on that curriculum, and uses common assessments for student evaluation.	In every core subject, the faculty follows a common curriculum, chooses instructional strategies based on that curriculum, and uses common assessments for student evaluation.	In every subject, the faculty adapts the common curriculum, chooses instructional strategies based on that curriculum, and uses common assessments for student evaluation.	In every subject, the faculty collaboratively adapts the common curriculum, chooses instructional strategies based on that curriculum, and creates common assessments for student evaluation.

EXHIBIT 4: RATE-OF-GROWTH CHARTING WITH LEADERSHIP PROJECTS

1. Generate a two-column table set up like the one below.

Key Activities or Accomplishments	Anticipated Date
A:	
B:	
C:	

2. In the left-hand column, list all of the key activities or accomplishments that you believe will need to occur for your initiative to realize its full potential. This list should not be considered final until after you have completed the development of your theory of action (Chapter 5).

3. In the right-hand column, place the date when each key activity or accomplishment should occur if your initiative is to realize its full potential in the allocated time.

4. Create a rate-of-growth chart. The horizontal axis is for plotting the elapsed time between the initiation of your project and the expected end date. On the vertical axis, you should list each of the key activities or accomplishments from your table.

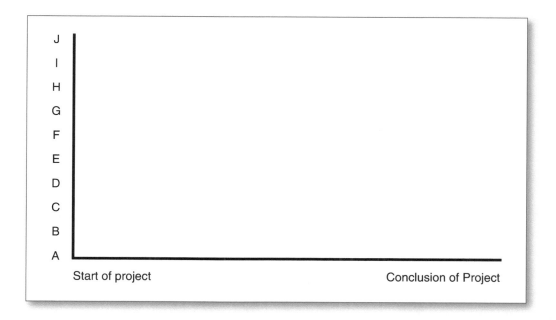

5. Draw a line graph reflecting the anticipated completion date for each key activity or accomplishment, as assigned on the table.

6. Periodically check in with key participants in your project regarding the status of each key activity or accomplishment, and indicate the date that activity actually occurred on the rate-of-growth chart.

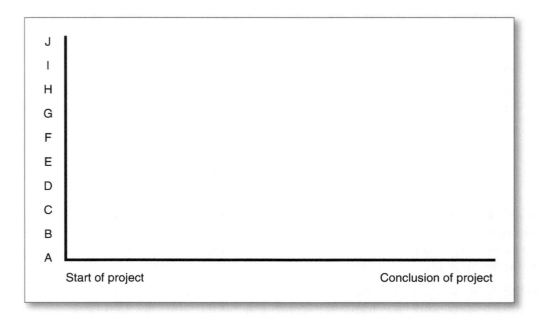

7. Connect the points indicating the actual dates of completion for the key activities or accomplishments of your project. That line represents your actual rate of growth. When the actual-rate-of-growth line is above your anticipated line (Step 5), it represents faster than expected rate of growth. When and if the *actual* line falls below the *anticipated* line, it reflects a slower-than-expected rate of growth.

EXHIBIT 5: USING THE TWO-STEP
WALK-THROUGH WITH A LEADERSHIP PROJECT

Below is Dr. Hernandez's graphic reconstruction of her plan to increase faculty collegiality by applying the two-step walk-through for the creation of research questions.

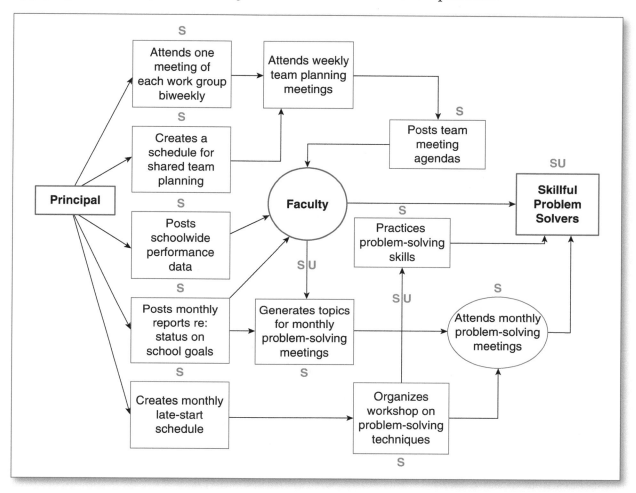

The two questions she asked of each assumption in the graphic reconstruction are as follows:

1. Is this factor, issue, variable, or relationship significant?

2. How confident am I regarding the workings of this factor, issue, variable, or relationship?

A yes answer to the first question is indicated with the letter *S* for *significance,* and a yes to the second question is indicated by a *U* for *uncertain.*

After taking her two-step walk-through, Dr. Hernandez listed all of the significant aspects of her theory, emphasizing in bold those aspects about which she had considerable uncertainty.

Significant Aspects of Theory

1. The principal attends meetings of each group biweekly.

2. The principal creates a schedule for shared team planning.

3. The principal posts schoolwide performance data.

4. The principal posts monthly reports on school goals.

5. The principal creates a monthly late-start schedule.

6. The principal organizes a workshop on problem solving.

7. The principal attends monthly problem-solving meeting.

8. The faculty generates topics for monthly problem-solving meetings.

9. Everyone attends monthly problem-solving meetings.

10. The faculty practices problem solving.

11. The faculty becomes skillful problem solvers.

Significant Relationships

1. The relationship between team meetings informed by data and the faculty's ability to generate meaningful topics for problem solving.

2. The relationship between problem-solving professional development and actual use of the skills.

3. The relationship between practicing problem solving and becoming skillful problem solvers.

Based upon this assessment, Dr. Hernandez generated the following three action research questions:

1. What was the nature of faculty development with problem-solving skills?

2. What factors influenced the faculty's decisions on topics for group problem solving?

3. In what ways did the principal's actions and professional development contribute to the development of faculty skills with problem solving?

EXHIBIT 6: DATA COLLECTION PLANNING MATRIX

Project Focus: Enhancing Faculty Collaboration

Research Question	Data Source 1	Data Source 2	Data Source 3
What was the nature of faculty development with problem-solving skills?	Faculty survey	Focus group interviews with each faculty work team	Video transcripts from problem-solving meetings
What factors influenced the faculty's decisions on topics for group problem solving?	Faculty survey	Focus group interviews with each faculty work team	Journal
In what ways did the principal's actions and professional development contribute to the development of faculty skills with problem solving?	Faculty survey	Focus group interviews with each faculty work team	Faculty response to the researcher's tentative assertions (member checking)

EXHIBIT 7: DATA COLLECTION PLANNING MATRIX (ACR QUESTIONS)

Project Focus: Enhancing Faculty Collaboration

Research Question	Data Source 1	Data Source 2	Data Source 3
What did I/we actually do?	Daily journal	Minutes from team meetings and faculty meetings	Materials produced as part of project
What improvements occurred on our/my achievement targets?	Faculty survey	Focus group interviews with each faculty work team	Contrast student performance data before and after each problem-solving session (pertaining to the problem focus)
How did our/my actions influence the changes in performance on the achievement targets?	Faculty survey	Focus group interviews with each faculty work team	Faculty response to my tentative assertions (member checking)

EXHIBIT 8: CREATING A COMPARISON GRAPH OF ACTUAL ENERGY EXPENDED

1. Consider the percentage of your (or your group's) total attention that you had expected (before the work started) this project would command.

2. Review your calendar, meeting agendas and minutes, and any other artifacts you have available regarding the work and energy that was ultimately expended on this project.

3. Based on your review of the data in Step 2, make a subjective judgment on the energy consumed by the project. Was it approximately what you had anticipated? Did you end up spending twice as much energy as you had anticipated on this? Did it garner only half the attention you thought it would? Or something else?

4. Make a list of all the significant *categories of action* that consumed attention from you or your group during the project.

5. If the total attention devoted to the project was less than anticipated, add an item to the list of *categories of action* (Step 4) titled "other priorities." If the attention devoted was approximately the same or more than you had anticipated (Step 1), do not add the "other priorities" category.

6. Assign percentages to the items on your list of *categories of action*. If you have a category for "other priorities," the percentage you should assign to that category should equal the loss of attention noted in Step 5. (For example, if you felt this project had only received half the attention you anticipated, then the category "other priorities" should be assigned 50 percent.) The percentage you assign to the remaining categories on your list should be based on your subjective judgment, after a careful review of your calendar and other artifacts.

7. Using the percentages assigned (Step 6), draw a pie chart illustrating your perception of the actual energy expended.

8. If you had determined that the total energy expended on this project was significantly in excess of what was anticipated (Step 5), that fact should be noted in the narrative comments you write explaining your two priority pies.

Resource D
Sample Abbreviated Action Research Reports

Exhibit 1: Dr. Hernandez's Project on Improving Collaborative Problem Solving

Exhibit 2: Mr. Johnson's Project on Leadership for Increasing Engagement

Exhibit 3: Ms. Montgomery's Project on Equitable Response Opportunities

Exhibit 4: Mr. Seeker's Project on Improving Persuasive Writing

Exhibit 5: Fifth-Grade PLC Team's Study of Student Engagement

EXHIBIT 1

Educator: Yolanda Hernandez

Action Research Project: Improving the quality of the collaborative problem solving engaged in by the Cesar Chavez High School faculty

Vision

I very much want to see our school become a genuinely collegial workplace. I believe a collegial work culture is essential if we are to become a school that is supportive of continuous progress toward universal excellence in student performance. My dream is to create a work environment at Cesar Chavez High School that is supportive of the professional needs of faculty and leads to high levels of staff morale. I want all of the Cesar Chavez teachers to feel part of a supportive faculty team so that whenever a student or program issue arises, they believe that together, we will be able to apply creative problem solving effectively and in a timely fashion. As our collegiality increases, I envision a tighter and tighter alignment of curriculum, instruction, and assessment. As I've reflected on the characteristics of such a school, it has appeared to me that a truly collegial high school faculty would demonstrate extraordinary performance across five particular traits:

- Universal student success
- High staff morale
- Collaborative team culture
- Skillful problem solving
- Tightly aligned curriculum

I then developed a rating scale that I could use for measuring our school's growth on each of those five traits as we worked toward becoming a collegial school. That complete rating scale is reprinted at the end of this project.

I have long felt that one of the most important elements of a successful collegial school was the ability and comfort of the faculty to collaboratively solve problems. For this reason, I decided to focus this action research study on my efforts to promote skillful collaborative problem solving by the Cesar Chavez faculty. My plan was to track our progress on the trait of skillful problem solving and then use those data as one measure of my success in promoting faculty development.

Trait	Emerging (1)	Basic (2)	Developing (3)	Proficient (4)	Fluent (5)
Faculty as skilled problem solvers	Teachers identify and articulate educational problems.	Teachers bring educational problems to the attention of other professionals.	Teachers routinely seek the input of colleagues when dealing with educational problems.	Teachers routinely seek the input of colleagues and collaboratively develop alternative approaches when dealing with educational problems.	Solutions to complex problems always involve solicitation of input, action research, and the collaborative development of alternatives.

Theory of Action

I began this part of the process by reflecting on what the most critical factors were that needed to be attended to if our faculty was to consistently engage in problem solving in the manner described as *fluent* on the above scale (i.e., *solutions to complex problems always involve solicitation of input, action research, and the collaborative development of alternatives*). I identified four factors that I deemed critical:

- Access to data
- Time to meet
- Focus on goals
- Limited partnerships

Since I believed my attention to these four factors would be the determining factor on whether the faculty became skillful collaborative problem solvers, I realized I would be well served to reflect more deeply on the importance of these four factors and how they interrelate. I did that through the use of two visual aids: the priority pie and the graphic reconstruction.

Priority Pie

I developed the pie chart and explanation printed below to clarify the relative importance of those four critical factors (access to data, time to meet, focus on goals, and limited partnerships)

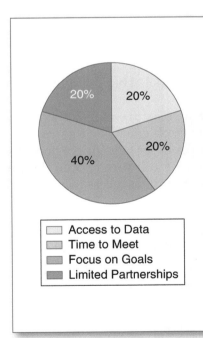

20% 20% 40% 20%

- Access to Data
- Time to Meet
- Focus on Goals
- Limited Partnerships

For the faculty to succeed in becoming an effective problem-solving team, I need to ensure that adequate time is provided for teachers to meet and work collaboratively. I also need to make sure that they have access to all the pertinent data and information needed to make successful decisions. Since a sense of common purpose is essential, I need to take steps to achieve clarity on our school goals and work at keeping our collective attention focused on schoolwide priorities. To build support for this process, I need to find a way to become a partner with each faculty work group as they work toward addressing a school goal.

I believe the most critical of all these actions will be my efforts to keep a clear and consistent focus on our school goals (40 percent). The three other critical factors that I must attend to as building principal are providing adequate and convenient times for problem-solving meetings (20 percent), ready access to all the pertinent student and school data (20 percent), and engaging every faculty work group as a limited partner (20 percent).

While I found the thinking involved in creating the priority pie quite helpful, I still felt I needed a more detailed road map laying out a viable strategy to get to schoolwide fluency with collaborative problem solving. To accomplish this, I created an implementation road map to further explain the actions I planned on taking as part of my effort to promote our faculty's development as collaborative problem solvers. My implementation road map is illustrated in the following graphic reconstruction.

Implementation Road Map

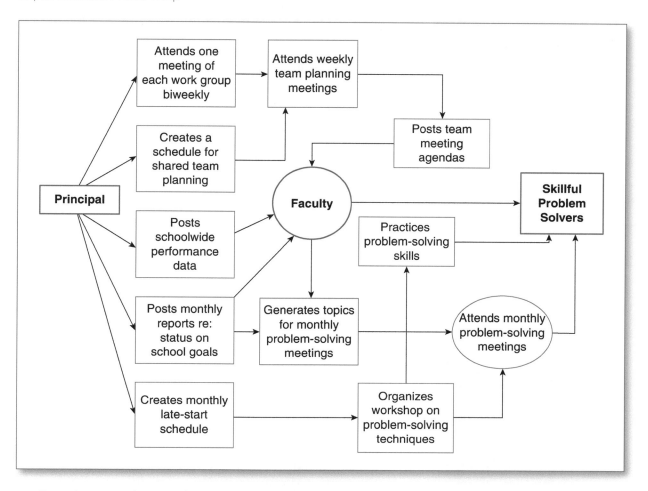

Based on my theory of action, if our faculty was to succeed in becoming skillful collaborative problem solvers, there were several things I would need to do. Specifically, I needed to attend meetings of each work group at least once every two weeks; I needed to create a schedule that was supportive of shared team planning; I would need to provide timely reports to faculty regarding schoolwide performance; each month, I needed to monitor the status on school goals and share those data with the faculty; and lastly, I needed to arrange for a late-start schedule to be used for professional development on collaborative problem solving.

In addition, I needed to make sure that the faculty had access to all of the pertinent data and information needed to make successful decisions. Since a sense of common purpose is clearly essential, I also needed to take steps to achieve clarity on our school goals and to see to it that our collective attention stayed focused on schoolwide priorities. To build support for this process, it was important that I enter into a partnership with each faculty work group as they did their work in furtherance of our school goals.

Research Design

To understand the adequacy of my theory and the effectiveness of my actions, I developed a plan to answer three key research questions. For my study, I decided to use as my research questions the three generic ACR questions described in *The Action Research Guidebook: A Process for Pursuing Equity and Excellence in Education*, third edition. The table below illustrates my triangulated data collection plan.

Yolanda Hernandez's Research Design

Research Question	Data Source 1	Data Source 2	Data Source 3
What did I/we actually do?	Daily journal	Minutes from team meetings and faculty meetings	Materials produced as part of project
What improvements occurred on our/my achievement targets?	Faculty survey	Focus group interviews with each faculty work team	Contrast student performance data before and after each problem-solving session (pertaining to the problem focus)
How did our/my actions influence the changes in performance on the achievement targets?	Faculty survey	Focus group interviews with each faculty work team	Faculty response to my tentative assertions (member checking)

Key Findings

I conducted my research over twenty consecutive weeks, running from October 15 through April 15.

- I attended twenty-four meetings of faculty work groups.
- We held seven problem-solving faculty meetings.
- Four reports (October, December, February, and April) were made on the status of school goals (had been scheduled monthly).
- Minutes were posted following 90 percent of team-meeting sessions. Eight teams posted 100 percent of their minutes.
- The faculty initially rated their collaborative problem solving as 2.7 (on a 5-point scale).
- In April, the faculty rated their collaborative problem solving as 3.9 (on a 5-point scale).
- Ninety-three percent of the faculty reported greater clarity on school goals at the end of the project.
- Eighty-five percent of the faculty rated the monthly problem-solving meetings as productive or highly productive.
- One hundred percent of the faculty reported that the professional-development workshop was very good or excellent.
- Ninety-three percent of the faculty reported seeing improvements in student performance following the monthly problem-solving meetings.

After my initial review of the data, I created a two-dimensional matrix for further sorting of the data. Since my project was aimed at developing the skills and attitudes of the faculty, I decided to re-sort the data by the dates they were collected. I thought this would help surface patterns and trends in the process of our development toward collegiality. After subjecting the data to this pattern analysis, I realized I could add these additional findings:

- Eighty percent (sixteen) of the comments on the April evaluation were positive.
- Fifty-five percent (eleven) of the comments in the September evaluation were positive.
- This was a typical comment from a fifth-grade teacher (April evaluation): "Honestly, I used to hate going to meetings at this school. I even dreaded reading the staff bulletin. Nothing that we ever did seemed relevant to me. But now, I look forward to working together; it has truly helped me to enjoy my job."
- Eighty percent (eight) of comments made by intermediate teachers in the September evaluation were negative in nature.

- Twenty percent (two) of the comments by the intermediate teachers in the April evaluation were negative in nature.
- Twelve comments on the April evaluation referred to positive actions taken by the principal.

Analysis and Conclusions

After reviewing all of the findings and analyzing the data, it appears to the faculty and me that the original theory of action illustrated on the implementation road map (graphic reconstruction) was fundamentally sound and provided a helpful structure for us. Consequently, we will be following the same theory of action next year as we proceed with our efforts to improve our collaborative problem solving.

However, when I reviewed the data on my time usage and expenditure of energy, it was clear that what actually transpired was significantly different from what I had anticipated.

I had intended to devote more time to compiling and sharing data with the faculty. I had committed myself to producing monthly reports (nine reports) on school goals yet only made four. I expected this to take 20 percent of my time, yet it turned out to be a far smaller percentage (10 percent).

In addition, my journal and calendar data reveal that the total time I spent on this project was about twice what had been anticipated. I had expected that 20 percent of my time and effort would be devoted to meeting with faculty work groups and forging limited partnerships. That work ended up consuming 55 percent of the total time spent on this initiative. Preparing for the problem-solving faculty meetings wasn't included in my original theory, yet I ended up spending 20 percent of my time and energy on this aspect of the project. As a result, the category *focus on goals* ended up receiving 15 percent of my attention. However, I realize that wasn't so bad since the majority of time spent on my limited partnership with the teams was indirectly focused on school goals.

The subsequent figures contrast my original view on the relative importance of the four critical areas with an honest report on the actual investment of time and energy with this project.

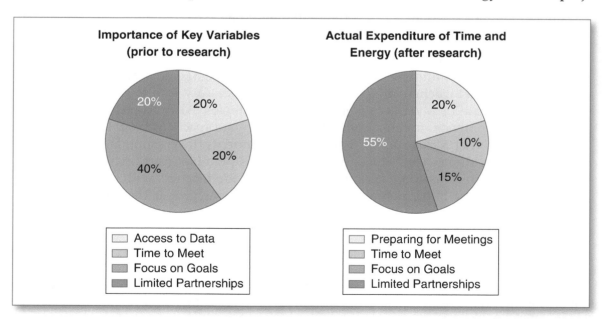

Based on this analysis and our continued commitment to making Cesar Chavez a collegial school, I intend to continue my work supporting the faculty with the development of their skills in collaborative problem solving. I will be following the same implementation road map; however, now being more mindful of the real demands on my time, I will do a better job of personal planning.

EXHIBIT 2

Educator: Franklin Johnson, principal of the AR Academy

Action Research Project: Increase engagement to promote equity and excellence in student participation and outcomes

Vision

Our school has rich racial and linguistic diversity, nestled in a low-income urban community in the Pacific Northwest. The school has experienced a reduction in resources, high staff turnover, and low morale. I surveyed staff to see what they wanted as a focus for their professional development. Overwhelmingly, teachers identified attacking student apathy and disengagement as priorities for professional development. Once we agreed to focus on engagement, I visited classrooms during the first weeks of school and to learn more about the staff concerns around student engagement. Students were, at best, passively engaged, with a few students dominating the discourse and a few students being disruptive and preferring to wander the halls. I met with the faculty to discuss the plan for addressing these concerns and offered the following vision:

> We should increase the quality, quantity, and equitable distribution of student engagement opportunities at AR Academy. We should create a shared concept of student engagement and its impact on the simultaneous goals of equity and excellence. And finally, I want to gain a clear picture of how my leadership practices support this vision.

Theory of Action

After engaging in a series of activities to identify variables that ultimately impact the goal of increasing student engagement, I crafted the following theory of action:

> In order to increase student engagement in my school, I need to work with the teachers to co-create a shared understanding of what student engagement actually means. I need to ensure that teachers are provided with the necessary training and support to implement the use of a variety of engagement strategies. Also, in order to promote sharing of best practices for engagement, I need to create space for them to collaborate and visit each other's classrooms. Teachers, like students, love exemplars, and I will provide them with models from as many sources as possible. And finally, I will conduct frequent mini–classroom observations and provide teachers with data and feedback specific to our implementation of engagement strategies at the individual and school level.

So I could better understand the relative importance of the key factors I would need to be attending to, I constructed a priority pie. That pie chart is reprinted below.

At this point, I began reflecting on how I might best leverage those four critical leadership actions (training and resources, classroom observations, collecting observation data and providing feedback, and collecting and analyzing student data). I wanted to develop a theory of action that would have a high probability of success. The graphic reconstruction shown below illustrates my full theory on how my leadership might be leveraged to produce higher levels of engagement.

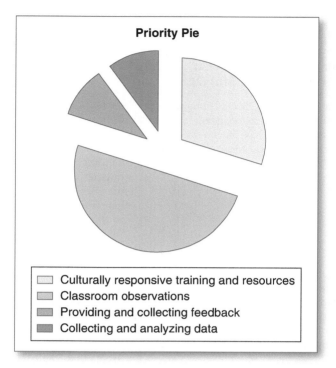

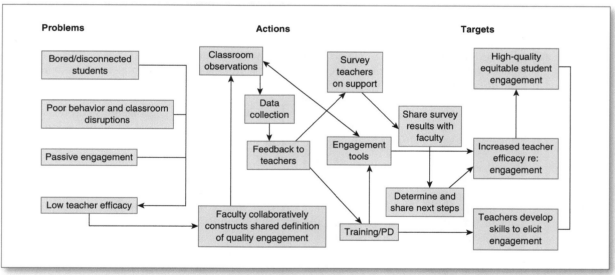

Research Questions and Data Collection

I conducted an analysis of my graphic reconstruction, called the two-step walk-through, to help me determine those significant issues about which I needed to learn more regarding this project. The two-step test helped me see that there were three key questions for which I both needed and wanted greater insight:

1. What does student engagement look like in our school?

2. What leadership practices move us closer to our ideal?

3. In what ways do these practices influence student engagement?

I then realized I would need an instrument for the teachers to use to provide me with continuous feedback on my leadership. For this purpose, I designed the following leadership rating scale.

LEADERSHIP RATING SCALE

	Minimally Helpful (1)	Somewhat Helpful (2)	Helpful (3)	Very Helpful (4)
Observation and feedback	Observations were minimal, and the feedback added some value.	Observations were inconsistent, but the feedback related to student engagement was somewhat useful.	Observations were consistent, and the feedback was clear and relevant and provided specific strategies for enhancing student engagement.	Observations were consistent, and the feedback was clear, thorough, and relevant; it provided specific strategies that would work in my classroom, enabling me to increase the quantity, quality, and equity of student engagement.
Training and support	Some training and support were provided. They provided some new information to improve my practice.	The training and support provided was acceptable, and I was able to find at least one strategy that will help with student engagement.	The training and support was timely, relevant, and well facilitated. The training and support provided new insights that I will use to improve student engagement.	Training and support were exceptional. This assistance was timely, was directly on point, and will enable me to make significant progress in the quality, quantity, and equity of student engagement in my classroom.
Materials and other resources	Some limited materials were made available to support student engagement.	When materials and other resources were provided, they added some value to my work on improving student engagement.	When materials and other resources were requested, high-quality materials and resources were promptly made available.	The leader effectively anticipated teacher needs and was able to provide high-quality materials and resources in a timely fashion so they could be used for planning purposes.
Response to teacher feedback	Feedback on leadership was solicited inconsistently, but it appears to have been received and accepted.	Feedback on leadership was solicited inconsistently, and it appears that occasionally, it resulted in changes in how leadership is handling the student engagement issue.	Feedback on leadership was consistently sought and incorporated into how leadership is handling the student engagement issue.	Feedback on leadership was consistently sought and incorporated into improved leadership behavior. The leadership of the student engagement initiative is being carried out with full transparency and disclosure.

I then designed the following triangulated data collection strategy to surface answers to the identified research questions:

Research Question	Data Source 1	Data Source 2	Data Source 3
1. *What does student engagement look like in our school?*	Principal classroom observations	Teacher observations	Document defining engagement, look-fors, and so on
2. *What leadership practices move us closer to our ideal?*	Principal notes	Teacher ratings of principal leadership	Faculty-meeting exit cards
3. *In what ways did those factors influence student engagement?*	Principal classroom observation data	Teacher surveys	Teacher interviews

Key Findings

The most significant findings from my action research were as follows:

1. I attended twenty-four grade-level PLC meetings.

2. I organized seven professional-development sessions on engagement strategies.

3. Student engagement data were collected weekly; disaggregated by race, gender, SPED, and ELL status; and shared at our regular monthly faculty meetings.

4. Each teacher conducted at least three peer observations.

5. Teachers valued collegial and administrator observation and feedback. They rated this as the most effective support.

6. Teachers appreciated having input and sharing responsibility for planning professional-development experiences.

7. Teachers appreciated my interest in learning what strategies they believed most enhanced their practice.

8. As the year progressed, the teachers increased their skills at critiquing their engagement practices through an equity lens and became more adept at addressing the unique needs of diverse students.

Analysis, Conclusions, and Action Plan

I had intended to devote fewer professional-development sessions to the focus on engagement strategies. I had committed myself to delivering two sessions during first quarter, accompanied by walk-throughs, with feedback provided to individual teachers in one-on-one conversations, along with brief engagement status updates on the project during faculty meetings. I expected this to take 20 percent of my time but recognized, based on teacher feedback and classroom observations, that more training was requested and needed. I added two additional training sessions, resulting in 40 percent of the time dedicated to the project. I also spent less time doing walk-throughs and providing feedback than expected. I originally planned on doing weekly scans of engagement per grade level; however, I wasn't able to follow through on this as I had intended due to a host of calendar interruptions. I hadn't anticipated needing to help teachers get prepared for the engagement training sessions, and as a result, that wasn't included in my original theory. The preparation for training ended up consuming 20 percent of the time and energy I devoted to this project.

After I presented the key project findings and my conclusions, the faculty identified several specific hurdles that they felt were still hindering our progress with student engagement. As a result, a team volunteered to identify additional culturally relevant resources to supplement the standard curriculum. The staff enthusiastically asked me to continue the project during the next school year.

EXHIBIT 3

Educator: Elaine Montgomery

Action Research Project: Equitable response opportunities to increase equitable engagement

Vision

William Butler Yeats stated, "Education is the not the filling of a pail but the lighting of a fire." This fire fueled my passion to become an educator. I wanted to make a difference for *every* student. I envisioned rich discussions, followed by deep reflective writing, spirited dialogue, and debates, with all, including me, leaving inspired, enlightened, and equipped for the next rigorous task. However, given my current reality, I was gravely concerned about the uneven participation of students in class discussions and the corresponding uneven performance on related follow-up activities. The gaps in participation and performance from students correlated with race, gender, SPED, ELL, and/or TAG status. I refused to accept the predictable disparity as the reality in my classroom. The training on culturally responsive pedagogy had been informative and inspiring, and I wanted to apply what I learned in a way that made a measurable difference for my students. Our school's focus on student engagement inspired me to focus on promoting equitable response opportunities from students to ensure all students knew I had high expectations for each of them. I created the following vision statement for my action research study:

> I want to increase the quality, quantity, and equitable distribution of response opportunities through effective question and discussion techniques.

Theory of Action

After engaging in a series of activities designed to identify the key variables that would likely have an impact on the achievement of my goal of improving response opportunities for students, I then crafted the following theory of action:

> I began this process by brainstorming what I thought were the key variables (areas for action) that I needed to attend to if my students and I were to realize our goal. I came up with four critical categories of action: time to think and reflect, time for classroom discussions, regularly tracking who is speaking and how often, and use of a variety of discussion structures and techniques. I then arranged these variables into a pie chart illustrating the relative importance of each item to the achievement of my goal.

When I reflected on my priority pie, several thoughts occurred to me. For my students to actively participate in class discussions at high levels, I needed to explicitly teach my expectations for classroom discussions. I also needed to make sure that the students had a proper amount of think time to process information and prepare their thoughts. Since response opportunities are an important component of displaying my expectations to a student, I was committed to finding ways to track and monitor the frequency and level of questions posed to all students in all groups. I committed myself to be intentional about planning questions ahead of time with each student in mind to ensure equitable participation. To build support for this process, I knew I would need to become a learner with my students, checking in as a class and with individual students to see how we were doing. Over a nine-week period, I made plans to hold at least five class meetings for eliciting feedback. My plan was to make feedback from students and my responses to patterns and themes in their feedback as transparent as possible. I felt this was the best way to create the safety and mutual respect needed to increase the frequency, as well as the depth and complexity, of response opportunities.

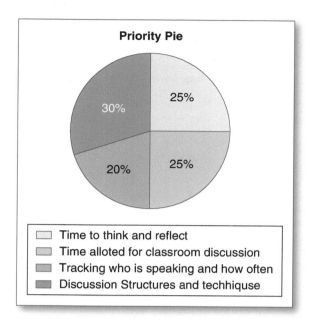

I then decided to turn that understanding into a road map illustrating my complete theory of action for enhancing response opportunities. The graphic reconstruction that follows illustrates my implementation road map.

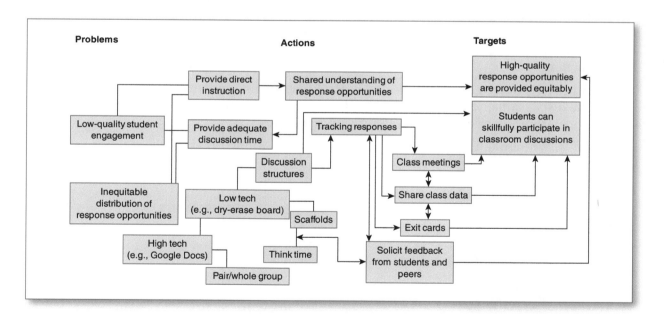

Research Questions and Data Collection

I then analyzed my theory of action (as depicted on the graphic reconstruction) using the two-step walk-through to see if I could distill a few important research questions. That analysis enabled me to come up with three meaningful questions:

1. What discussion structures promote equitable responses from students?

2. How did the class meetings on response opportunities impact student participation?

3. In what ways did enhancing response opportunities influence academic performance?

I then produced the following table to flesh out a triangulated data collection strategy that I could use to answer my research questions.

Research Question	Data Source 1	Data Source 2	Data Source 3
How has this effort influenced the provision of high quality equitable response opportunities?	Response tracking sheets	Exit cards	Student surveys and interviews
How did the class meetings on response opportunities impact student participation?	Meeting notes	Surveys and interviews	Recordings of meetings and lessons
In what manner did emphasizing discussion structures influence the ability of students to skillfully participate in class discussions?	Grade book	Student portfolios	Student surveys and interviews

Findings

The findings were as follows:

1. Student responses increased in frequency and depth when the topic was controversial or relevant.

2. My consistency in tracking student responses had a significant impact on the distribution of responses and whether students thought I was being fair.

3. The most favorable responses from the class were from student-led discussions. All three student-led discussion days ranked the highest in student engagement and satisfaction.

4. Student grouping was an issue on several days when students were not satisfied with the discussions. Students reported not working well with a partner for various reasons, and careful planning led to better group dynamics.

5. Boys, who initially reported I had a bias toward calling on girls, shared that I showed much improvement each term.

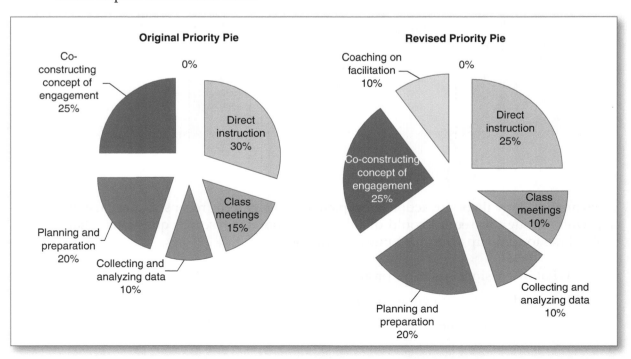

6. Think–pair–share activities generated the most ELL dialogue and overall student participation.

7. Students preferred a balance of teacher- and student-mediated dialogue.

After reviewing and analyzing all of my data, I decided to use what I learned to revise my theory of action. I did this first by baking another priority pie, but this time, I based it on what I had learned from my study. In what follows, you will see my two pies, side by side. The one I prepared before doing research, and the other was informed by my data.

When looking at my two pie charts side by side, you will see, based on the data from my action research, I realized I needed to create an entirely new category of action: *coaching students on leading and facilitating discussions*. You will also note that I found the time for this new activity by reducing some of the time I had previously devoted to class meetings.

Then, based upon what I learned, I created a second graphic reconstruction. These are subsequently reprinted.

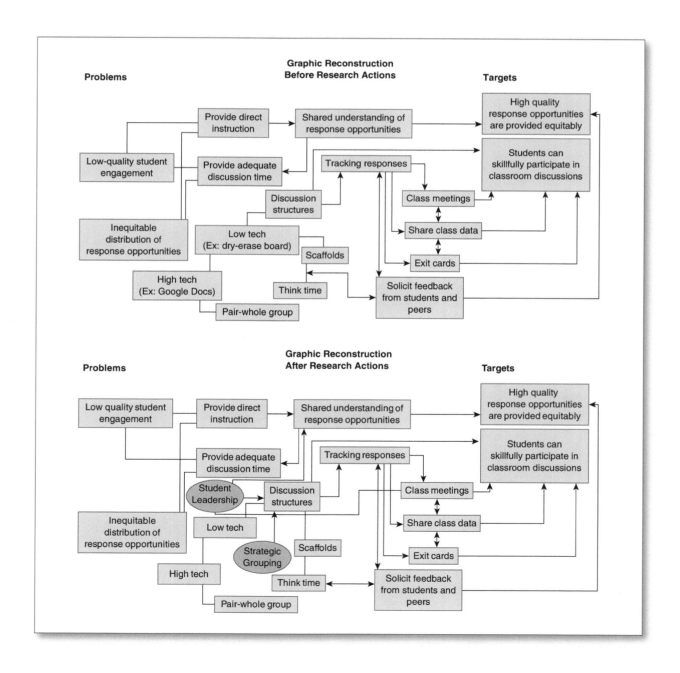

On first examination, these two pictures of my theory of action, before and after research, may not seem that different. However, upon closer inspection, you will see that I added two things: student leadership and strategic grouping. These changes were based on data.

1. **Student leadership**. Prior to conducting my research, I felt it was a good idea for the teacher to mediate most early class discussions to ensure that each student truly had equitable response opportunities. But the data from student exit cards after the class meetings revealed clearly that students, at both the group and class level, wanted to lead and facilitate their own discussions earlier in the process.

2. **Strategic Grouping**. Prior to conducting my research, I felt it was a good idea to randomly group and regroup students periodically as a way to enhance discussions. But the data revealed a significant disparity between the functioning of the different groups. It seemed that random assignments often didn't result in groups with a productive chemistry. Based on this finding, I now believe that student groups will function better when I strategically assign students based on their strengths and needs.

After presenting the research to my administrator and colleagues, I asked for a peer and an administrator to observe my class to confirm my findings using the scale I generated for the project. As a wonderful and unintended consequence, three of my colleagues are now either formally or informally monitoring response opportunities in their classrooms, and I am continuing to refine my techniques to push for deeper learning and understanding for all of my students.

EXHIBIT 4

Educator: Allen Seeker

Action Research Project: Improving the quality of student writing: the five-paragraph persuasive essay

Vision

I have been teaching the required sophomore English class at Hoodland High School for the past eight years. This has been both a pleasurable and frustrating experience for me. If there is one aspect of the English curriculum that I have always been particularly drawn to, it is the teaching of writing. I deeply believe that helping students become proficient writers is the most effective way I can help them become good thinkers. Students who have learned to organize their thoughts and present those thoughts clearly and convincingly have a transferrable skill set that will empower them for the rest of their lives, regardless of which career path or personal avenues they pursue. For the eight years that I've taught this course, I have come to believe that the development of student proficiency with one particular writing genre, the persuasive essay, was especially critical for realizing this goal. I believe this is because a well-done persuasive essay requires an organized presentation of an argument, the use of logic and evidence to support that argument, and effective word choice to make a convincing argument.

My frustration comes from my lack of success in motivating my students to do their very best with the required writing assignments, most notably, when we are doing the unit on persuasion. In the past, when teaching the persuasive essay, I have been frustrated by what appears to me to be a decided lack of student effort and emotional engagement. That frustration was what motivated me to use action research to monitor and explore how I could improve my teaching of the five-paragraph persuasive essay. I hoped to find out if, by making some changes to my instructional process, I could increase student motivation, foster greater engagement, elicit greater effort, and ultimately improve their persuasive writing.

Theory of Action

I began the action research process by attempting to flesh out what I have come to understand to be the key variables I would need to focus on if my students were to be motivated to do what it takes to write a proficient five-paragraph persuasive essay. Based on my years of experience, what I had gathered from the graduate courses I've taken and the articles I've read, as well as recent discussions I've had with colleagues, I concluded that there were five critical skills that my students needed to master. In addition, I believe it is crucial that I provide the students with continuous quality feedback. The five critical skills the students needed to master were as follows:

- Organization
- Persuasive voice
- Editing
- Vocabulary
- Grammar and mechanics

Priority Pie

I then decided to visually display my emerging theory using the priority pie process. My pie is illustrated next.

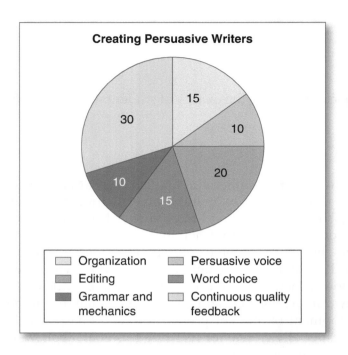

As I reflected on what it would take to help my students become proficient writers of persuasive essays, I concluded that the most critical factor was the quality and amount of feedback I provided. I felt that if the feedback were provided properly, that variable would be responsible for 30 percent of the student's ultimate success. The second-most-critical factor was the development of editing skills by the students, at 20 percent. I theorized that learning to edit their own work would, in the long run, enable them to be less dependent on my feedback. The skills of organization and word choice (vocabulary) were the next most critical, at 15 percent, followed by the development of a persuasive voice and grammar and mechanics at 10 percent each.

I then asked myself, Based on the importance of those six variables, when doing my lesson planning, how should class time be allocated? The chart that follows illustrates my theory on how I should budget time for the major activities (individual writing and editing, peer editing, direct instruction, and feedback) during the persuasive-writing unit.

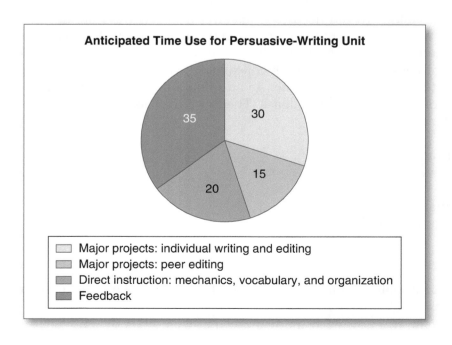

This pie chart represents my belief that attending to the critical factor of timely quality teacher feedback would probably consume 35 percent of my time and energy. The second-most-time-consuming element of this process would be the time the students spent drafting and editing their own work (30 percent). Providing direct instruction on writing skills—mechanics, vocabulary, and organization—is essential for student success and likely will take 20 percent of my time and energy. In my opinion, it will be valuable for students to collaborate and get a second opinion when editing. Therefore, I expect that peer editing will take 15 percent of the class time we spend on this unit.

Graphic Reconstruction

To further clarify my theory of action, I then drew up a graphic reconstruction to illustrate more precisely how I intended to organize the classroom and my instruction during the unit on the persuasive essay. My graphic reconstruction is shown in the chart that follows.

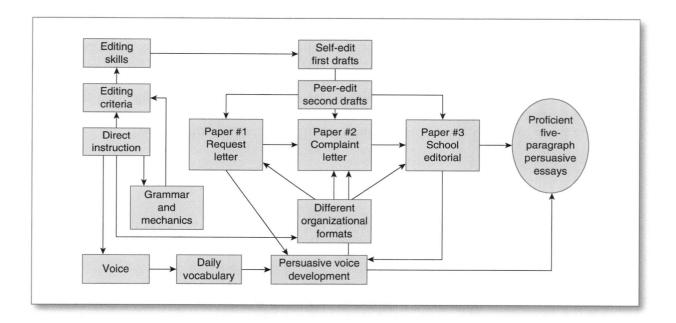

The graphic reconstruction reflects my plans for teaching these critical skills. According to my theory of action, the development of the skill of using persuasive voice and vocabulary will be fostered by direct instruction and our daily vocabulary exercise. The students will be given the opportunity to practice these skills, as well as writing in different organizational formats, and the skills of editing while producing three required papers (the request letter, the complaint letter, and the school editorial). Each paper will require a minimum of three drafts. Students will be expected to edit their own first drafts (the sloppy copy) and then have a peer or peers edit the second draft. If my theory turns out to be sound, at the end of this unit and upon completion of the three papers, the students will be able to write proficient five-paragraph persuasive essays, as measured by the English Department rubric.

Research Design

I decided to conduct this action research study by organizing my data collection around the three ACR questions. An outline of my data collection plan follows.

Research Question	Data Source 1	Data Source 2	Data Source 3
1. What did I/we do?	Teacher's plan book	Weekly student assessments	Student portfolios
2. What changes occurred on my achievement targets?	Assessments of three student assignments using the English Department rubric	Students' self-assessments of their writing using the English department rubric	Weekly student assessments
3. How did my actions affect any changes in performance?	Teacher's journal	Student interviews	Weekly student assessments

My intention was to chronicle what the students and I actually did by using information from my plan book, a weekly student survey in which students assessed the class at the close of the week each Friday, and my review of the work they placed in their portfolios.

To determine our success in hitting the achievement target (specifically, increased writing proficiency), I planned on evaluating all three of the student papers using the department's rubric, comparing those assessments with the students' self-evaluations (using the departmental rubric), and then analyzing all of these performance data in relation to the data obtained from the students' weekly assessments of my teaching. Finally, I hoped to get a handle on the role of my teaching on changes in their writing proficiency by reviewing the data from my daily journal, contrasting it with the data from the students' weekly assessments, and further comparing those to the data obtained through group interviews with students.

Findings

Question 1: What Did I/We Do?

As for the first research question, "What did we/I do?" that story is told by contrasting the pie chart on anticipated time use with the chart on actual time spent.

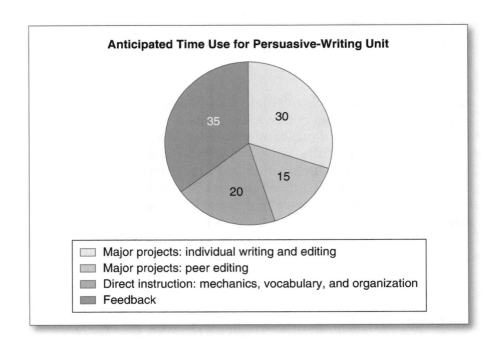

Anticipated Time Use for Persuasive-Writing Unit

35   30   15   20

☐ Major projects: individual writing and editing
☐ Major projects: peer editing
☐ Direct instruction: mechanics, vocabulary, and organization
☐ Feedback

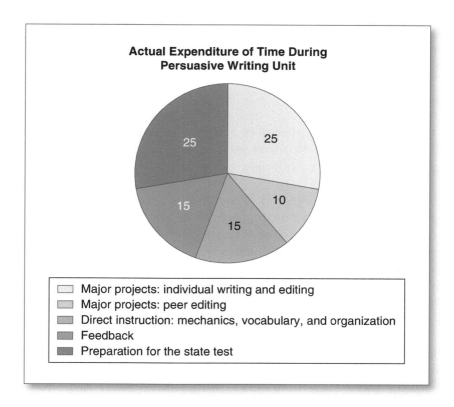

Actual Expenditure of Time During Persuasive Writing Unit

- Major projects: individual writing and editing
- Major projects: peer editing
- Direct instruction: mechanics, vocabulary, and organization
- Feedback
- Preparation for the state test

Well, things didn't go as I had expected. My original thinking on time allocation had me spending 35 percent of class time providing feedback for my students. However, the data showed I spent less than half that time on feedback (15 percent). Likewise, the time I devoted to direct instruction was less than anticipated (from 20 percent down to 15 percent). I was pleased to note that in actuality, we spent the same time on the major projects that we expected (25 percent for individual work and 10 percent for peer editing). Finally and surprisingly, these data reflected that 25 percent of class time ended up being devoted to preparation for the state competency exam, a category of action that I hadn't even considered when originally planning my action research on this unit.

Question 2: What Changes Occurred on the Achievement Targets?

There were far more data collected in answer to this question than I have space for in this abbreviated report. I will list some of the more significant findings here and will be happy to provide access to the other data and further information upon request.

- Average class performance declined during the period of preparation for the state exam.
- Average performance of the boys declined sharply during the period of preparation for the state exam.
- The performance of the average- and low-performing students declined during the period of preparation for the state exam.
- There was no significant change in performance of the high-achieving students during the period of preparation for the state exam.
- There was a slight improvement in performance of the girls during the period of preparation for the state exam.

- Class discussions were held following the return of each major writing assignment.
- On seven occasions, I made note of the need to spend an entire class period reviewing previously taught material.
- On four of the five times that peer editing was used, it took at least twice the amount of time allocated.

It appeared that the process (my theory of action) was working, to a point. I arrived at this conclusion by observing several trends that were repeated throughout the period of data collection. Those trends reflected several things:

- On most measures, the girls scored higher than the boys.
- Both boys and girls reported putting forth more effort each week up until Week 6.
- Both boys and girls did demonstrably better on the second paper (the complaint letter) than the first paper (the request letter).
- The upward trends in both attitude and performance switched in Week 6 (when we began two weeks of prep for the state exam) and continued through Week 7.
- In the last two weeks of the unit, when we were working on the school editorial, performance rebounded but not as significantly for the boys as the girls.

A window into those five trends listed can be observed in the three graphs that follow, detailing data from student self-reports for "Effort Expended" and "How Much I Learned" and a composite of the teacher's and students' ratings of the major papers using the departmental rubric.

Question 3: What Was the Relationship Between My Actions and Changes on the Performance Targets?

Based on my analysis of all of the available data, it appeared to me that the drop in average performance (both academic and attitudinal performance) in Week 6 appeared to be a reflection of a decline in student motivation created by a shift of classroom focus from the writing process to review for the state exam. This documented drop in performance was most pronounced with the boys and with students with a history of moderate and low performance. I suspect the reason why there wasn't a comparable decline in the performance of the high achievers was that these kids have become accustomed to doing what is required to receive good grades so that it didn't matter to them if the work was particularly motivating or interesting. The girls in this class are a very cooperative and responsible group, and this may explain why they continued to put forth considerable effort even though their feedback made it clear that they found the work to be less than stimulating. My guess is that the slight improvement in the girls' performance (even though they didn't like it) was due to this.

Conclusions and Action Plan

Conclusions

After reviewing the findings from this project and member checking those findings with the students, I concluded that my theory of action (as illustrated in the graphic reconstruction) was fundamentally sound. Specifically, all of the following were true:

- For the overwhelming number of students, the sequencing of the three persuasive essays resulted in improved scores with each successive assignment.

Student Weekly Assessment: Effort Expended

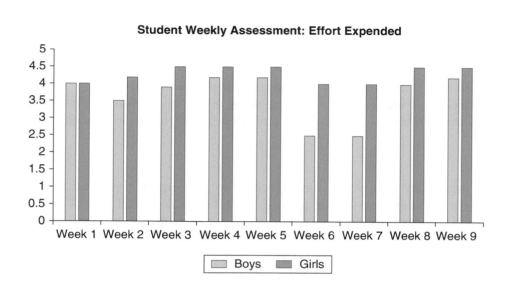

Boys   Girls

Student Weekly Assessment: "How Much I Learned"

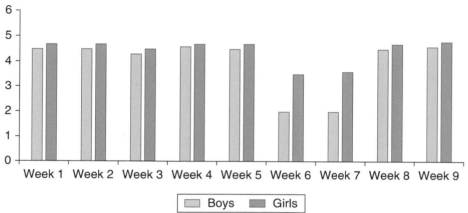

Boys   Girls

Performance Across Major Assignments

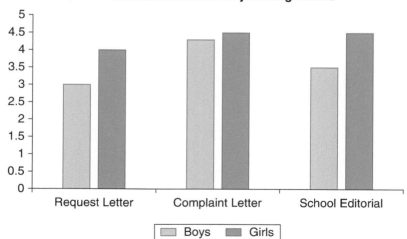

Boys   Girls

- One hundred percent of the students reported enjoying the fact that all three of the assignments had them dealing with real-world issues.
- Evidence from the student surveys and assessments of the improvement in their work on later drafts established the value of the time that was devoted to peer editing.
- The patterns I detected in the grammatical and mechanical mistakes made by students were evidence that they needed some more instruction in this area.
- Many students continued to make the same errors on each major paper, which indicated to me that the students would have benefited from more teacher feedback.

Action Plan

As a result of this action research, I have decided to implement the same theory next year when teaching the persuasive-essay unit. I will, however, make certain that I do a better job of following through on my commitments—specifically, providing direct instruction on writing skills and providing timely effective feedback. Lastly, I shared with my department the data regarding the negative impact that interrupting instruction for state test preparation had on my students. Many of them said they sensed the same thing, and consequently, we decided to find another way to conduct preparation for the state exam. Right now, the two things we are considering are either organizing our units next year so that state exam prep will not interrupt any regular units or my recommendation that we imbed preparation for the state exam into our regular instruction, thereby avoiding any disruption in the flow of positive momentum for our most vulnerable students.

EXHIBIT 5

Educators: AR Academy Fifth-Grade PLC Team

Action Research Project: All students actively and productively engaged

Vision

While many of us often feel overwhelmed by the challenges presented at The AR Academy, we, the fifth-grade PLC team, were excited last fall about working collaboratively to learn how to better meet the diverse needs of our students. Each of us came to this process with a smattering of strategies that we had learned at various professional-development training sessions and through initiatives, all of which promised better outcomes for our students.

While each of us brought different perspectives to this process, we agreed on the fundamental problem: Too many of our students were disconnected and appeared bored by our content. Frequent behavioral disruptions, likely influenced by the high degree of student boredom and lack of engagement, occurred in each of our classes. Finally, all of us had become sensitive to the fact that many of our students were not represented in the curriculum we used, and when they were present, far too often, it was through a deficit-based portrayal.

We were equally clear about what we wanted to see in our classrooms. We wanted to see classrooms filled with academically competent, confident, and enthusiastic students. We wanted to see students actively engaged in classroom environments, where one would see frequent and high-quality student-generated questions, student-mediated dialogue, and examination of lessons and curricula through multiple relevant perspectives. Lastly, we wanted high-performing classrooms where there was no discernable difference in engagement based on racial, linguistic, or other indicators.

Upon further dialogue, we crafted the following concise vision for our PLC's action research project:

> We want to ensure that all groups of students are engaged with their learning at a rate commensurate with their high-performing peers and, ultimately, that traditionally underperforming students experience academic success at a rate commensurate with their high-performing peers.

Theory of Action

We began this part of our project by using a set of strategies designed to help develop a theory of action. Specifically, we wanted to clarify our perspective on what would likely be required if we were to fully realize our vision.

The process began with our brainstorming whatever factors we considered critical for enhancing quality student engagement. We quickly surfaced four specific factors we deemed critical:
- High-interest, culturally relevant curriculum
- Classroom organization and management
- Personalized and differentiated instruction
- Appropriate instructional strategies

At that point, we constructed a priority pie to illustrate the perceived relative importance of those four key variables. Our priority pie is illustrated below.

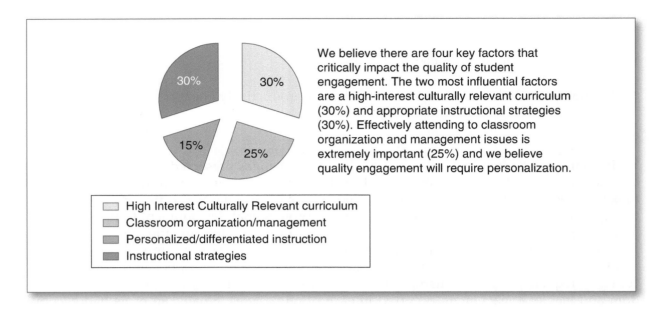

We believe there are four key factors that critically impact the quality of student engagement. The two most influential factors are a high-interest culturally relevant curriculum (30%) and appropriate instructional strategies (30%). Effectively attending to classroom organization and management issues is extremely important (25%) and we believe quality engagement will require personalization.

- ☐ High Interest Culturally Relevant curriculum
- ☐ Classroom organization/management
- ☐ Personalized/differentiated instruction
- ☐ Instructional strategies

This brought us to the second phase of the development of our theory of action: a graphic reconstruction. At this point, we felt good that we had successfully identified the critical variables, but we still needed to understand how those variables related to each other and specifically how we would need to organize ourselves and our classrooms if we were to fully realize our vision. The graphic reconstruction reprinted below is actually our comprehensive plan or road map, prepared to show the route that we believed needed to be followed if we were to realize our ultimate vision of *all students actively and productively engaged.*

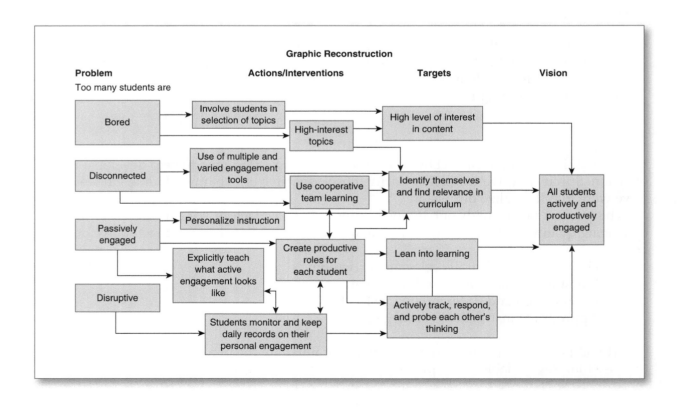

Statement of Theory

Our theory of action was built upon the following two big assumptions:

1. When students get to experience classrooms marked by high levels of interest in the content being studied, where students can readily identify themselves and find relevance in the curriculum; regularly track, respond to, and probe each other's thinking; and consistently find themselves leaning into learning, then we expect those students will be actively and productively engaged.

2. There is a set of activities that, when strategically used in classrooms, leads to high-quality engagement. Specifically, we believe meeting our achievement targets will require engaging students in describing what active engagement means to them, making use of cooperative-team-learning structures, having students monitor and keep daily records on their engagement, engaging students in high-interest topics, involving students in the selection of topics to be studied, making use of a multitude of varied engagement tools, personalizing instruction, and creating productive classroom roles for students.

Research Questions and Data Collection

We decided to focus our research and test our theory of action by collecting data in response to the three generic ACR (action, change, relationship) questions:

1. What specifically did we do?

2. What improvement occurred for our students?

3. What was the relationship between our actions and changes in performance?

The following table illustrates our triangulated data collection strategy. Once these data were collected, it was our intent to further disaggregate the findings by racial and ethnic group, as well as by ELL, TAG, and special education status.

Research Question	Data Source 1	Data Source 2	Data Source 3
What specifically did we do?	Classroom walk-throughs	Lesson plans	Student surveys and selected student interviews
What improvement occurred for our students?	Classroom walk-throughs	Student and teacher daily records on engagement	Student surveys and selected student interviews
What was the relationship between our actions and changes in performance?	Classroom walk-throughs	Correlated lesson plans with daily records on engagement	Student surveys and selected student interviews

Key Findings

We learned a great deal in this study, and much of our data are still being analyzed. However, certain key findings jumped out right away and are as follows:

1. The rates of productive engagement increased significantly from the first to second quarter for each racial category studied: African American, Latino, Native American and Pacific Islander, and white.

2. The largest increase was with the Native American and Pacific Islander students, whose scores increased 1.2 points (2.0 to 3.2). African American students gained 0.5 points (2.5 to 3.0), Latino students gained 0.4 (2.4 to 2.8), and white students gained 0.2 (3.5 to 3.7).

3. The largest racial gap between groups (in engagement) was cut from 1.5 to 0.9.

4. The overall rate of productive engagement increased for all students (from 2.5 to 3.2).

5. The subcategories of ELL students, TAG students, and special education students all showed significant increases in productive engagement.

6. The largest increase by subcategory was with the special education students, who posted a 1.1 increase (2.0 to 3.1) followed by the TAG students with 0.8 (3.0 to 3.8), and the ELL students with 0.6 (2.4 to 3.0).

7. We surveyed a total of 124 students, 90 percent of whom reported learning more, being more challenged, and enjoying our classes more after our study.

8. All eighty-one students of color reported learning more, being more challenged, and enjoying our classes more after we introduced the new model.

9. All special education and ELL students (thirty-two students) reported learning more, being more challenged, and enjoying our classes more after we introduced the new model.

Conclusion

After reviewing all the data from this project, including our teacher journals, we reflected on the experience during this past semester. Then, based upon what we learned, we drew a priority pie for the second time, this one illustrating our current beliefs regarding the importance of the four critical variables. In what follows, you can see our *before* priority pie (theory) next to our *after* pie.

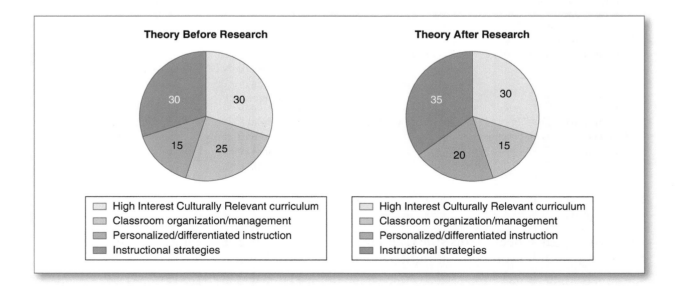

These before and after pies illustrate what we've learned through this process. We now believe that classroom management simply isn't as important as we once thought. When students are meaningfully engaged, classroom management basically appears to be less of an issue. However, both our data and this experience have convinced us that if we want to make further advances in the productive engagement of our students, we would be wise to make bigger investments in our repertoire of instructional strategies and skill sets with personalizing instruction.

Action Plan

We presented these preliminary findings and then solicited written input from the rest of our school's faculty at the end of the semester. Based upon an analysis of our findings and the assessment of our colleagues, we decided to expand our grade-level focus on enhancing engagement by concentrating on higher-level questioning. Toward this end, we have decided as a group to supplement our teaching and questioning skills through additional professional development, specifically SIOP (Sheltered Instruction Observation Protocol). After that training, it is our intent to redraw a new graphic reconstruction, adding any new insights we gain. Then, our plan is to repeat the action research process again, following our "new and improved" theory of action.

Glossary

This is a listing of terms used throughout this book, many of which have more than one meaning, even within the field of action research. This glossary defines these words and phrases as they are used in this book.

academic postmortem A comprehensive review of the educational and instructional activities that preceded and likely contributed to a particular educational outcome

achievement target A performance or outcome that one believes can be influenced by the actions of educators

adequate yearly progress (AYP) The rate of growth expected of a student or group of students over the course of a school year

analytic discourse The process of being interviewed by a group of colleagues to assist in articulating, clarifying, and deepening one's perspective on an issue

boundaries Limits placed on the scope of an inquiry or activity to assist in maintaining focus

cause and effect A supposition that a particular action is responsible for producing a specified result

context Factors found in an environment that may have an influence on what works or doesn't work in that environment

culturally responsive pedagogy A pedagogy that rests on three criteria or propositions: (a) Students must experience academic success; (b) students must develop and/or maintain cultural competence; and (c) students must develop a critical consciousness through which they challenge the status quo of the current social order (Ladson-Billings, 1995)

dependent variable The behavior, outcome, or performance that one expects to see changed as a result of targeted action

descriptive research An inquiry or study that seeks to answer the question of what is currently going on in a specified arena

educated hypothesis An assumption or prediction regarding what will result from a particular action based upon past experience

emergent theory of action The beginnings of a theory of action that is still under development

extraneous variable A factor that has nothing to do with the phenomenon under study (the relationships between the dependent and independent variables) and exerts its own separate effect on the dependent variable

face validity Something that seems obvious or true based on simply looking at it

hypothesis A prediction of what will result from an action or set of actions

intervening variable A phenomenon that has its own relationship with the independent variable and has a separate influence on the dependent variable

literature review A systematic examination of what has been written or reported on a phenomenon

operative theory of action The approach currently in use and the rationale behind that approach

performance targets Particular skills, outcomes, or performances that one would like to see improved

principal investigator (PI) The person with primary leadership responsibility for a research project. This individual sets the focus, articulates the theory, and establishes the research design that guides the study.

process targets Professional techniques, actions, or procedures that one would like to see improved

qualitative data Material that is collected or assembled pertaining to a phenomenon being studied, made up of descriptions, opinions, artifacts, or some combination of these—frequently subjective in nature

quantitative data Material that is collected or assembled pertaining to the phenomenon being studied that is made up of objective ratings or scores that can be expressed mathematically

quasi-experimental research An inquiry or investigation that infers a relationship between an action or set of actions and a defined target (dependent variable)

rate of growth The speed at which progress is being made on an achievement target

rating scale A pre-established continuum of performance that can be used to reliably determine a level of performance on an achievement target (also referred to as a rubric)

reflective interview A discourse with a colleague designed to identify and explore a potential action research focus

relationship A pattern of consistent influence between factors, variables, programs, or actions

reliability The accuracy of the data

research assistant (RA) An individual who assists in carrying out an investigation or study as a subordinate to the principal investigator (PI)

researcher's journal Notes kept by an action researcher for the purpose of tracking events that transpire during the course of research, especially any deviations from a pre-established theory of action

spreadsheet An expandable record-keeping matrix (either paper or electronic) that enables a researcher to assemble data on numerous variables across a large number of subjects

team reflection A process for a work group to deliberate in an effort to arrive at a collective research focus

tentative assertions Statements regarding patterns or trends that surfaced during the analysis of action research data

theory of action The rationale behind the actions to be taken by a practitioner and the particular inferences that back up that rationale

trend analysis A search for patterns in data over time to identify any relationships between changes in performance and specific actions and events

universal student success All students meeting academic expectations without gaps in performance due to demographic or socioeconomic factors

validity The truthfulness of data; whether the data do, in fact, represent what they purport to represent

vision The overall picture of what one would like to see accomplished as a result of action

References

Aronson, J., Zimmerman, J., & Carlos, L. (1998). *Improving student achievement by extending school: Is it just a matter of time?* San Francisco, CA: WestEd. Retrieved from https://www.wested.org/online_pubs/po-98-02.pdf

Barth, R. S. (1980). *Run school run.* Cambridge, MA: Harvard University Press.

Brown, M., & Macatangay, A. (2002). The impact of action research for professional development: Case studies in two Manchester schools. *Westminster Studies in Education, 25*(1), 35–45.

Caro-Bruce, C., & Zeichner, K. (1998). The nature and impact of an action research professional development program in one urban school district. Madison, WI: Madison Metropolitan School District.

Century, J., Freeman, C., Rudnick, M., & Leslie, D. (2008). *Rigorous measurement of fidelity of implementation of instructional materials.* Baltimore, MD: National Association for Research in Science Teaching.

Curtis-Fields, F. E. (2010). *The impact of self-efficacy, locus of control, and perceived parental influence on the academic performance of low and high achieving African-American high school students with low socioeconomic status* (Doctoral dissertation). Wayne State University, Detroit, MI.

Deming, W. E. (2000). *Out of the crisis.* Cambridge, MA: MIT Press. (Original work published 1986)

De Pree, M. (1997). *Leading without power: Finding hope in serving community.* San Francisco, CA: Jossey-Bass.

Dilworth, M. E. (Ed.). (1997). *Being responsive to cultural differences: How teachers learn.* Thousand Oaks, CA: Corwin.

Dufour, R., Dufour, R., & Eaker, R. (2008). *Revisiting professional learning communities at work: New insights for improving schools.* Bloomington, IN: Solution Tree Press.

Fishman, B. J., Marx, R. W., Best, S., & Tal, R. T. (2003). Linking teacher and student learning to improve professional development in systemic reform. *Teaching and Teacher Education, 19,* 643–658.

Fullan, M. (2001). *Leading in a culture of change.* San Francisco, CA: Jossey-Bass.

Gardner, H., Csikszentmihalyi, M., & Damon, W. (2001). *Good work: When excellence and ethics meet.* New York, NY: Basic Books.

Gay, G. (2000). *Culturally responsive teaching: Theory, research, & practice.* New York, NY: Teachers College Press.

Hale, J. A. (2008). *A guide to curriculum mapping: Planning, implementing, and sustaining the process.* Thousand Oaks, CA: Corwin.

Hargreaves, A. (1991). Teaching and guilt: Exploring the emotions of teaching. *Teaching and Teacher Education, 7*(5/6), 491–505.

Hattie, J. (2008). *Visible learning: A synthesis of over 800 meta-analyses relating to achievement.* New York, NY: Routledge.

Hersey, P., & Blanchard, K. H. (1993). *Management of organizational behavior: Utilizing human resources* (6th ed.). Englewood Cliffs, NJ: Prentice Hall.

Hord, S. M. (1997). *Professional learning communities: Communities of continuous inquiry and improvement.* Austin, TX: Southwest Educational Development Laboratory.

Hubbard, R. S., & Powers, B. M. (1999). *Living the questions: A guide for teacher-researchers.* Portland, ME: Stenhouse.

Jacobs, H. H. (1997). *Mapping the big picture: Integrating curriculum and assessment K–12.* Alexandria, VA: Association for Supervision and Curriculum Development.

Joyce, B., & Calhoun, E. (Eds.). (1996). *Learning experience in school renewal: An exploration of five successful programs.* Eugene, OR: ERIC Clearinghouse on Educational Management.

Kemmis, S., & McTaggart, R. (Eds.). (1988). *The action research planner.* Victoria, Canada: Deakin University Press.

Ladson-Billings, G. (1995). But that's just good teaching! The case for culturally relevant pedagogy. *Theory Into Practice, 34*(3), 159–165.

Little, J. W. (1982). Norms of collegiality and experimentation: Workplace conditions of school success. *American Educational Research Journal, 19,* 325–340.

Los Angeles Unified School District. (2010). Fidelity of implementation. Retrieved from http://www.lausd.k12.ca.us/lausd/offices/hep/news/fidelity.html

Miles, M., & Huberman, A. M. (1994*). Qualitative data analysis: An expanded sourcebook* (2nd ed.). Thousand Oaks, CA: Sage.

Nir, A. E., & Bogler, R. (2008). The antecedents of teacher satisfaction with professional development programs. *Teaching and Teacher Education, 24*(2), 377–386.

O'Donnell, C. L. (2006). Fidelity of implementation in scaling up highly rated science curriculum units. In A. E. Benbow (Ed.), *NSF K–12 mathematics, science, and technology curriculum developers' conference 2005: Dealing with challenges to effective and widespread implementation of IMD curricula.* Alexandria, VA: American Geological Institute.

Reeves, D. B. (2008*). Reframing teacher leadership to improve your school.* Arlington, VA: Association for Supervision and Curriculum Development.

Reeves, D. B. (2010). *Transforming professional development into student results.* Alexandria, VA: Association for Supervision and Curriculum Development.

Robins, K. N., Lindsey, R. B., Lindsey, D. B., & Terrell, R. D. (2002). *Culturally proficient instruction: A guide for people who teach.* Thousand Oaks, CA: Corwin.

Rosenholtz, S. J. (1989). *Teachers' workplace: The social organization of schools.* New York, NY: Longman.

Sagor, R. (1995). Overcoming the one-solution syndrome. *Educational Leadership, 52*(7), 24–27.

Sagor, R. (2003). *Motivating students and teachers in an era of standards.* Alexandria, VA: Association for Supervision and Curriculum Development.

Sagor, R. (2010). *Collaborative action research for professional learning communities.* Bloomington, IN: Solution Tree.

Sagor, R., & Cox J. (2004). *At-risk students: Reaching and teaching them* (2nd ed.). Larchmont, NY: Eye on Education, 2004.

Sagor, R. & Curley, J. (1991, April). *Can collaborative action research improve school effectiveness?* Paper presented at the American Education Research Association annual meeting, Chicago, IL.

Sagor, R., & Rickey, D. (2012). *The relentless pursuit of excellence: Lessons from a transformational leader.* Thousand Oaks, CA: Corwin.

Schlecty, P. C., & Vance, V. S. (1983). Recruitment, selection, and retention: The shape of the teaching force. *Elementary School Journal, 83,* 469–487.

Senge, P. M. (1990). *The fifth discipline: The art and practice of the learning organization.* New York, NY: Doubleday Currency.

Singleton, G. E., & Linton, C. (2006). *Courageous conversations about race: A field guide for achieving equity in schools.* Thousand Oaks, CA: Corwin.

Shepherd, S., Owen, D., Fitch, T. J., & Marshall, J. L. (2006). Locus of control and academic achievement in high school students. *Psychological Reports, 98*(2), 318–322.

Sizer, T. R. (1984). *Horace's compromise: The dilemma of the American high school.* New York, NY: Houghton Mifflin.

Stanley, K. R., Spradlin, T. E., & Plucker, J. A. (2007). The daily schedule: A look at the relationship between time and academic achievement. *CEEP Education Policy Brief, 5*(6), 1–7.

U.S. Census Bureau. (2015, March 3). New Census Bureau report analyzes U.S. population projections. Retrieved from http://www.census.gov/newsroom/press-releases/2015/cb15-tps16.html

Index

Abstracts
  creating bank of, 191–194
  samples, 193
  300-Word Action Research Abstract
    Worksheet, 194
  writing prompts, 193
Achievement targets
  analysis of changes regarding,
    143–146
  relationship between actions taken and
    changes in, 149–153
Action
  implementing, 8, 11
  planning informed, 8–9, 11
  research question focusing on, 92–96
  tendencies and, 157
Action plans
  data-based decision making,
    172–176
  modifying the theory of action,
    167–172
  project on improving persuasive
    writing, 240
  project on improving student
    engagement, 245
  project on promoting leadership on
    increasing student engagement, 227
  in quality action research project, 205
  revised theory of action 2, 182–183
  soliciting and brainstorming action
    alternatives, 178–179
  turning findings into, 167–183
  turning findings into ed specs, 176–178
  using ed specs to evaluate action
    alternatives, 179–181
  using ed specs to evaluate action
    alternatives for schoolwide projects,
    181–182
Action research. *See also* Focus; Sample
    abbreviated action research reports
  categories of, 9
  characteristics of quality project,
    203–205
  continuous improvement and, 59–60
  defined, 1, 6–7

  ethic of, 198–200
  reasons to conduct, 1–2
  stages of, 4–5, 7–9
  transformation of teacher working
    conditions and, 5
Action research cycle, 9, 183
Action Research Journal Sheet, 27
Action Research Report Checklist, 191, 192
Action taken
  data analysis of, 131–143
  relationship to changes in performance
    on targets, 149–153
  research questions and, 92–96
Activity Analysis Form, 140
Adequate yearly progress (AYP). *See also*
    Rate of growth
  determining in real time, 54–56
  as value judgment, 57
Affective performance targets, 20
Agenda, for reflective interviewing, 29, 30
Analytic discourse, 31
  ground rules for, 31
Assessment criteria, weighing, 176
Assumptions, confidence in, 102–104
Audiences
  for action research, 185–187
  for graphic reconstruction, 87

Behavioral performance targets, 20
Behavioral ratings, keeping running
    records of, 120–125
Bins and matrixes method
  creating bins for data, 158–160
  low-tech strategies for, 160–162
  qualitative data analysis using, 158–160
  using computer for, 162–166
Boundaries
  around action research inquiries, 64
  for reflective writing, 16
  when using journal to find action
    research focus, 25
Brainstorming
  action alternatives, 178–179
  critical independent variables,
    67–68, 72

data collection planning and, 114
variables, actions, and ideas in graphic reconstruction, 84

Carbonless paper form, 119
Carbonless paper strategy, 118–120, 121, 125
Causal language, avoiding, 105
Causal relation, tentative assertions and, 154
Changes regarding achievement targets
  data analysis of, 143–146
  relationship between actions taken and, 149–153
  research question focusing on, 96–98
Code numbers, for bins and matrixes, 162
Cognitive performance targets, 20
Coherence, in education, 197–198
Collaborative AR Group Focus Worksheet, 32
Collaborative problem solving, sample action research report on, 219–223
Colleague Interview Guide, 40, 41–42, 43
Colleagues, comparing experiences with, 39–40
Collegial school, rating scale for, 209–210
Columbus, Christopher, 75–77, 78, 168
Commercial programs, for educational program improvement, 43–45
Computer
  grade books on, 125–126
  using for bins and matrixes, 162–166
Conclusions
  drawing tentative, 166
  project on improving collaborative problem solving, 223
  project on improving persuasive writing, 238–240
  project on improving student engagement, 244–245
  project on promoting leadership on increasing student engagement, 227
Confidence in assumptions, 102–104
Conflict, evaluating action alternatives using ed specs and minimization of, 182
Congruence, in education, 197–198
Context
  explanation of, 203
  tendencies and, 157
Continua, creating performance rating scale, 49–50
Continuous improvement, action research and, 59–60
Correlation, tentative assertions and, 154
Creating a Comparison Graph of Actual Energy Expended, 217

Credibility
  using member checking to add to findings, 166
  using member checking to add to tentative assertions, 155–156
Criteria
  to measure changes with priority achievement targets, 45–47
  research evaluation, 195
  weighing assessment, 176
Curriculum maps, 93
Cutting and pasting, in bins method, 162

Data analysis, 128–166
  of changes occurring regarding achievement targets, 143–146
  disaggregation and, 146
  drawing tentative assertions, 153–154
  low-tech strategies for bins and matrixes, 160–162
  project on improving collaborative problem solving, 223
  project on promoting leadership on increasing student engagement, 227
  qualitative data analysis using bins and a matrix, 158–160
  in quality action research project, 205
  of relationship between actions taken and changes in performance on targets, 149–153
  of research goals, 131–143
  tools for qualitative data analysis, 156–158
  trend analysis, 129–131
  using computers for bins and matrixes, 162–166
  using member checking, 155–156
Data-based decision making, 172–176
  ed specs and school facilities, 174–175
  ed specs for purchasing computers, 175–176
  scoring action alternatives, 181
  use of ed specs in, 172–174
  weighing assessment criteria, 176
Data collection, 8, 11, 107–127
  building triangulated data collection plan, 113–116
  competing demands for time and, 107–108
  data in descriptive research, 109
  data in quasi-experimental research, 109–110
  in data-rich environments, 111–112
  definition of data and, 109
  integrating efficiencies into, 117–125
  journaling and, 26
  for leadership projects, 116–117
  precision concerns and, 110–111
  project on improving student engagement, 243

project on increasing equitable response opportunities, 229
project on promoting leadership on increasing student engagement, 225
reliability and, 110–111
research assistants and, 112–113
researcher's journal, 126–127
research questions and, 91, 93–98
teaching and, 108–109
using technology to compile and assemble action research data, 125–126
validity and, 110–111
Data Collection Planning Matrix, 215
Data Collection Planning Matrix (ACR Questions), 216
Decision making
action research informing, 187, 188
data-based, 172–176
Degree of detail, in action research reports, 187–189
Deming, W. Edwards, 59
Demographics of American schools, 5
Demonstrative performance targets, 20
Dependent variables, 64–65
relationship with independent, 64–65, 98–99
Descriptive research, 9, 10–12
data in, 109
graphic reconstructions with, 80–90
using priority pie with, 71–72
Dickens, Charles, 196
Direct instruction, 108
Disaggregation, 146, 163
District archive, of action research, 195
Diversity of student needs, 5–6

Educational specifications (ed specs)
for computer purchase, 175–176
evaluating action alternatives for schoolwide projects using, 181–182
evaluating action alternatives using, 179–181
school facilities and, 174–175
turning findings into, 176–178
use in data-based decision making, 172–176
weighing assessment criteria, 176
Educator frustration
complexity of routine instructional decisions and, 2–4
diversity of student needs and, 5–6
organization of teacher work and, 4–5
Educators, reflective writing and setting annual goals, 18–20. *See also* Teachers
Efficiencies, integrated into data collection work, 117–125
Empowerment, action research and teacher, 7

Energy expended
comparison graph of, 217
contrasting anticipated and actual, 133–139
Equitable response opportunities, sample action research report on, 228–232
Equity and excellence, as educational goals, 2, 63, 146, 196, 197, 199, 224
Ethic of action research, 198–200
European explorers, as action researchers, 74–77
Every Student Succeeds Act, 63
Expectation for universal student success, 1–2, 12–13
Explanation of context, problem or issues, in quality action research project, 203
Extraneous variables, 99

Face validity, graphic reconstruction and, 74
Facilitators, teachers as, 108
Factoids, from information in bins, 163–165
Feedback forms, 124, 201–202
Feedback Summary Form, 124
Findings, 137–139. *See also* Reporting and sharing action research
modifying the theory of action and, 168–172
project on improving collaborative problem solving, 222–223
project on improving persuasive writing, 236–238
project on improving student engagement, 243–244
project on increasing equitable response opportunities, 230–231
project on promoting leadership on increasing student engagement, 227
reporting, 155
turning into action plans (*See* Action plans)
turning into ed specs, 176–178
using member checking to add credibility to, 166
Focus, action research
analytic discourse, 31
performance target, 46
priority achievement targets by school leaders and, 22–24
process target, 46
program target, 46
reflective interviews and, 29–31
team reflection and, 31–33
using journal to identify, 24–29
using reflective writing to find, 15–22
zeroing in on priorities, 14–15

Focus, refining action research, 34–58
  assessing rate of growth, 54
  comparing own experience with others', 39–45
  conducting instructional postmortem, 36–38
  creating performance rating scales, 47–50
  determining adequate yearly progress, 54–56
  developing criteria to measure changes, 45–47
  long-range goals and, 53–54
  producing rate-of-growth charts, 56–58
  rate of growth in leadership projects, 58
  rating scales and program action research, 50–52
  taking stock of recent leadership experience, 39
  visualizing success, 35–36
Formats for reporting, 189–191
Fullan, Michael, 158

Goals
  educator annual, 18–19
  problem of long-range, 53–54
Grade books, computer, 125–126
Graphic reconstruction, 66, 72, 73–90
  after walk-through, 103–104
  audiences for, 87
  brainstorm variables, actions, and ideas, 84
  building, 77–78
  comparing before and after research versions, 231–232
  for descriptive research, 80–90
  European explorers as action researchers, 74–77
  face validity, 74
  grouping and sorting variables, actions, and ideas, 84–85
  implementation road map, 74, 221
  importance of visual planning and, 80–83
  leadership projects and, 88–89
  making program clear to stakeholders, 78, 80
  modifying theory of action and before and after, 168–169, 171
  project on improving persuasive writing, 235
  project on improving student engagement, 242
  project on increasing equitable response opportunities, 229, 231
  project on promoting leadership on increasing student engagement, 225
  proofing road map, 88–89
  providing guidance to others, 78, 79

  providing insights into process, 78, 79–80
  for quasi-experimental research, 78–80
  reviewing final product, 89–90
  sequencing parts logically, 85–87
  sequential steps in, 82–90
  two-step walk-through and, 213
Graph of operant theory, 70–71
Grouping/sorting, of variables, ideas, and actions in graphic reconstruction, 84–85
Growth
  rate of, 54
  rate-of-growth charting with leadership projects, 211–212
Guidance, using graphic reconstruction to provide, 78, 79
Guilt, public school teachers and, 2

Handouts, action research report, 189
Hargreaves, Andy, 2
Highlighters, use in bins method, 162
Hillel, 61
Historical world maps, 75–77, 168, 169, 170
Huberman, A. M., 158

Illustrative factoids, 164
Implementation dip, 158
Implementation road map, 74
  for project on improving collaborative problem solving, 221
Independent variables, 64–65
  brainstorming critical, 67–68, 72
  inferring, 65–66
  relationship with dependent variables, 64–65, 98–99
  summarizing, 68–69, 72
  using priority pie to identify, clarify, and weigh, 66–71
Insights into process, using graphic reconstruction to provide, 78, 79–80
Instructional decisions, complexity of, 2–4
Instructional postmortem, conducting, 36–38
Instructional Postmortem Form, 37–38
Instructional strategies, graphic reconstruction and, 78
Internal locus of control, 122
Internet, literature review on, 43
Interpretations, soliciting, of findings, 155–156
Intervening variables, 99
Interviews, reflective, 29–30
Intuitive regression analysis
  conducting, 69, 70
  modifying the theory of action and, 172
Intuitive Regression Analysis Form, 173

Intuitive Regressive Analysis Worksheet, 69
Isolation, reflective interviewing and, 30–31

Journal, using to identify action research foci, 24–29
    researcher's journal and, 126–127
    sample journal entry, 25–26
    team action research and, 26
    writing prompt for, 25
Journal Analysis Form, 28, 29
Journaling, as data collection strategy, 26

Kemmis, S., 7
Knowledge base, articulating a theory of action and, 60–61
Knowledge workers, students as, 108

Leadership experience, taking stock of, 39
Leadership projects
    applications for, 206–217
    contrasting anticipated and actual energy expended in, 133–139
    data collection planning for, 116–117
    for increasing engagement, sample action research report on, 224–227
    proofing theory of action for, 88–89
    rate of growth in, 58
    surfacing research questions for, 106
Leadership Rating Scale, 226
Learning, relation of time to, 66–67
Line graphs
    time allocation, 133
    trend analysis and, 130
Literature review, 40–43
Literature Review Planning Form, 43, 44
Long-range goals, 53–54
Low-tech strategies for bins and matrixes, 160–162

Maps. See also Graphic reconstruction
    curriculum, 93
    historical world, 75–77, 168, 169, 170
    implementation road, 74
Martellus, Henricus, 75, 77, 168, 169
Matrix. See Bins and matrixes method
McAuliffe, Christa, 200
McTaggart, R., 7
Member checking
    to add credibility to findings, 166
    to add credibility to tentative assertions, 155–156
Mileposts, creating, on route to mastery, 65
Miles, M., 158
Myth of homogeneity, 6

Narrative
    creating, 141
    keeping file copies of, 117–120
No Child Left Behind Act, 54, 63

Online research, tips for conducting, 43
Open-ended questions, 104–105
Operant theory, 71
    graphing, 70–71, 72
Organization of teacher work, 4–5
Outline, action research report, 189

Patterns, data analysis and, 139–141
Performance
    changes in, 96–98
    relationship between actions taken and changes in, 98–99
Performance rating scales, 47–50, 96
    for collegial school, 209–210
    creating continua for, 49–50
    identifying traits, 49
    program action research and, 50–52
    visualizing excellent achievement, 48–49
Performance targets, 20
    action research by school leaders and, 22–24
    categories of, 20
    foci for, 46
    for leadership projects, 207
Persuasive writing, sample action research report on improving, 233–240
Planning time, 4
Plan of action, 71
PLC (professional learning community) team study of student engagement, 241–245
Polo, Marco, 76
Portland (OR) Public Schools, 199–200
Post Hoc Analysis of Leadership Form, 39, 208
Precision, data collection and, 110–111
Priorities, research focus and, 14–15
Priority achievement targets, 20–22. See also Performance targets; Process targets; Program targets
    creating mileposts for, 65
    developing criteria to measure changes with, 45–47
    school leaders and, 22–24
Priority pies, 131–132
    brainstorming critical independent variables, 67–68, 72
    comparing revised and original, 230, 244–245
    graphing operant theory, 70–71, 72
    intuitive regression analysis, 69, 72
    modifying the theory of action and updating, 172, 174
    project on improving collaborative problem solving, 220–221
    project on improving persuasive writing, 233–235, 236, 237
    project on improving student engagement, 242, 244

project on increasing equitable response opportunities, 229, 230
project on promoting leadership on increasing student engagement, 225
summarizing independent variables, 68–69, 72
using to identify, clarify, and weigh independent variables, 66–71
using with descriptive research, 71–72
Problem, explanation of, 203
Process targets, 20
   action research by school leaders and, 22–24
   foci for, 46
   for leadership projects, 207
Program action research, rating scales and, 50–52
Program targets, 20
   action research by school leaders and, 22–24
   foci for, 46
   for leadership projects, 207
Prompts
   for abstract writing, 193
   for journal writing, 25
   for reflective writing, 16
Proofing graphic reconstruction, 88–89
Proven practices, articulating a theory of action and, 61–64
Purpose, of action research report, 187, 188

Qualitative data
   additional tools for, 156–158
   analysis using bins and a matrix, 158–160
Qualitative research, 12
Quantitative research, 12
Quantitative terms, converting qualitative data into, 158–160
Quasi-experimental research, 9–10, 11
   data in, 109–110
   graphic reconstruction for, 78–80, 89
Questions. *See also* Research questions
   in analytic discourse, 31
   open-ended, 104–105

Rate of growth
   adequate yearly progress (AYP), 54–56
   assessing, 54
   in leadership projects, 58, 211–212
Rate-of-Growth Charting with Leadership Projects, 211–212
Rate-of-growth charts, 96
   with leadership projects, 211–212
   producing, 56–58
Rating scales, performance, 47–50, 96
   for a collegial school, 209–210
   program action research and, 50–52
   of reading proficiency, 52
   tips on creating, 52

Rating-Scale Worksheet, 50, 51
Recruitment, of educators, 197
Reflection
   on data, 8–9, 11
   instructional postmortem, 36–38
   team, 31–33
Reflective interviews, 29–30
   agenda for, 29, 30
   problem of isolation and, 30–31
Reflective writing, 15–22
   identification of priority achievement targets, 20–22
   prompts for, 16
   sample prompt response, 17–18
Reflective Writing Worksheet, 19
Regression analysis. *See* Intuitive regression analysis
Relationship between action and performance change, research question focusing on, 98–99
Relationships, significant, 105
Reliability, data collection and, 110–111
Reporting and sharing action research, 184–195. *See also* Sample abbreviated action research reports
   abstract bank, 191–194
   audience for, 185–187
   creating district archive, 195
   degree of detail, 187–189
   evaluation criteria, 195
   purpose of, 187, 188
   reasons for, 184–185
   reporting formats, 189–191
Report Planning Form, 190
Research. *See also* Action research
   descriptive, 9, 10–12
   qualitative, 12
   quantitative, 12
   quasi-experimental, 9–10, 11
Research assistants, 112–113
Research design
   project on improving collaborative problem solving, 221–222
   project on improving persuasive writing, 235–236
   in quality action research project, 204
Researcher's journal, 126–127, 133
Research for action, 7
Research in action, 7
Research of action, 7
Research questions, 91–106
   data collection and, 91, 93–98
   data collection planning and, 216
   developing own, 100
   drafting questions, 104–106
   framing, 105–106
   generic action research questions, 92–100
   for leadership projects, 106
   open-ended, 104–105

project on improving student engagement, 243
project on increasing equitable response opportunities, 229–230
project on promoting leadership on increasing student engagement, 225–226
two-step walk-through, 100–104
what changes occurred regarding performance on targets, 96–98
what was actually done, 92–96
what were relationships between actions taken and changes in performance, 98–99
Responses
   sample action research report on equitable response opportunities, 228–232
   tendencies and, 157
Rubric, 47

Sagor-Williams reading program, 79
Sample abbreviated action research reports
   Dr. Hernandez's project on improving collaborative problem solving, 219–223
   fifth-grade PLC team's study of student engagement, 241–245
   Mr. Johnson's project on leadership for increasing engagement, 224–227
   Mr. Seeker's project on improving persuasive writing, 233–240
   Ms. Montgomery's project on equitable response opportunities, 228–232
Sample Action Alternatives Poster, 180
School as learning organization, 196–200
   coherence and congruence and, 197–198
   institutionalizing ethic of action research, 198–200
School leaders. *See also* Leadership projects
   priority achievement targets and, 22–24
   taking stock of recent leadership experience, 39
Schoolwide projects, using ed specs to evaluate action alternatives for, 181–182
Scientifically proven practice, 61
Scouting, 156
Sequence of action, graphic reconstruction and, 77
Sequencing item, in graphic reconstruction, 85–87
Significance, determining, 101–102
Sizer, Ted, 108
Sort command, for bins and matrixes, 162–163
Speed, John, 75, 76
Sphere of influence, of teachers, 7

Stakeholders, graphic representation and, 78
Statement of theory, project on improving student engagement, 243
Statistical factoids, 163
Stickney, Jane, 198
Student engagement
   sample action research report on increasing, 224–227
   sample action research report on PLC team's study of, 241–245
Students
   diversity of needs of, 5–6
   as knowledge workers, 108
   as research assistants, 113
Summary reports, use of, 202
Summary Time Priority Form, 134, 137
Support staff, 4

Target Identification Form, 20–22, 24, 29
Target Identification Form for Leaders, 207
Targets. *See* Priority achievement targets
Teachers
   complexity of instructional decisions and, 2–4
   diversity of student needs and, 5–6
   as facilitators, 108
   guilt and, 2
   setting annual goals, 18–20
   sphere of influence, 7
   work context for, 4–5
Teaching, data collection and, 108–109
Team action research, journaling and, 26
Team reflection, to find action research focus, 31–33
Technology, use of, to compile and assemble action research data, 125–126
Tendencies, 156–157
Tentative assertions
   drawing, 153–154
   modifying the theory of action and, 168–172
   using member checking to add credibility to, 155–156
Tentative conclusions, drawing, 166
Theoretical perspective, in quality action research project, 204
Theory, articulating, 8, 11
Theory of action, 8, 10
   drawing (*See* Graphic reconstruction)
   modifying, 167–172
   project on improving collaborative problem solving, 220
   project on improving persuasive writing, 233
   project on improving student engagement, 241–242
   project on increasing equitable response opportunities, 228–229

project on promoting leadership on
  increasing student engagement, 224
revised, 182–183
significant aspects of, 105
Theory of action, articulating, 59–72
  building theory of action, 61–64
  inferring independent variables, 65–66
  knowledge base for, 60–61
  mileposts towards mastery, 65
  two kinds of variables, 64–65
  using priority pie to clarify and weigh
    independent variables, 66–71
  using priority pie with descriptive
    research, 71–72
300-Word Action Research Abstract
  Worksheet, 194
Time
  data collection and competing demands
    for, 107–108
  modifying the theory of action and
    reconsidering issue of, 172
  relation to learning, 66–67
Time allocation
  data analysis and, 133–139
  graph, 133, 135
Time line, creating, 141–143
Time Priority Tracking Form,
  96, 97, 133, 172
Traits, identifying performance rating
  scale, 49
Trend analysis, 129–131
  comparing and contrasting,
    144–145
Trend graph, 141
Trends in Time Use Form, 136
Triangulated data collection plan,
  113–116
Triangulation, 98
Triangulation Matrix, 111, 114, 117
Triangulation Worksheet, 118
Turning Research Findings into Ed Specs
  Form, 177

Universal student success, 1–2, 12–13
Using the Two-Step Walk-Through with a
  Leadership Project, 213–214

Validity, data collection and, 110–111
Variables
  dependent, 64–65, 98–99
  extraneous, 99
  independent (*See* Independent variables)
  intervening, 99
Vision
  action research and clarifying, 8, 11
  project on improving persuasive
    writing, 233
  project on improving student
    engagement, 241
  project on increasing equitable response
    opportunities, 228
  project on promoting leadership on
    increasing student engagement, 224
Visualizing excellent achievement, for
  performance rating scales, 48–49
Visualizing success, 35–36
Visual planning, graphic reconstructions
  and, 80–83

Waldseemüller, Martin, 168, 170
Walk-through, using two-step walk-
  through with a leadership project,
  213–214
Washoe County School District (Nevada),
  199, 200
Weighing assessment criteria, 176
Willamette Primary School (West Linn,
  Oregon), 198–199
Work context, for teachers, 4–5
Writing, sample action research report on
  improving persuasive, 233–240
Writing prompts
  for abstract writing, 193
  for journal writing, 25
  for reflective writing, 16

CORWIN

A SAGE Publishing Company

Helping educators make the greatest impact

CORWIN HAS ONE MISSION: to enhance education through intentional professional learning.

We build long-term relationships with our authors, educators, clients, and associations who partner with us to develop and continuously improve the best evidence-based practices that establish and support lifelong learning.

Solutions you want. Experts you trust. Results you need.

AUTHOR CONSULTING

Author Consulting

On-site professional learning with sustainable results! Let us help you design a professional learning plan to meet the unique needs of your school or district. www.corwin.com/pd

INSTITUTES

Institutes

Corwin Institutes provide collaborative learning experiences that equip your team with tools and action plans ready for immediate implementation. www.corwin.com/institutes

ECOURSES

eCourses

Practical, flexible online professional learning designed to let you go at your own pace. www.corwin.com/ecourses

READ2EARN

Read2Earn

Did you know you can earn graduate credit for reading this book? Find out how: www.corwin.com/read2earn

Contact an account manager at (800) 831-6640 or visit **www.corwin.com** for more information.